The Task of the Interpreter

The *Task*
of the
Interpreter

Text, Meaning, and Negotiation

Pol Vandevelde

University of Pittsburgh Press

Published by the University of Pittsburgh Press, Pittsburgh, Pa., 15260
Copyright © 2005, University of Pittsburgh Press
All rights reserved
Manufactured in the United States of America
Printed on acid-free paper
10 9 8 7 6 5 4 3 2 1

Library of Congress Cataloging-in-Publication Data

Vandevelde, Pol.
    The task of the interpreter : text, meaning, and negotiation / Pol
Vandevelde.
        p. cm.
    Includes bibliographical references and index.
    ISBN 0-8229-4263-1 (hardcover : alk. paper) — ISBN 0-8229-5884-8
(pbk. : alk. paper)
        1. Criticism. 2. Hermeneutics. 3. Criticism (Philosophy) I. Title.
    PN81.V28 2005
    801'.95—dc22

                                    2005006832

To Nicholas and Henry

Contents

Acknowledgments

Some of the material in this book has appeared in other publications. I thank the editors and publishers for granting permission to use these publications.

The first section of chapter 2 is a significant reformulation of views presented in 2002. "L'interprétation comme acte de conscience et comme évènement. Une critique de Gadamer." In *Littérature et savoir(s)*, ed. S. Klimis and L. Van Eynde, 41–64. Bruxelles: Publications des Facultés universitaires Saint-Louis.

The second section of chapter 2 is a reformulation of views presented in 2005. "A Pragmatic Critique of Pluralism in Text Interpretation." In *Metaphilosophy* 36: 501–21.

Some of the material used in chapter 3 was used with another purpose in 1998. "La traduction comme interprétation. Une comparaison et quelques répercussions théoriques." In *Existentia* 1–4:1–26.

Some of the material used in chapter 4 was used, with significant differences, in 2003a. "*Divina eloquia cum legente crescunt.* Does Gregory Mean a Subjective or an Objective Growth?" *Rivista di storia della filosofia* 4:611–37.

Some of the material used in section 2 of chapter 5 was also used, although differently, in 1996. "Ontologie et récit selon Ricoeur. Une application a 187 à Günter Grass, *Les années de chien.*" In *Les Études de Lettres* 3–4:195–213.

Some of the material used in chapter 6 was used, with a different purpose, in 2003b. "Literatur und Wahrheit am Beispiel Ernesto Sabatos." In *Literatur als Phänomenalisierung*, ed. H. R. Sepp and J. Trinks, 30–63. Vienna: Turia & Kant.

Many friends gave me their professional opinions on specific points and commented on previous drafts of some of the chapters. My thanks to John Meech and Thomas Prendergast, who gave me their critical comments on a draft of the second section of chapter 2; Armel Job, who provided many valuable insights regarding Homer's text and its difficulties in chapter 3; and Father Roland Teske, Father Pierre Bogaert, and Lance Richey, who made useful comments on the section on Gregory the Great in chapter 4. Terri Hennings read the whole manuscript, provided many valuable insights, and made a number of excellent suggestions. Gregory Traylor helped me organize and harmonize the whole text and proofread the manuscript. I also benefited from the editorial skills of Alice VanBenthuysen, Kyle McNeel, and Cristina Bucur. I am also grateful for the judicious suggestions made by two anonymous readers of Pittsburgh University Press.

The Department of Philosophy, the College of Arts and Sciences, and the Graduate School at Marquette University provided significant financial support for writing the manuscript through a summer fellowship, several travel and research grants, and several research assistantships.

Finally, I thank Dominique Poncelet, my wife, for her constant support and judicious advice.

The Task of the Interpreter

1

The Debate between Monism
and Pluralism

∾

The term "interpretation" can be applied to a wide range of activities. Biologists interpret data, and journalists interpret events. Similarly, any object of interest can be considered to be a text to be deciphered, whether it is nature created by God (the famous book of nature for the medieval fathers of the church), the structures of kinship (Lévi-Strauss 1967, Bourdieu 1977), or a landscape to be painted. Furthermore, interpreters can decide how to treat their object of interest: Homer's *Iliad* was taken as a topographic manual by Heinrich Schliemann in his search for the city of Troy (1976), the Gospels have been submitted to a psychoanalytic reading (Dolto 1977), and many novels have been analyzed as a manifestation of male prejudices against women (for example, Morris 1993). It comes as no surprise that many trends in the theory of interpretation have subscribed to a form of relativism: any interpretation makes use of notions, values, and interests that are cultural, so that an interpretation can only be relative to a framework, which is specified historically and culturally. Such a view, which takes the possibility of multiple interpretations of the same text as a given and which in addition rejects the possibility of an ultimate court of appeal that could adjudicate the validity of an interpretation, is defended in both the continental and analytic philosophical traditions.

Hans-Georg Gadamer, following Martin Heidegger, claims that there is something absurd in the idea of one correct interpretation of a text (1998, 120). This view has become almost standard in the tradition of philosophical hermeneutic. "Hermeneutic thinkers are . . . multiplists insofar as they hold that there can be a number of different true interpretations of the entities studied by the human sciences" (Guignon, 2002, 280). In the contemporary debate on interpretation, this view has received different labels with different emphases: critical pluralism, multiplism, constructivism. Critical pluralism holds that there are a multiplicity of equally valid interpretations, resulting from the different backgrounds of interpreters who do not read with the same interests, concerns, and knowledge. Michael Krausz defines what he calls multiplism as "the ideal of a multiplicity of admissible interpretations," while singularism is "the ideal of a single admissible interpretation" (2002b, 1). Constructivism, according to Torsten Pettersson, "holds that interpretations of literary works are not accounts of their objects but projections from critical stances and sets of values" (2002, 217). Stanley Fish is one of the most vocal representatives of such a view. In his book *Is There a Text in this Class?* he grants communities of readers the power not only to read, but in reading to construe the objects of interpretation so that readers or interpreters "do not decode poems, they make them" (1980, 327). The text does not provide any anchor for agreement among readers on what the text means. Interpretive communities come to a text with their strategies of reading, and the text serves as an occasion for those strategies to play out.

The reason for such a possible multiplicity of equally valid interpretations lies in the nature of the object of interpretation. As Joseph Margolis puts it, "the problem of interpretation is precisely what it is because there is no formal demarcation line between what is describably present in a work and what may be interpretively imputed to it" (1980, 127). Since cultural objects have many properties, the existence of which depends on the background against which they emerge (Margolis 1974), there is no stable framework in which the truth or falsity of an interpretation can be decided. Margolis defends what he calls a robust relativism: the claim that interpretations are not submitted to truth values does not amount to the claim that interpretations are epistemically indeterminate. Interpretations have "to meet criteria of critical plausibility which entails (a) compatibility with the describable features of given artworks and (b) conformability with relativized canons of interpretation that themselves fall within the tolerance of an historically continuous tradition of interpretation" (Margolis 1980, 163). As David Novitz concludes, "Since these properties are discerned only in terms of certain historically located cultural principles, both Krausz and Margolis believe that there can be no neutral way of deciding between competing interpretations as there are 'preferred' (Margolis) or 'pertinent' (Krausz) cultural principles in terms of which the work may be interpreted. . . . And since there may be different yet undeniably pertinent or preferred cultural principles, it follows that there is no single right interpretation of a cultural object" (2002, 118).

Opposed to pluralism in interpretation, critical monism or singularism defends the view that for a given text there is ideally only one correct interpretation. A version of monism specifies the correct interpretation as the author's intention. Monists can claim to discover the psychological states of the writer and thus attempt to relive what the author experienced while creating the text, as Friedrich Schleiermacher, the founder of romantic hermeneutics, believes they do (1977); or, following E. D. Hirsch's views as influenced by Edmund Husserl, monists can claim to access the idealities that writers put into words (1967). These two types of monism would fall under what Noël Carroll calls actual intentionalists as opposed to the hypothetical intentionalists (2000, 2002). The former "contend that the authorial intentions that are relevant to the interpretations of artworks are the actual intentions of the pertinent artists," while the latter "claim that what is relevant for interpretation is merely our best-warranted hypotheses concerning the intentions of actual authors" (Carroll 2002, 321–22).

What is remarkable is the fact that the views defended by critical monism and critical pluralism are from a theoretical point of view almost mutually exclusive, while in the practice of interpreters they have cohabited somewhat peacefully. Most interpreters in their practice would assent to points made by monists and pluralists alike. With the pluralists, they would assent to the possibility of multiple interpretations of the same text.

Usually interpreters do not claim that a particular text means this and that without qualification, but are careful to specify the type of meaning they are interested in, the perspective they take, and the methods they use. In addition, interpreters can pursue different goals, take different perspectives, and use different methods. It would thus be difficult to argue, for example, that a feminist reading of Ernest Hemingway's *Farewell to Arms* invalidates a structuralist reading of the same novel. Most interpreters would agree with the pluralists that the two readings can be legitimate. In Margolis's words, "The collective practice of critics shows a distributed tolerance for competing canons—without any loss of rigor" (1980, 157).

However, while recognizing a disseminating factor, most interpreters in their practice would also side with the monists and claim that, with the aim they have and the method they use, and the perspective they take, what they

offer is the best interpretation they can think of. Furthermore, if interpreters claim validity for an interpretation, they have to make clear to others what the object of interpretation is, and, in the case of texts, they can
only define or identify the object by using the author: this novel by Hemingway or those texts by German romantic novelists. Interpreters have to
posit an intention behind the object of interpretation, even if it is a minimal intention—having written the text—and even if it is to dismiss it,
because they are interested in figures of style or in a Freudian unconscious
or in cultural stereotypes. Even those who interpret a champion of indeterminacy of meaning such as Jacques Derrida are very careful to explain a text
by Derrida through the use of other texts by the same Derrida, and not by
appealing to a speech by Tony Blair or NASA's pictures of the planet Mars.

I take this capacity for monism and pluralism to cohabit at the empirical level of the practice of interpretation as an indication that the debate
between monism and pluralism is formulated in the wrong terms. The two
positions constitute not a dichotomy but rather two theoretical positions
on two different aspects of interpretation. I call these two aspects act and
event. By event I mean the fact that we as speakers and interpreters partic-
ipate in a culture and a language that carry with them concepts, values, and
habits of which we might not be aware, so that our interpretation is also
something taking place in a tradition. By act, I mean an act of consciousness: someone interpreting a text makes a statement or an utterance and
through his or her act is committed regarding the truth of what is said, his
or her truthfulness, and the rightness or appropriateness of what is said, so
that, if prompted, the interpreter must be ready to defend the interpretation made regarding these three claims.

As an event, interpretation is situated in a cultural and historical framework where historical writer, interpreter, audience, and text are parameters
of something that happens. Situated in a particular period and permeated
by cultural and historical forces, interpreters come to a text with questions,
concerns, and methods of which they are not fully conscious, so that they
are instances of cultural forces and historical trends: we do not interpret
Homer now as he was interpreted in the eighteenth century, because we do
not share the worldview of the eighteenth century.

The second aspect of interpretation tempers the historicism or relativism that seems intrinsic to an exclusive focus on interpretation as an
event. Interpretation is also an act of consciousness where an intention is
expressed through statements, so that interpretation is a performance by a
real person who relates to other people. Through their performance (writ-

ing a series of statements, presenting those statements in an ordered fashion, justifying the validity of those statements, etc.), interpreters are implicitly bound by what they wrote and committed to their audience, so that, if prompted, they must be ready to justify their interpretation. The mistake of many advocates of pluralism is to focus exclusively on the event of interpretation and overlook the pragmatic aspect of interpretation as an act. They take a third-person perspective on what happens when an interpretation takes place, and from this perspective they can assess or make assumptions about what influenced interpreters and the prejudices they had. If we take the first-person perspective of the interpreter when presenting a new interpretation, we see that the interpreter does not have available a knowledge of the influences and prejudices marring the enterprise of interpretation.

My intent is to illustrate the way monism and pluralism play out and cohabit in the practice of interpretation and to offer an appraisal of monism and pluralism. I confine my investigation to the interpretation of texts and take no position on what is at stake in other types of interpretation, such as psychoanalysis or legal hermeneutics.

Any study of what interpretation is faces external and internal difficulties that need to be recognized. The external difficulties have to do with the way disciplines of knowledge are structured in academe and the different traditions that have taken possession of the ways and means to approach a problem. The internal difficulties concern the different levels of meaning lying in a text.

Most disciplines in human sciences are interpretive and have developed their own methods, so that practitioners of theology, for example, can perform their task successfully while ignoring the reflection on interpretation developed in literary criticism or philosophy. Or a practitioner can make an ad hoc use of a theoretician or philosopher by applying selected concepts of such a theorist without having to deal with the whole theory defended by this theorist. When, for example, Hirsch (1967) makes use of Ferdinand de Saussure or Husserl, but only selectively, it is not an easy conceptual task to try to find out what other elements of Saussure or Husserl, if any, Hirsch also accepts or rejects. Many philosophers, for their part, have the bad habit of presenting their arguments without making sure that the subtle conceptual distinctions they draw correspond to real differences that are relevant in the practice of interpretation. Furthermore, they often content themselves with some short examples, which can only appear terse to practitioners of interpretation, who could meaningfully ask, would this example hold true for the interpretation of the whole novel?

This tendency of philosophers is not alleviated by the use ad nauseam of the same examples. The opposite interpretations Cleanth Brooks and F. W. Bateson gave of Wordsworth's poem "A Slumber Did My Spirit Seal" have become a topos of interpretation theory, the equivalent of "the cat is on the mat" of philosophy of language. (After Hirsch 1967, 227–28, this example can be found in Margolis 1980, 115; Krausz 1992, 161; Levinson 1992, 239; Beardsley 1992, 29–31; and Stecker 1997, 209–11.)

Because of the different methods used in literary criticism, theology, and philosophy—methods that function as many codes of the profession— it is not easy to develop a theory of interpretation that would be recognized by all interpretive disciplines as relevant or convincing. That means also that practitioners in one discipline can somewhat easily dismiss theoretical reflections coming from other quarters on the basis that these reflections do not account for the specificities of their discipline.

In addition to the different interests at play in various disciplines, a difficulty more specific to philosophy consists in its division into several traditions that tend to ignore each other at best or dismiss each other at worst. Two prominent traditions are continental and analytic-pragmatic philosophy. There are of course many philosophers who have bridged these traditions or belong to both. Karl-Otto Apel, Jürgen Habermas, Paul Ricoeur, and Richard Rorty were in this sense pioneers in opening new avenues for doing philosophy. But despite the many researchers nurtured in both traditions, the divide remains quite strong in academe. Emblematic of this mutual ignorance is Peter Carruthers's preface: "I ignore the small minority who attempt to do philosophy in Continental mode—they will not, in any case, read this" (1996, xii).

These two traditions use different approaches and different conceptual frameworks, so that the phenomenon of interpretation receives radically different treatments in the continental than in the analytic-pragmatic tradition. Influenced by Heidegger, for whom interpretation is an existential dimension of human existence, the continental tradition tends to treat interpretation in quasi-metaphysical terms: one speaks of "the sense of understanding" (Figal 1996) or "the ontology of the work of art" (Gadamer 1998). Interpretation is almost immediately categorized as belonging to the discipline of hermeneutics, with the accusation by the other tradition of indulging in generalizations and speculations. In the analytic-pragmatic tradition, interpretation is approached through multiple conceptual distinctions about the authorial intention (hypothetical vs. actual intentionalism and its "anti-intentionalism"), the possibility of multiple interpretations (monism or singularism vs. pluralism or multiplism or their subcategories), the types of interpretation (meaning vs. relational, description vs. interpretation, etc.), or about the logical status of interpreters' statements. One of the common accusations made by the other tradition is that the analytic-pragmatic tradition unnecessarily multiplies distinctions that do not bear on real differences. Trying to solve the thought experiment that a monkey typed Hamlet before Shakespeare (Gracia 2002, 178–80) or that waves of the ocean composed a text on the shore similar to a poem by Wordsworth (Knapp and Michaels 1992) are not of much help in dealing with the actual and concrete problems interpreters encounter in their practice.

Not only does the phenomenon of interpretation appear quite different when analyzed in either tradition, but it is also very difficult for those who try to bridge the two traditions to be recognized by or even receive a hearing from practitioners of either tradition. For many reasons, one of them probably being intellectual comfort, some theorists in each tradition have adopted the habit of simply ignoring what other theorists in the other tradition do. Robert Stecker, for example, in *Artworks* (1997), discusses the issue of meaning and interpretation, but focuses exclusively on the contemporary discussion in analytic and pragmatic circles. There is not a single mention of Anglo-American authors who deal with interpretation in the continental tradition and no mention of classical continental theoreticians of interpretation such as Gadamer or Ricoeur. In addition, there is no mention of any work not written in English. We can find the same attitude in the continental tradition. In *Der Sinn des Verstehens* (1996), Günter Figal only deals with theorists of the continental tradition, most of them German, without any mention of the rich and sophisticated reflection made in the analytic-pragmatic tradition.

The unfortunate consequence of such an academic schizophrenia is that it perpetuates itself through students and publishing policies targeting specific audiences. The irony is that the most innovative works in the past twenty years or so have been made by those people who have crossed disciplines and traditions, both on the European and the American sides. These include Ricoeur, Habermas, Apel, and Rorty, who each in his own way formulated new problems and provided a new vocabulary for dealing with them.

Faced with these external difficulties, I have opted for a method that calls for crossing disciplines and traditions. Since the problem I am dealing with is interpretation, it would be irresponsible to ignore what other disciplines do and how particular practices of interpretation work. A study of interpretation is only credible if it is about the way actual interpretations are performed by real practitioners. Similarly, what theorists have said about interpretation cannot be ignored simply because they belong to a specific tradition. I appeal to theorists because of their views, regardless of the tradition from which they come. Although I had to choose among them, they were chosen on their merits.

Besides these external difficulties, there are internal ones as well. What is the question of the meaning that an interpreter tries to bring to the fore? Monroe Beardsley answered quite concisely: "He tells us what a literary work means. . . . So what the interpreter reveals is the meaning of a text" (1992, 24–25). The problem with this statement is the vagueness of meaning, already identified by Goethe in this ironic exchange with Johann Peter Eckermann: "There they come and ask: What idea did I try to incorporate in my *Faust*? As if I myself knew it and could express it! 'From heaven through the world to hell'—that would already be something, if need be. But that's no idea; it's the course of the plot. And further, 'that the devil loses the bet and that a man is to be redeemed who from grave mistakes constantly aspires to something better.' That's quite a powerful good, and very enlightening thought. But that's not an idea that lies at the basis of the whole play and of each individual scene" (cited in Kayser 1992, 219; my translation).

What Goethe's impatience points to is that the meaning of a text is not a monolithic entity. Most interpreters heed Goethe's suspicion and do not even use this kind of blanket formulation that, for example, *Faust* means this and that.

In the tradition of text interpretation, several levels of text meaning have always been differentiated. One of the most famous distinctions was made in biblical interpretation between three and sometimes four levels of meaning. In contemporary discussion three levels of meaning are usually mentioned: (1) the meaning of the one who wrote, what we usually call the author's intention; (2) the meaning of the text, in the sense of what its words and sentences say; and (3) the meaning that readers see in the text, that is, what they take the text to mean or the representative content of the text. While most theorists would agree with the distinction of these three levels, none to my knowledge shows the interaction between the three. They usually equate two of the three or disqualify one of them. Schleiermacher distinguishes the grammatical from the psychological interpretations, each requiring its own method (1977), but he does not consider seriously level three. Novitz draws an analogous distinction between elaborative interpretations, which "gratuitously elaborate by 'filling in' the indeterminacies of a work," and elucidatory interpretations, which "seek specifically to understand and to explain" (2002, 106).

A similar distinction can be found in the work of Jorge Gracia, who differentiates meaning interpretation, the aim of which "is to provide an understanding of the meaning of the text," from relational interpretation, which provides "an understanding of the relation of a text or its meaning to something else" (2000, 47). A Marxist or feminist interpretation of Thomas Aquinas's *Summa Theologiae* would be an example of a relational interpretation. But these theorists do not distinguish the link between levels one and two. The dispute between actual and hypothetical intentionalists concerns the first level, what an author meant. But they conflate what an author meant with what a text means. Hirsch, who can be called an actual intentionalist (although with some qualifications), distinguishes between verbal meaning and significance, but he equates verbal meaning with author's intention, level one, while significance is level three. Beardsley calls Hirsch's position the identity thesis: "that what a literary work means is identical to what its author meant in composing it" (1992, 25). When Margolis defends his robust relativism on the basis of the fact that it is very difficult to demarcate a description of the features of the text from an interpretation of the features imputed to the text, he considers only levels two and three.

I consider the interaction among these three levels of meaning to be central to a theory of interpretation as well as to the practice of interpretation. It is my contention that much of the disagreement among theorists, especially monists and pluralists, comes from their simplified understanding of what an intention is and what a text's meaning is.

The three notions of author's intention, literal meaning, and representative content constitute in an ascending order what we encounter when we interpret. When we read a text, we treat it as an entity, and we can only do that when we presuppose that it conveys something. It must be the embodiment of an intention, whatever that intention may be and whatever we may decide to do with it. It only means that, if I read a text, I treat it differently than I would treat scrambled passages or letters put randomly on a page. (And if I try to interpret scrambled passages, I will try to find out the intention of someone who wanted to write a scrambled passage—such as a psychologist writing a psychological test for aphasia—or the intention of someone who wanted to convey something—like some Broca's aphasia patients who have lost the capacity to represent grammatical links.) What is puzzling regarding this notion of intention is that very few theorists seem aware of the distinction made by Schleiermacher, Wilhelm Dilthey, and later Husserl between an intention that is a psychological moment—what is going on in the author's mind—and an intention that is a publicly available moment once this intention has been formed and articulated, in our case through words. The latter was what Schleiermacher, Dilthey, and Husserl focused on.

When Gadamer dismisses the author's intention, he only considers the psychological and private intentional moment. After him a whole generation of theorists in the continental tradition adopted this view as a canon. Replying to the view I defend in this book, a representative from this tradition once conveyed to me quite forcefully that Gadamer and Derrida had clearly undermined the notion of author's intention.

When I consider a text as conveying something, I must have understood a minimal level of meaning. It is what our mastery of language allows us to grasp immediately: what the sequences of words mean, given the meaning of the individual words and the grammar of the language, even if we may decide to modify this level of meaning, because of an interest in cultural or individual unconscious, or downplay it to focus on ideas and concepts. Regarding this level of meaning—what a text means—theorists for the most part do not take into consideration the difference between what a sentence means in terms of what its components mean and what a sentence means in terms of the intentional state it expresses. Saussure is the linguist who most clearly showed that there is a level of meaning at the semiotic level of words distinguishable from the level of meaning of an intentional state. By the words I use I can convey an attitude of disrespect or of lack of sensitivity without being consciously aware of it at the level of what I mean. Regarding intentional states, John Searle has convincingly demonstrated their public character in his reflections on speech acts and intentionality such that, when I speak, I make use of a "fungible" intentionality.

When we put together these two levels of meaning, semiotic and intentional, it appears that these two levels of meaning in one sense precede the speaker: she has to make use of words as existing in her language and she has to borrow what are acceptable intentional states in her community; however, because there is on her part a choice both of words and intentional states, she is accountable for what she said and expressed. When we apply these considerations to a text, its meaning cannot just be either what the words and sentences mean or what the author meant. Meaning, in other words, cannot just be either semiotic (language speaks) or mental (the author's thought). The meaning of the text is both semiotic and mental: it is what the sentences mean as made up of the words written and as chosen by the author as conveying those intentional states that a speaker of this language would understand. Because we have this interaction between two levels of meaning in the text itself, we cannot simply distinguish between two moments—for example, a verbal meaning and the significance this meaning has for readers—as Hirsch does, or between what lies in the text and what we impute to the text, as in Margolis. Before any significance (Hirsch) or imputation (Margolis), we already have two moments, semiotic and mental. The significance or imputation is in fact a third level of meaning, what I call the representative content of the text.

In addition to the literal meaning, we need to understand what is said in the sense of what is represented. For sometimes we wonder what a sentence means—"His theological position is a round square"—or what a text means: we understand the sentences of Franz Kafka's *Trial* and still remain puzzled as to what it all means. In most types of texts, the authors try to be as clear as possible so that readers can move smoothly from what the words and sentences mean to what the text represents. There are, however, other texts, such as literary fictions, which offer an opaque representation or invite several possible readings, as in the case of Kafka. We say that they are susceptible to multiple readings. That does not mean, however, that a self-identical meaning can be extracted from the text and then applied. We do not have, as in Margolis, an opposition or competition between the text's meaning and what readers impute to the text, but an interaction. Furthermore, it is not an interaction between two levels of meaning, but three: (1) the author's intention—what someone meant by writing the text to be interpreted; (2) the literal meaning—what the text says, given the individual meanings of words and the composed meanings of sentences; (3) the representative content—what the text as a whole means in the sense of what it represents.

Because we have an interaction—philosophers of old would say a dialectic—we avoid Margolis's relativism, however robust he claimed it to be: it is not as if one level is relative to another, since none of these levels has an independent existence. Neither of these levels can be identified independently of the others. We also avoid the choice Jerrold Levinson believes is necessary when we ask the question of what literary texts mean: "I think there are only four models to choose from in answer. One is that such meaning is akin to word-sequence (e.g., sentence) meaning *simpliciter*.

Another is that it is akin to the utterer's (author's) meaning on a given occasion. A third assimilates it to the utterance meaning generated on a given occasion in specific circumstances. And a last model pictures it, most liberally, in terms of what may be called ludic meaning" (1992, 222). If we distinguish the three levels of meaning we can see how these four models are compatible without entailing any relativism.

Since interpretation of necessity has to deal with these three fluctuating levels, what gives stability to an interpretation is not one level of meaning that would anchor interpretation, but something in the process of interpretation itself, what I call the claims made by interpreters, which force interpreters into a narrative of justification. Within this process of justification, the author's intention is a necessary device not of interpretation itself (interpreters can decide to ignore an author's intention and focus on style, vocabulary, what is described, or the collective unconscious of a culture), but of the justification of the validity of an interpretation: a case has to be made as to why an interpreter can decide to leave aside the author's intention.

I understand these levels of meaning as what interpretation encounters and do not claim that they are components of a text. Rather than belonging to any ontology of the text they are categories of interpretation. A text obviously includes other features: it belongs to a genre, it has stylistic features, contains intertextual references (Kristeva 1986; Guillén 1993), and so on. These three components of what interpretation encounters are three levels at which interpreters have to make decisions and must be ready to justify these decisions: how to treat the intention, how to understand the literal meaning, and how to construe the content of what the text represents.

To counter the view that my distinctions are mere philosophical speculations, I test them against concrete practices of interpretation. Do we find any evidence that practitioners of interpretation make use of the three levels of meaning I distinguish? I examine three practices of interpretation: translation, biblical interpretation, and interpretation of novels. These practices individually illustrate best the three levels of meaning I have presented: almost by definition translation has to take a stance on what the author intended or be denied its status as translation; biblical interpretation, which usually treats its object as originating from a divine source, has to account for the status of a level of meaning that lies in the words written; and the interpretation of novels, which are mostly fictional texts not referring to real events, is the best candidate to illustrate the status of what is represented and the manner in which it matters to us.

I do not purport to offer a new method for translating, interpreting the Bible, or interpreting events in the world or literature. Rather, I take a meta-critical or philosophical position in the sense that, instead of offering a method for interpreting texts, I examine what is involved in interpretation, what kind of decisions have to be made by interpreters, what the goals are when someone interprets a particular text, and how the validity of an interpretation can be assessed. Although I cross disciplines and bridge different traditions, the metacritical position I take is phenomenological in nature: I start with an investigation of a particular practice of interpretation, describe this practice, and then examine its rules and regularities. Thus, in addition to the claim to explain, I make a stronger claim that the description corresponds to what is accomplished at the empirical level of what an interpretation does: I show how different practices such as translation, biblical interpretation, and interpretation of literature each have their own method for determining what validity means and how to assess it.

I thus do not believe that we can lump together all forms of interpretation and subsume them under a unique schema to reconstruct in a rational manner what interpretation is and involves. Annette Barnes (1988) follows such a procedure, grouping together all types of interpretation of the arts and investigating the logical status of interpretive remarks, asking whether these are statements and whether they are defeasible. Similarly, Patrick Hogan (1996), Wolfgang Iser (2000), and Paul Thom (2000) attempt to outline the general structure common to all forms of interpretation, from literary criticism to executing a piece of music. Hogan and Thom even claim that interpretations in the humanities and in the natural sciences have the same structure. Diverging from these approaches, my goal is not to construe the knowledge necessary for understanding what interpreters do, but to account for the specific manner in which interpreters actually perform their task and do justice to the specific areas of interpretation. Although I acknowledge that there is a sort of family kinship among the different forms of interpretation, I try to show how translatability into another register takes different forms in different areas of interpretation. We cannot, as Barnes, Iser, Hogan, and Thom argue, compare, for example, the discourse of ethnography or the execution of a piece of music with the interpretation of literary documents. A translator does not interpret in the same way as one reads the Bible or a piece of literary fiction.

In the second chapter I present the argument in philosophical terms through a discussion of Hans-Georg Gadamer. In the third chapter I examine the notion of author's intention through an evaluation of the positions of monism and pluralism. I discuss the views of E. D. Hirsch and Alexander Nehamas and test these two notions by comparing fifty translations in English, French, and German of a passage from Homer's *Odyssey*. In the fourth chapter I examine the status of the literal meaning. I discuss the views of Gregory the Great and John Searle on the interaction between literal meaning and background.

In chapters 5 and 6 I turn to the practice of interpreting novels and examine the notion of representative content or the status of the story told. I discuss two versions of the content of representation, which are not mutually exclusive: when we read we construe narratives or we construe intentional states. In chapter 5 I analyze the first version. I discuss Paul Ricoeur's views on the role of literature and illustrate these views through an analysis of the novel *Dog Years* by the German writer Günter Grass. In chapter 6 I turn to the second version of the representative content. I examine the claim made by the Argentinian writer Ernesto Sabato that the duty of a writer of fiction is to tell the truth. I analyze his novel *On Heroes and Tombs* and discuss John Searle's understanding of fiction as a pretended speech act.

2

Interpretation as Event

A Critique of Gadamer's Critical Pluralism

In 1960 Hans-Georg Gadamer published what was to become his master-work, *Truth and Method.* Building on Heidegger's reformulation of phenomenology in terms of hermeneutics, Gadamer offers an alternative to Dilthey's foundation of the human sciences. Instead of being governed by a method that allows objectivity, as in the case of the natural sciences, human sciences are concerned with the truth that lies outside the scope of any method. In the investigations proper to human sciences, the fact that the investigator belongs to a tradition and performs his task within a tradition is of paramount importance. Interpretation is thus, before being an act, an event that takes place within history of which the interpreter is more a parameter than an agent.

Gadamer's views have had a tremendous influence in all fields of the human sciences. He provided not just a philosophy of interpretation but a foundation for the project of human sciences in contrast to the model of natural sciences. He rejuvenated the discipline of philosophical hermeneutics and offered what has become in continental philosophy the canonic model of interpretation.

Some Ambiguities in *Truth and Method*

At the beginning of *Truth and Method,* Gadamer insists that he does not propose a new technique of interpretation, but a reflection on what happens in the act of interpreting: "The hermeneutics developed here is not . . . a methodology of the human sciences, but an attempt to understand what the human sciences truly are, beyond their methodological self-conscious-ness, and what connects them with the totality of our experience of the world. If we make understanding the object of our reflection, the aim is not an art or technique of understanding, such as traditional literary and the-ological hermeneutics sought to be" (1998, xxiii).

Or, as he puts it in the preface to the second German edition: "The pur-pose of my investigation is not to offer a general theory of interpretation and a differential account of its methods . . . but to discover what is com-mon to all modes of understanding. . ." (1998, xxxi). He repeats and stress-es the specificity of his perspective in "Hermeneutics and Historicism," originally published in 1965: "Fundamentally . . . I am describing what is the case. That it is as I describe it cannot, I think, be seriously questioned. . . . I am trying . . . to envisage in a fundamentally universal way what always happens" (1998, 512).

Gadamer's starting point is thus strictly phenomenological. He intends to find out what different ways of understanding have in common. Such a position commits him to avoid a rational reconstruction of what interpre-tation means, which would be an account explaining how interpretation works, without being accountable to the concrete ways acts of interpreta-tion are performed in everyday experience. As suggested by Hubert Drey-fus, Donald Davidson is a remarkable representative of the reconstruction school. In his investigation of the question of meaning, Davidson (2001) attempts to make the functioning of language intelligible by determining the knowledge that is necessary for understanding the sentences of that language. Since he is not interested in describing a usage as it is practiced, but only the knowledge necessary for understanding this language, the question of whether actual speakers of that language have that knowledge is irrelevant. Davidson (1984) gives this example: "'Es schneit' is true (in German) for a speaker x at time t if and only if it is snowing at t (and near x)." Here, the right-hand side of the biconditional is a sentence in the lan-guage of the descriptor expressing the belief the descriptor would have, if he were in the vicinity of x at time t. What matters is thus not what x actu-ally means but the knowledge that is necessary for making sense of the noises x makes.

One of the requirements for a theory of meaning is that "knowledge of the theory suffices for understanding the utterances of speakers" (Davidson 1984, 215). The reconstruction consists in correlating noises made by x on particular occasions with beliefs caused by the environment on those particular occasions, which a normal speaker would form. "We must view meaning itself as a theoretical construction. Like any construct, it is arbitrary except for the formal and empirical constraints we impose on it. In the case of meaning, the constraints cannot uniquely fix the theory of interpretation" (Davidson 1980, 256–57). The difference between the phenomenological perspective and reconstruction lies in part in the ways theories can be refuted. In phenomenology, a theory is refuted through its inadequacy—its lack of harmony—with what is described as it gives itself in experience; in a reconstruction, through its internal incoherence or low explanatory power.

Gadamer's phenomenological project commits him to avoid rational reconstructions and to provide evidence supporting the proposed thesis, a commitment he does not satisfy. Furthermore—and this is linked to the first problem, either as its cause or its consequence—he does not always provide detailed arguments for his views but instead just asserts them, which makes it difficult to delineate exactly his position. He asserts, for example, that his views do not lead to relativism, but he does not supply the criteria that would prevent the derivation of relativism from his views. He asserts that he does not conceive of language as the acting subject imposing constraints on human beings but does not show the difference between this and his own position.

Gadamer often presents his thoughts as lying between two extremes, as if these two extremes constituted a necessary polarity, an either/or. To present a third view, as he does, would indeed offer an original position that would be justified *a contrario* by refusing the polarity. However, this strategy so dear to Gadamer only works if the two poles between which he wants to drive a wedge indeed constitute a true dichotomy, that is, if they are two mutually exclusive positions. For if a mean position is possible, Gadamer must offer a justification for his views other than the refusal of the polarity, lest his views become vaguely situated on a continuum without clear indication of where he stands and how far he wants to go in one direction or the other.

The result is not that Gadamer contradicts himself or that he can be refuted. Rather, his views are largely ambiguous, which leaves interpreters in the infelicitous position of either attacking Gadamer, as does Habermas (1977), or choosing the apologetic approach, selecting one option as the most plausible candidate for what Gadamer really meant, as sympathetic commentators have done. I focus here on some of these ambiguities, revolving around three fundamental themes in Gadamer's hermeneutics: the fusion of horizons, the active role of the interpreter, and the status of language.

The Fusion of Horizons

From the beginning Gadamer rejects the methods of sciences that claim to retrieve the meaning of a text in its pristine state, before and independently of a tradition that has continued since this meaning arose. "Understanding is certainly not concerned with 'understanding historically'—i.e., reconstructing the way the text came into being. Rather, one intends to understand the text itself. But this means that the interpreter's own thoughts too have gone into re-awakening the text's meaning" (1998, 388). The participation of the interpreter in the process of interpretation and the identification of the object is called a fusion of horizons, in which the interpreter starts from where she is, with her cultural background in what Gadamer calls a tradition, and moves toward a text that may have been produced in another horizon of the tradition. The interpreter's horizon fuses with the horizon of what is to be interpreted in such a way that a third horizon is created. This is the event of interpretation. At this moment the tradition becomes richer and moves forward, because a link has been established between a text from the past and an interpreter from the present.

To the extent that Gadamer recognizes that interpretation is an act performed by an interpreter, he remains within the phenomenological line of thought: interpreting is an act of consciousness. The fact that there is a fusion, however, makes interpretation an event (*Geschehen*; 1998, xxiii). The concept of fusion of horizons presents itself implicitly as crossing between a Husserlian phenomenological perspective and a perspective pertaining to Heidegger's transformation of phenomenology into a hermeneutics: the act cannot be separated from the horizon from which it arises, so that an act, such as an interpretation, is an event in which an identity can be found for both the act and the object.

Gadamer thus stretches the phenomenological principle according to which a meaning is always for consciousness. He integrates a historical perspective: a meaning is for historically situated consciousness. This stretching or reformulation of the phenomenological principle leads him, however, to make assertions of general scope that are not self-evident. It also leads him to use strong terms for which he does not offer a justification, so that these terms can be understood either as outlandish literal assertions or as forgivable exaggerations because they are tempered by other, tamer passages. Gadamer writes, for example, "[There is] an insuperable difference between the interpreter and the author that is created by historical distance. Every age has to understand a transmitted text in its own way. . . . The real meaning of a text . . . is always co-determined also by the historical situation of the interpreter and hence by the totality of the objective course of history. . . . Not just occasionally but always, the meaning of a text goes beyond its author. That is why understanding is not merely a reproductive but always a productive [*produktiv*] activity as well" (1998, 296).

The terminology Gadamer uses in this quotation raises a significant and rather strong claim that he must defend in order to justify the use of these terms. For one does not readily see why there is necessarily an insuperable distance between an interpreter and an author of the past, or why it is necessary for an era to understand a text in its own way, and even less self-evident is the claim that an interpretation is always productive. It would be quite acceptable, but also somewhat trivial, to transform the necessity into a contingency: "There may be cases where there is an insuperable difference between the interpreter and the author," and so on.

Gadamer summarizes his views in the famous formula, "We understand in a different way, if we understand at all" (1998, 297). We understand in a different way because our consciousness, which is anchored in history, transposes itself with its horizon in the object or person to be understood. "Transposing ourselves consists neither in the empathy of one individual for another nor in subordinating another person to our own standards; rather, it always involves rising to a higher universality that overcomes not only our own particularity but also that of the other" (1998, 305). Here again one does not immediately see why it is necessary to understand a text differently nor does one see the ground of the general scope of the proposition.

Now, instead of redeeming his strong assertions by providing us with evidence, Gadamer hastens to temper his own views, obviously in order to prevent misunderstandings. "It is constantly necessary to guard against overhastily assimilating the past to our own expectations of meaning. Only then can we listen to tradition in a way that permits it to make its own meaning heard" (1998, 305). Or again: "The interpreter's own horizon is decisive, yet not as a personal standpoint that he maintains or enforces, but more as an opinion and a possibility that one brings into play and puts at risk, and that helps one truly to make one's own what the text says" (1998, 388).

On the one hand, Gadamer denies our capacity to retrieve the meaning of a text in its original state. Given that we are necessarily anchored in a tradition, we color the meaning of the text to be interpreted and thus intervene in the genesis of this meaning. But on the other hand, we must believe Gadamer that this does not amount to simply imposing our own views and expectations on the text of the past, but rather leads to the creation of a space where the alterity of the text can speak to us.

Gadamer asks us to believe a position that is surely attractive but difficult to defend, if mechanisms are not provided to prevent the fusion of horizons from devastating the text, or understanding from becoming mere projection or speculation. The difficulty is that, in a fusion of horizons, the horizons in question are always moving and can only be identified after the fusion has taken place. Gadamer acknowledges that the fusion does not take place between two horizons that could exist independently of one another. "If, however, there is no such thing as these distinct horizons, why do we speak of the fusion of horizons and not simply of the formation of one horizon, whose bounds are set in the depths of tradition?" (1998, 306). The reason for this, Gadamer continues, lies in the fact that historical consciousness, the one that transposes itself into another horizon, is itself "only something superimposed upon continuing tradition" (306). The interpreter is himself situated in the tradition and it is from his own position in the tradition that he participates in and even causes a process of fusion to start. "In the process of understanding, a real fusing of horizons occurs—which means that as the historical horizon is projected, it is simultaneously superseded" (307).

Gadamer characterizes this demand for fusion as a claim (*Anspruch*) that the tradition makes to the interpreter. "I must allow tradition's claim to validity, not in the sense of simply acknowledging the past in its otherness, but in such a way that it has something to say to me" (1998, 361). This claim that the tradition makes to the interpreter takes the form of a question. Gadamer calls this the logic of question and answer, which governs any process of interpretation and understanding. "That a historical text is made the object of interpretation means that it puts a question to the interpreter. . . . To understand a text means to understand this question" (369–70). To recover this question, one has to go beneath what the text says; one has to reconstruct the question, not yet formulated, starting with the answer formulated in the text to be interpreted. Since the question formulated in the text can only be grasped by entering the horizon of the text, one has to enter that horizon guided by anticipation or by a question that originates with the interpreter. There are thus two questions that set the act of interpreting into motion: (1) the question to which the text responds—that which is beneath the text, prior to its materialization, and which can only be grasped in (2) the question that the interpreter asks the text—that which is beyond the text, deriving from the text.

Gadamer writes, "Thus a person who wants to understand must question what lies *behind* what is said. He must understand it as an answer to a question. If we go back behind what is said, then we inevitably ask questions *beyond* what is said. We understand the sense of the text only by acquiring the horizon of the question—a horizon that, as such, necessarily includes other possible answers. Thus the meaning of a sentence is relative to the question to which it is a reply, but that implies that its meaning necessarily exceeds what is said in it" (1998, 370).

Although he characterizes the understanding of the question to which a given text gives an answer as a *Rekonstruktion* (reconstruction), Gadamer also claims that "in the beginning there is the question that the text puts to us" (1998, 373; translation modified). The only explanation he gives is that we have been reached by the word of the tradition (*das betroffensein von dem Wort der Überlieferung*; 373; translation modified) or addressed by such a word (*das uns anspricht*). From the claim (*Anspruch*) the tradition makes to us or this right that the tradition exercises over us, we reconstruct the question to which the text has to respond. Understanding is thus a reconstructed question: "Reconstructing the question to which the text is presumed to be the answer itself takes place within a process of questioning through which we try to answer the question that the tradition asks us" (374; translation modified). This dialectic of question and answer, which precedes the dialectic of interpretation, "is what determines understanding as an event [*Geschehen*]" (472).

Gadamer thereby describes in a judicious and attractive manner an intermingling of questions that sets in motion a dialectic between the text and the interpreter. But he does not show exactly how this dialectic gains its momentum between the two questions, the one the text asks the interpreter as a claim made by the tradition and the one the interpreter asks the text as the response to that claim. What are the mechanisms that would prevent an interpreter from using the text for her own purposes, or at least that would allow a second interpreter to say that the first one missed the text? In short, Gadamer does not indicate how this dialectic permits one to say, "This is what the text means," instead of, "This is what I find in it." The former statement includes a claim to validity, whereas the latter does not.

As for the danger of arbitrariness, Gadamer contents himself with a mere assertion: "This is not to open the door to arbitrariness in interpretation but to reveal what always takes place" (1998, 374). This is again the phenomenological claim to describe and to be accountable to what is. But the only proof of adequacy confines itself to a mere assertion: "It is . . . indubitable that it remains the same work whose fullness of meaning is realized in the changing process of understanding" (373).

The Active Role of the Interpreter

One can best see the ambiguity of Gadamer's position in the way he characterizes the active role of the interpreter in the act of interpretation. Understanding is "always a productive activity" (1998, 296). Negatively, he means that "understanding is always more than merely reproducing [*Nachvollziehen*] someone else's meaning" (375). He also uses the term "re-creating" (*Nachschaffen*): "In a certain sense interpretation probably is re-creation [*Nachschaffen*], but this is a re-creation not of the creative act but of the created work, which has to be brought to representation in accord with the meaning the interpreter finds in it" (119). Sometimes he has recourse to the term "reproduction" (*Nachbilden*) in the case of translation, which is a case of understanding and interpretation. "Here no one can doubt that the translation of a text, however the translator may have dwelt with and empathized with his author, cannot be simply a reawakening [*Wiedererweckung*] of the original process in the writer's mind; rather it is necessarily a reproduction [*Nachbildung*] of the text guided by the way the translator understands what it says. No one can doubt that what we are dealing with here is interpretation and not simply a reeffectuation [*Mitvollzug*]" (385–86; translation modified).

Because of this difference, a translator can only offer a compromise, despite the fact that he tries "to transpose himself completely into his author" (Gadamer 1998, 386). Gadamer even says that interpretation is a new creation, because the interpreter speaks from her own milieu and language. "For the interpreting word is the word of the interpreter; it is not the language and the dictionary of the interpreted text. This means that assimilation [*Aneignung*] is no mere reproduction [*Nachvollzug*] or repetition [*Nachreden*] of the traditionary text; it is a new creation [*neue Schöpfung*] of understanding" (473). Interpretation is a new creation because the text has meaning when it is related to the subject who understands and not to the subject who wrote the text. "If emphasis has been—rightly—placed on the fact that all meaning is related to the I, this means, as far as the hermeneutical experience is concerned, that all the meaning of what is handed down to us finds its concretion (i.e., is understood) in its relation to the understanding I—and not in reconstructing [*Rekonstruktion*] the originally intending I" (473).

Here again Gadamer uses a powerful formula, new creation, to characterize the act of interpreting, while at the same time defending a more mitigated position: "Only that translator can truly render [*nachbilden*] a text who brings into language the subject matter that the text points to; but this means finding a language that is not only his but also appropriate to the original" (1998, 387; translation modified). When Gadamer says that the interpretation is productive, he means that the behavior of the interpreter takes place in a conversation (*Gespräch*) with a mutual exchange between text and interpreter. The logic of conversation is the logic of question and answer, and the productive character of interpretation results from such a logic. For in this conversation the interpreter is the one who has the initiative, given the fact that the text only speaks if the interpreter gives it voice: "It is true that a text does not speak to us in the same way as does a Thou. We who are attempting to understand must ourselves make it speak" (377). It is because he is "reached" (*erreicht*) and "called upon" (*aufgerufen*) that the interpreter can question the text, so that making the text speak is nothing else than formulating the response that we expect from the text according to the question that we put to the text. This manner of giving voice in interpreting "as a question . . . is related to the answer that is expected in the text" (377). Gadamer quickly asserts that "this kind of understanding, 'making the text speak,' is not an arbitrary procedure that we undertake on our own initiative" (377). To lend voice to the text is the manner in which the interpreter responds to the claim (*Anspruch*) of the tradition.

But is this a sufficient justification? An interpreter who would use the text and manipulate it for personal, activist, revisionist, or political goals could borrow Gadamer's vocabulary of new creation and production. She could justify her manipulation by the Gadamerian principle that "one partner in the hermeneutical conversation, the text, speaks only through the other partner, the interpreter. Only through him are the written marks changed into meaning" (1998, 387). Gadamer clearly would not agree with the arbitrary use of a text. It would thus be pointless to accuse him of arbitrariness. Yet he only offers dogmatic assertions against arbitrariness. On what basis could Gadamer say to that interpreter who misuses the text that she is wrong, that what she does is not interpreting? What are the criteria of the validity of an interpretation?

The ambivalence in Gadamer is that he uses powerful formulas to describe the active role of the interpreter and, to temper this aspect of intervention, adds that such an intervention is what the text asks for or what the tradition demands. This leads Gadamer to take a rather radical position regarding the validity of an interpretation: "Understanding is not a psychic transposition. The horizon of understanding cannot be limited either by what the writer originally had in mind or by the horizon of the person to whom the text was originally addressed" (1998, 395). The hermeneutic rule of introducing nothing into a text that the author or first readers could not have had in mind is quite reasonable, Gadamer acknowledges, and even largely accepted, but it only applies in extreme cases. Texts, Gadamer says, do not ask to be understood as living expressions of the subjectivity of the author. "What is fixed in writing has detached itself from the contingency of its origin and its author and made itself free for new relationships. Normative concepts such as the author's meaning or the original reader's understanding in fact represent only an empty space that is filled from time to time in understanding" (395).

Since we can appeal neither to the author nor to the first audience, and since the text has gained a life of its own at the moment it was written and circulated, the conclusion follows: "There cannot, therefore, be any single interpretation that is correct 'in itself,' precisely because every interpretation is concerned with the text itself. The historical life of a tradition depends on being constantly assimilated and interpreted. An interpretation that was correct in itself would be a foolish ideal that mistook the nature of tradition" (Gadamer 1998, 397).

Gadamer goes even further: "In view of the finitude of our historical existence, it would seem that there is something absurd about the whole idea of a unique, correct interpretation" (1998, 120). The absence of correctness in itself is due to the dependence of interpretation on the situation, and, Gadamer claims, "Being bound by the situation does not mean that the claim to correctness [*der Anspruch auf Richtigkeit*] that every interpretation must make is dissolved into the subjective or the occasional" (397).

Besides the dogmatic aspect of Gadamer's denials of arbitrariness and relativism, his rejection of the author's role seems to rely on a narrow understanding of what author means. "Our understanding of written tradition per se is not such that we can simply presuppose that the meaning we discover in it agrees with what its author intended" (1998, 372). What the author intended is what happens in the author's mind, which leads to the aporia of historicism: "Reconstructing what the author really had in mind is a limited undertaking. Historicism tempts us to regard such a reduction as a scientific virtue and to regard understanding as a kind of reconstruction which in effect repeats the process whereby the text came into being" (373). This goal of understanding as reconstruction was the ideal of romantic hermeneutics, which Gadamer vehemently criticizes: "Understanding is not based on transposing oneself into another person, on one person's immediate participation with another. To understand what a person says is . . . not to get inside another person and relive his experiences" (383). What matters in interpretation is "the substantive rightness of his opinion," and for grasping it, "we do not relate the other's opinion to him but to our own opinions and views" (385).

Gadamer thereby concocts an opposite view that he refutes without realizing that this opposite view is so caricatural that refuting it neither clarifies nor supports his own views. He thinks that the only alternative to his views is a return to the reliving (*Nacherlebnis*) or reproducing (*Nachvollziehen*) as advocated by Dilthey and Schleiermacher. Since this alternative is not acceptable, Gadamer seems to argue, the only viable option is to discard the author's experience as telos and norm. And doing so, he adds, does not amount to arbitrarily projecting what the interpreter wants to see or hear in the work. "But the fact that the representation is bound to the work is not lessened by the fact that this bond can have no fixed criterion. Thus we do not allow the interpretation of a piece of music or a drama the freedom to take the fixed 'text' as a basis for arbitrary, ad-lib effects, and yet we would regard the canonization of a particular interpretation—e.g., in a recorded performance conducted by the composer, or the detailed notes on performance which come from the canonized first performance—as a failure to appreciate the real task of interpretation" (1998, 119).

The analogy between an author writing a text and knowing what he means and a composer writing down his music and playing it may be misleading. First, the relation between intending and writing is not analogous to the relation between composing a piece of music and playing it. It is well known that a composer can be a bad performer, so that a piano player can perform a composer's piece better than the composer himself can. It would thus be odd to claim that the mistakes made by the composer when performing his own music are part of what the piece of music means. So, in general, Gadamer is right that the composer's performance of his own music is no necessary standard for how to play it. But the same does not transfer directly to a writer. While a composer can be a poor performer, a writer cannot easily have good meaning-intentions and be bad at writing, since it is the writing that makes him a writer, not his intentions. As Stéphane Mallarmé reminded Edgar Degas, who complained that he had difficulty writing poetry although he had ideas, poetry is made of words, not ideas.

A second difference between composer and writer lies in the type of articulation they provide. While a composer has to follow rules of harmony, genres, and so on for composing, a writer has to follow more than the rules of grammar for writing. Although it has sometimes been argued that music is a language, a sequence of notes does not represent as articulated a level of meaning as a sequence of words. Words before being used are already endowed with a meaning within the sociolinguistic sphere, and sentences in order to be meaningful must express intentional states that are possible within a linguistic community. The writer selects not just words and sequences of words but also the meanings that go with those words and sequences of words. His intention is thus more articulated than the intention of a composer and, because of that, more easily identifiable. While one can see in Ludwig van Beethoven's *Moonlight Sonata* an evocation of romantic moonlight or a hymn to sadness, a text offers more constraints on interpreters in the sense that they have to take into account the customary meaning of words and sentences. For example, an interpreter cannot claim without further justification that Henry James's sentence at the end of *The Portrait of a Lady*, "She walked him away with her . . . as if she had given him now the key to patience," means that a war is going to break out. The relationship between a composer to the performance of his music is thus significantly different from the relationship of a writer to his text. Dismissing the original performance of a piece of music as canonic does not entail the dismissal of the intention of a text's author. In his legitimate effort to show the active role of interpreters, Gadamer excludes the author from the equation of meaning without any serious justification.

The Status of Language

A final ambiguity pertains to the role of language and Gadamer's notion of application. "To understand what a person says is . . . to come to an agreement in a language. . . . We emphasized that the experience [*Erfahrung*] of meaning that takes place in understanding always includes application. Now we are to note that this whole process is verbal. . . . Language is the medium in which substantive understanding and agreement take place among people" (1998, 383–84; translation modified). By language, Gadamer does not only mean that the agreement needs a medium, for example in the form of arguments, but rather and especially the fact that what exists is, in its ontological status, linked to language. There is an "enigmatic intimacy" between thinking and speaking that "conceals the role of language in thought" (389).

This enigmatic intimacy is not just the fact that a language, with its syntactic and lexical resources, is "a process which has no single knowing and choosing consciousness standing over against it. (Thus it is literally more correct to say that language speaks us, rather than that we speak it)" (Gadamer 1998, 463). More important is the fact that language is "the hermeneutical event proper" that consists "in the coming into language of what has been said in the tradition. . . . Thus here it really is true to say that this event is not our action upon the thing, but the act of the thing itself" (463).

Language mediates what we say, so that the act, for example, an act of interpretation, becomes an event of which we are a parameter rather than an agent. This allows Gadamer to claim that it is language that acts. Because it allows a tradition to live, language pertains to the ontological constitution of what is, of the interpreter and of things in the world. Language, Gadamer says, "is a medium where I and world meet or, rather, manifest their original belonging together" (1998, 474). Language is that space of presentation or that event in which "a coming into language of a totality of meaning" occurs (474). To the extent that everything toward which understanding turns is permeated by language, language pertains to a universal ontological structure. Gadamer gathers his views in another powerful formula: "Being that can be understood is language" (474). Things become meaningful only when they can be understood, and they can be understood only when they can be brought to language. Language is thus not only what allows things to manifest their ontological status but also what, literally, constitutes their ontological status. The ontological constitution of what is understood is "in a universal sense . . . language" (475), and the relationship we have to beings is an interpretation. "Thus we speak not only of a language of art but also of a language of nature—in short, of any language that things have" (475).

This prominence of language, Gadamer believes, does not amount to a hypostatization of language: "Language is not the subject eventually found of all the processes and actions that take place in society and in history, the subject that would present itself, with the totality of its activities and objectifications, to our gaze as analysts. Language is rather the play in which we are all partners, without any of us having priority over the others" (1999, 98). Analogously, Gadamer says that a claim to truth is still very much in place in such a view of language: "That this does not in the least relativize the claim to truth [*Wahrheitsanspruch*] of every interpretation is seen from the fact that all interpretation is essentially verbal" (1998, 398). As for relativism, Gadamer stresses that language does not imprison those who speak: "But the fact that we live entirely in language is not a relativism, because we are absolutely not imprisoned in a language—not even in our native language" (1999, 43).

As with the fusion of horizons and the active role of the interpreter, Gadamer asserts his rejection of relativism but does not offer a model that would allow invalidation of an arbitrary interpretation. So, what is missing in his model? What could avoid the risks of arbitrariness and relativism?

Interpretation as Act

As a rational reconstruction of the process of interpretation, Gadamer's views offer a clear and attractive explanation of the fact that interpretation is an event. But to the extent that he wants to describe what happens in the process of interpretation, Gadamer wants more. From a phenomenological point of view, Gadamer misses a fundamental component of interpretation: it is an act performed by someone who believes he knows what he does and intends to take responsibility for what he says. Any interpreter of texts would accept the proposition that he speaks from his own cultural background when, for example, approaching a text from a different cultural horizon. In this sense interpretation is an event that takes place in a specific culture at a specific historical time. This same interpreter would probably accept the fact that he only offers the best approximation of which he is capable, leaving the door open to better future interpretations. I doubt, however, that the majority of interpreters would accept Gadamer's conclusion that they only offer a fusion of horizons and do not render the original text in what this text actually says.

What makes Gadamer's account unsatisfactory is the fact that interpreters, at the moment they offer an interpretation, usually do not themselves say that what they offer is a compromise, a new creation, or a production, to use Gadamerian formulas, even if, to repeat, they would have no problem using these qualifications to describe the interpretations of those who preceded them or of some of their contemporaries. On this point I agree with P. D. Juhl: "Critics who propose and defend an interpretation of a work do not usually claim merely that their reading is possible or plausible; rather, they typically claim implicitly, if not explicitly, that it is more likely to be correct than the various other interpretations which they have considered in determining what the text means" (1980, 213). If an interpreter wants to convince a publisher to print a new interpretation of the *Odyssey*, he must claim that his interpretation is better than existing ones or is original in some respect. As soon as a claim is made, the interpreter is engaged in his responsibility to defend his interpretation, if prompted—and very often interpreters do this unprompted in order to be published.

There is thus a capital difference between the historical or cultural perspective that describes the process of interpretation as an event and the perspective of the one who performs an act in interpreting and, by so doing, engages his responsibility. The former perspective can be called the third-person perspective and the latter the first-person perspective. One could also call the former the descriptive perspective (of the one who observes from the outside) and the latter the pragmatic perspective (since the latter is anchored in the practice). Gadamer only considers the descriptive, or third-person, perspective and does not take into account the pragmatic, or first-person, perspective. When he qualifies interpretation unilaterally, although accompanied by tempering formulations, as an event, he misses the component of act in the phenomenon of interpretation. A phenomenological perspective, which claims to describe what takes place in interpretation, as Gadamer does, must give an account of both aspects, act and event, to do justice to the phenomenon of interpretation. In this sense, Gadamer only gives us a reconstruction, which, as such, remains attractive and of significant interest. Where he fails, however, is precisely in his phenomenological claim to account for what takes place in the process of interpretation.

Gadamer gives an example of fusion of horizons: "In fifty or a hundred years, anybody who reads the history of these tribes [what he calls the Eskimo] as it is written today will not only find it outdated (for in the meantime he will know more or interpret the sources more correctly); he will also be able to see that in the 1960s people read the sources differently because they were moved by different questions, prejudices, and interests" (Gadamer 1998, xxxii).

As a reconstruction of what happens to most historical writings, Gadamer is right. There is, however, no necessity for a historical account to become obsolete, let alone refuted. Gadamer makes this generalization: most interpretations of the past have become outmoded, if not false, so all interpretations will become outmoded, if not false. Two replies are available. First, Gadamer has not demonstrated and does not even claim that all past interpretations have become outmoded, if not false. His argument cannot thus rely on inductive generalization. Second, it is empirical evidence about past interpretations—they missed their object or grasped it only from one vantage point—that allows us to make these judgments. Unless we have empirical proofs that present and future historical accounts will become obsolete or false, there is no basis for asserting that in principle that will be the case. It would be paradoxical for a historian, for example, to claim at the same time that she contributes to the knowledge of the past and that her present interpretation will be false fifty years from now, unless she demonstrates why this will be the case. Without further justification other than such was the fate of most interpretations, most readers of this historical account would at best not understand why this author herself belittles the relevance of her work and at worst not even bother to read these investigations the very author of which already considers to bear the potential to be outmoded and false.

To speak of a fusion of horizons is only legitimate when we take a descriptive. or third-person, perspective and on the basis of some evidence that interpreters extrapolated and projected their cultural values or prejudices into the object to be interpreted. Fusion suggests that, from a mutual give-and-take, a third milieu arises that is neither that of the original alone nor that of the interpreter alone. As an empirical result, such a fusion is most likely what happens in an interpretation. From a retrospective stance we can qualify most interpretations of the past as such a fusion between what the text offered and what readers could find intelligible in it, since we know that for most interpretations belonging to the past, better ones followed that provided evidence of the partial failures of the previous ones. In this sense, a fusion of horizons holds as an empirical statement about what happens to most interpretations.

The fusion of horizons does not account, however, for the pragmatic aspect of an interpreter presenting his interpretation. An interpreter cannot himself judge his own present work from a future point of view he cannot presently occupy. When interpreters interpret, they do not have the future perspective of a better interpretation available, from which it could be seen that the present interpretation is just a fusion of horizons. This would mean to commit what I call the future-perfect fallacy, consisting in speaking in the future perfect: "I now qualify what I say because, fifty years from now, it will have been shown that I fused my horizon with the horizon of the text." This future perspective, strictly speaking, cannot belong to interpreters. Thus, an interpreter cannot say, at the price of sinking into pragmatic difficulties, "My interpretation is true, but of course I can be wrong." To such an interpreter it could be replied that he does not know what true means, that he does not master what Ludwig Wittgenstein would call the grammar of the term true.

At the moment someone presents a new interpretation, this person performs an act and thereby is committed to defend the validity of what she says. This pragmatic aspect surfaces in the warnings and disclaimers that researchers make when presenting the results of their research, so that they do not claim more than what they can support.

The pragmatic aspect of interpretation can be described through four parameters of interpretation. The act performed by an interpreter (1) involves claims, (2) is linguistic in nature (writing or uttering statements), (3) is situated in particular discourses with their rules and goals, and (4) is part of a conversation within a community of interpreters and readers. The first of these components is the notion of claim at the heart of what the performance of an act involves.

The Claims of a Speech Act

Common sense and theorists of language agree that speakers when saying something claim to do something. Implicitly, we take a person who publicly outlines an interpretation to say, "This is what I believe," so that we believe the person to be truthful. Since the person says something about something, we take that person to refer to a specific object and to say implicitly, "What I say is true," so that the person claims to tell the truth. In addition, since the person says something to somebody and thus interacts with others, we take the person also to say implicitly, "What I say is right and just and appropriate given the set of present circumstances," so that the person makes a claim to rightness.

The claims to truth and truthfulness have been put at the core of what it means to make an utterance or to perform a speech act by people as different as Paul Grice (2001), through his cooperative principle; Searle (1979), through his rules of illocutionary acts; the German linguist Karl Bühler

(1965), through his connection among the expressive realm, the representative realm, and the normative realm; and Apel (1980, 1998) and Habermas (1984), through their validity claims.

Grice explains the cooperative principle as a set of rules that participants in a conversation ought to follow for the conversation to be such. Borrowing from Kant, he spells out four categories of rules, including one or several maxims (2001, 167–70). The category of quantity includes the amount of information to be provided. The maxim says, "Make your contribution as informative as is required." The category of quality includes the maxims "Do not say what you believe to be false" and "Do not say that for which you lack adequate evidence." The category of relation includes the maxim "Be relevant." Finally, the category of manner includes the maxims "Avoid obscurity of expression," "Avoid ambiguity," "Be brief," and "Be orderly." Grice also mentions other sorts of maxims, aesthetic, social, or moral, such as "Be polite."

Searle, expanding the program of J. L. Austin, refines Grice's views and attempts to determine the different types of illocutionary acts. He finds five types: assertive, directive, declarative, commissive, and expressive (Searle 1979, 12–20). For each of these types he attempts to spell out all the rules necessary for the success of the illocutionary act. For example, an act of assertion, such as "It is raining," is governed by four rules, in which we can see an obvious overlap with Grice's cooperative principle. (1) I commit myself to the truth of what I say. This is the essential condition and not satisfying it amounts to telling something false. (2) I claim to be in a position to provide evidence or reasons for the truth of what I say. Not being in such a position amounts to making unsubstantiated claims. (3) I claim to have a point, namely that what I say is not obviously true to the person I talk to. Not to fulfill that claim means to make a pointless statement. (4) I commit myself to believing that what I say is true and thus being truthful. This is the sincerity condition and not fulfilling it amounts to lying (62). Let us note that the truth condition is different from the sincerity condition, since a person can tell something false while believing it is true.

Writing long before Austin, Grice, and Searle, Bühler, in his book *Sprachtheorie* of 1934, distinguishes three components in language that correspond to the three parameters of language: sender, addressee, and things. To the sender there corresponds in language the function of expression (*Ausdruck*), which links what is said to the internal field of the speaker. To things there corresponds the function of representation (*Darstellung*), which links what is said to the external world. And to the addressee there corresponds the function of appeal (*Appell*), which links what is said to those to whom it is said (1965, 29). Regarding this last term, Bühler notes, "the Latin word *appellare* (English: appeal, German: *ansprechen*) is appropriate" (29; my translation). This last component does not receive much attention in Austin and Searle, although Grice mentions a category of morality: when speaking, the speaker is engaged in the normative or ethical realm of the community in the sense that what he says is intended to have an effect on someone else.

Habermas and Apel combine the views of Bühler, on the one hand, and Austin and Searle, on the other, and offer an original reformulation of the speech-act theory in pragmatic terms. When speaking, speakers not only do something with words, as Austin and Searle showed, but are committed to other human beings as well, as Bühler claims (Apel 1976, 53–80; 1980, 54–55; 1998, 238–39; Habermas 1984, 307–8). Apel and Habermas show that the act of speaking is a full-blown action involving speakers not only as instances of illocutionary acts but also as real agents intervening in the world through their utterance. The claims or commitments that Searle sees as constitutive of the linguistic act are now constitutive of the engagement between the speaking person and a real community. When people communicatively interact, they make validity claims either implicitly or explicitly. The fact that an act is performed establishes a relationship among the internal expressive realm of the person who wants to say something, the external objective realm of things in the world, and the social normative realm of the people with whom a communication takes place.

Without discussing any further the differences among Searle, Bühler, Apel, and Habermas, I retain the thrust of their views: claims bind the speaker to justify the validity of what is said, so that the claim, which is present in any speech act, is also, once a speech act is performed, a personal commitment of a real person. Claims conflate an instance of speech with the real flesh-and-blood person who speaks. Such a commitment is realized in providing arguments supporting what is said. The act of speaking, when it presents itself as intelligible and rational, commits the speaker to argumentation, to the extent that the claim binds the speaker to abide by it, to defend it, and in short to interact with others on the basis of what is said. When performing a rational and intelligible speech act, I in fact argue (Apel 1996, 317; 1994, 156). Failing to satisfy any of these validity claims amounts to what Apel calls a performative contradiction, in the sense that the speaker, by not living up to the claim implicitly made and the commitment that goes with the claim, would thereby deny the very condition for the possibility of uttering what he says. In a performative contradiction, the propositional content of one's claim is contradicted by the claim involved in the very speech act conveying such a proposition. Apel gives several examples of such performative contradictions: "I hereby assert that I do not exist," "I hereby assert as true (i.e., intersubjectively valid) that a consensus regarding that which I assert cannot be expected in principle." Besides committing a performative contradiction, the person, as Habermas has shown, might be resorting to a strategic action where the goal is not to pursue a rational communication but to use communication for a specific effect sought, or the person might just break communication altogether.

Since interpretation takes the form of making statements outlining the content of the interpretation, and since making statements is an act, the act, like any speech act, commits interpreters to follow up on their claims if they claim any validity for their interpretation. Of course, interpreters can just enjoy a work, find inspiration in it, arbitrarily select some passages of a text, and so on. But when doing so, they cannot and usually do not ascribe to the text what they construe out of it. When claiming validity, their act of interpreting turns the claims they make into a personal commitment to redeem those claims, if asked. To interpret therefore amounts to being committed to providing arguments supporting what is said.

Several claims are involved in interpretation. There is first a claim to intelligibility, which binds the interpreter not only to speak in an intelligible manner but also to have a point in presenting an interpretation. In other words, the interpretation is not a statement of the obvious but pertains to the current conversation. The second claim binds interpreters to tell the truth, so that they implicitly accept that their interpretation will be tested for its validity, given the current state of knowledge and the methodology available. By claiming that an interpretation is true, interpreters accept arguing for it, defending it, in short, entering into a discussion with others, thereby accepting indirectly that what is presented can in principle be falsified. The third claim, to be truthful, binds interpreters regarding their own attitude toward the interpretation. They implicitly claim that they are not trying to deceive or manipulate, that the data have not been forged, that the results have not been stolen from colleagues, in short that, to the best of their knowledge, what is presented is accurate. Last, the claim to rightness commits interpreters to the larger community in which they live. They implicitly claim that the interpretation presented fits the available pragmatic circumstances, for example, that it is not harmful to others or libelous and that it will not cause social unrest or, on the contrary, that the interpretation presented aims at causing social unrest, as in the case of some artists in dictatorial regimes. Such an ambivalence of the claim to rightness, that it cannot be right to cause social unrest or that it is right to cause social unrest, indicates, first, that it does not belong to the same level as the other three claims and, second, that the rightness does not prejudge any content the claim might have.

Through all these claims interpreters, if prompted, have to engage in a narrative of justification. While any original intention coming from the text tends to be disseminated by the various perspectives on a text that interpreters can take, given their background, the claims made by interpreters unify the task of interpretation by linking them to an ongoing conversation with other interpreters or readers: through the claims they make, interpreters accept the fact that they have to justify the validity of their interpretation and situate what they do by anchoring their interpretation in a genre of discourse: academic literary criticism, scientific research, journalism, casual discussion, and so forth, and specify the kind of relevance they want for their interpretation, whether it is an adaptation, a rendition for the specific purpose of serving as the scenario for a movie, or an academic interpretation.

By their claims, interpreters situate themselves in a process in which different interpretations can be evaluated and which thus leads to progress. The progress in question, however, is merely formal or procedural. The claims made by interpreters in principle bind them to account for what they did and give reasons for why we should pay attention to what they provide. For example, within the institution of higher education, with its genre of academic discourse, it is not yet readily acceptable for faculty members to use their position in the classroom to pursue a social and political agenda by trying to shape the ways students think about specific issues. By speaking in the genre of academic discourse, the claims commit speakers to abide by the rules of such a genre of discourse. Not abiding by them, as in the example above, can lead to the charge that the faculty members are not truthful or that what they did is inappropriate.

The existence of different genres of discourse, however, testifies to the fact that claims can take a different slant depending on the genre in which they are made. The claim to truthfulness does not have the same weight and, if broken, the same consequences in a casual chat as in professional journalism. Fabricating a story during a casual supper with relatives and fabricating a story in the *Boston Globe* or the *New York Times* are not treated the same way (several journalists lost their jobs for doing the latter). The genres of discourse can also change over time. North American academic discourses in the humanities have integrated a wide array of new subjects (gay studies, women's studies, multicultural studies, feminist studies) that their western European counterparts have been reluctant to accept. Despite these variations in how claims are involved, claims regulate the conversation that takes place, in the sense that interpreters have to be ready to provide a narrative justifying what they do.

The first consequence of the claims implied in the act of interpretation involves identifying the object of interpretation by doing justice to that object. Although anything, even a natural phenomenon, can be treated as a text, the claims the interpreter makes force him to justify how the object of interpretation is to be treated. Regarding this treatment it is reasonable to believe that some objects of interpretation are intentional and others non-intentional.

When an intention permeates an object, as in the case of a text in the narrow sense of a written document, the intention is part of the definition of the object: it is because of an intention that we have a text, and it is because of an intention that we treat it as a text. Marks on rocks caused by erosion do not require the positing of an intention for explaining their production and do not require an intention for identifying them as marks. Thus, to say that scientists interpret marks left on rocks by erosion indicates that the interpretation they perform is weaker than the interpretation of the Constitution a judge performs for deciding a case. The realization that the channels and canyons on the planet Mars were the result of huge floods caused some people some disappointment, since these phenomena could be explained as natural occurrences and not as products of intelligence. Thus, if marks on rocks are interpreted in the strong sense as a text, say by a poet, a case has to be made as to why an intention is posited behind these marks. If a poem tells us that "Spring is like a perhaps hand/(which comes carefully/out of Nowhere) arranging/a window, into which people look" (Cummings 1994, 20), a case has to be made why an intention is posited behind the spring (in the case of poetry, it is because the poet, speaking in the poetic discourse, is not bound to tell scientific truths). Similarly, if an object permeated by an intention, such as the Gospels, is interpreted without regard to the original intention, then in a weak sense, the interpreter has to justify why the intentional character can be bracketed, downplayed, or even ignored, and why, for example, the Gospels can be interpreted in the light of Freudian psychoanalysis or used as a document about the flora that existed in the first century AD.

As a result, unless the goal of interpretation is just to consume and enjoy the work—in which case there is no effort and no need to justify the validity of the reading—every interpretation of an intentional object has to posit an intention behind the object of interpretation, even if it is a minimal intention—having written the text—and even if it is to dismiss it, because interpreters are interested in figures of style or in a Freudian unconscious or in cultural stereotypes or in topographic information, as in the case of Schliemann. But even those who dismiss the original intention or modify it do not deny it. They presuppose an intention behind the *Iliad*: that it was written intelligibly by someone at a certain time for certain purposes, that the sentences mean something in the original Greek language, that the story made of those sentences means something, even if after those presuppositions there is disagreement on the identity of the one who wrote, on the right sequence of verses, on the specific meaning of the sentences, and on the specific meaning of the story.

Without the presupposition of an original intention, there would be no basis for even disagreeing. Interpreters not only would talk past each other but would not even be interpreters. Even someone like Derrida, who championed the indeterminacy of meaning, wanted his position to be accurately represented and became angry and aggressive if he believed that his opponent adulterated his views. When Michel Foucault in *The Order of Things* (1970) uses works of economics, biology, medicine, and philology of the Renaissance and the seventeenth and eighteenth centuries as documents or monuments (sets of statements) testifying to the structures of knowledge governing the different ways a specific individual intention in a given period (in an *episteme*) is to be articulated, without individuals being aware of those structures at the time of articulating their intentions, he presupposes that these works were endowed with an original intention by their authors. It is precisely that presupposition that makes his work so fascinating: an order of knowledge precedes the actual intentions of authors. Deconstruction, feminism, and cultural studies followed suit and made talk of rereading, deconstructing, or disseminating fashionable and rejoiced in what they—mistakenly, in my view—took to be the death of the author.

If the original intention is presupposed in any interpretation of an intentional object (even provisionally in order to be put aside), then such an intention first has to be located and identified. Anti-intentionalists only oppose a psychological version of intention and do not seem aware of a distinction established long ago between what happens in the author's head—

the private psychological intention—and the publicly available content of intention. Schleiermacher makes such a distinction. The goal of an interpreter is indeed to transpose herself (*sich verwandeln*; Schleiermacher 1990, 169) into the author—this is the method of divination—but this transposition does not aim at recovering the private psychological persona of the author. "The task is to be formulated as follows: 'To understand the text at first as well as and then even better than its author.' Since we have no direct knowledge of what was in the author's mind, we must try to become aware of many things of which he himself may have been unconscious" (Schleiermacher 1977, 112).

Because the intention is mediated through discourse, the object of interpretation is the author not as a person but as crafter of a speech. A discourse is made both of language and of the thought someone had. Thus, "All understanding consists in the two moments of understanding the discourse [*Rede*] as cut out of the language and understanding such a discourse as a fact of thinking" (Schleiermacher 1990, 77; my translation). As was common in German romanticism, Schleiermacher speaks of an interaction in the text between discourse and spirit (*Rede und Geist*). We cannot understand the spirit if we do not take into consideration the discourse in which this spirit manifested itself, because the passage through language modifies the spirit (1996, 947). But a discourse is also not understood "when it is not understood as a fact of the spirit" (947; my translation). This is the reason the grammatical interpretation—figuring out what the text says—and the psychological interpretation—understanding the thought—have to work together: "Without words the thought is not yet formed and clear. Since hermeneutics must lead to an understanding of the content of thought, but the content of thought is only real through language, hermeneutics relies on grammar as the knowledge of language" (1990, 77; my translation). Since the author's intention is made of both spirit and discourse, what I can understand is not his private psychology—he might not know it either—but the public aspect of that private individual: "To the extent that I know the author, I know him as he contributes something in a language. . . . In the same way, to the extent that I know the linguistic field, I know the language as the author is its product and stands under its power. The two sides are the same, only seen from different perspectives" (Schleiermacher 1990, 167; my translation).

Dilthey expands the views of Schleiermacher. For him, understanding is a process through which we use external signs manifested by a person to know something internal of that person. The specific task of interpretation is to focus on expressions of life, but these expressions are essentially public. "What is internal in a human being only finds in language its complete, exhaustive and objectively intelligible expression" (1924, 319; my translation). This qualifies the notion of experience (*Erlebnis*), which is the minimal unit of the object of interpretation: experience is not privately subjective but in a way objectively subjective. Following Schleiermacher, Dilthey speaks of the spirit of an epoch (*der Geist einer Zeit*), such as the spirit of the Middle Ages or the spirit of the Enlightenment (177; my translation), which determines human experience: how people think and feel. Individuals are maintained and bound "in a certain circle of modifications of conceptions, formation of values and setting of goals" (178; my translation). The existence of such a spirit guarantees a commonality between interpreter and objects of interpretation. "Each space planted with trees, each room in which seats are set up has been intelligible to us from the perspective of kids' legs, because the way human beings set goals, organize things, determine values is something common that has assigned its place to each space and each object" (208; my translation).

The "connection of life" (*Lebenszusammenhang*) the interpreter tries to relive (*nacherleben*) is thus a public phenomenon. In the case of literature, for example, "the lyric poem allows in the deployment of its verses the reliving of a connection of experience: not of the real connection of experience which motivated the poet, but of what, on the basis of this connection, the poet put in the mouth of an ideal person" (Dilthey 1924, 214; my translation). The notions of reliving or reproducing (*Nacherzeugen*; 234), thus, against all of Gadamer's misunderstandings, and almost the whole post-Heideggerean tradition in the United States, do not mean a recovery of what was going on in the head of a single person. It rather means the possibility, for example, to put oneself in the circumstances of Luther, through his letters, through a study of the controversies of the time and the import of the scriptures in daily life, and try to understand what he thought. Despite the empirical difficulties, "I can re-live what he experienced" (*aber nacherleben kann ich ihn* [Luther]): "I transport myself in his circumstances. . . . I see in the monasteries a technique for dealing with the invisible world, which gives the monks' souls the constant direction of their gaze toward otherworldly things: the theological controversies become here questions of the inner existence. . . . And thus this process opens up for us the religious world of Luther and his contemporaries, of the first Reformation times, which broadens our horizon in possibilities of human life, which becomes only thus accessible to us" (216; my translation).

It is quite remarkable that now Schleiermacher and Dilthey are brand-ed as proponents of psychologism, which they explicitly rejected. Also remarkable is the fact that now the author's intention is presented as being either what was in the head of the person who wrote the text or a construct made by readers of what they take the writer to have meant. Margolis is one of the few contemporary theorists of interpretation who do justice to Dilthey and show the simplification made by those who dismiss the author's intention, as do William Wimsatt and Beardsley in their "Inten-tional Fallacy" (1946): "It may, in fact, be fairly claimed that 'The Intention-al Fallacy' conflates and confuses what Dilthey originally distinguished as the psychological and the hermeneutic conceptions of intentions. . . . What Dilthey meant by a hermeneutic understanding of intentions was an inter-pretation of texts, actions, and expressive behavior in terms of the public intentional structures of the cultural life of an historical community, not the putatively private, inchoate, or inaccessible psychological states of par-ticular persons" (Margolis 1980, 175; for a detailed critique of Beardsley, see Carroll 1992).

Husserl was influenced by Dilthey and refined his notion of *Erlebnis*. Parallel to Gottlob Frege (2001), who had the merit of conceptualizing the distinction between the psychological moment of a meaning—what he calls a *Vorstellung*—and its logical moment—what he calls the *Sinn*, Husserl (1913) uses a similar distinction, with different terms, and applies such a distinction to intention, which has a psychological aspect as well as a logical aspect. This distinction can also be found in Hirsch (1967), who was influenced by Husserl, and Searle (1983), who took it from Frege: for both Hirsch and Searle, although with quite different emphasis, the inten-tion that matters, the only one available, is the publicly available intention, articulated in language.

I consider this distinction between a private psychological moment and a public mental moment to be crucial for interpretation theory. While the psychological version of an intentional state is individual and private, the public version is available in a community, manifested by narratives, cus-toms, habits, manners of speaking and behaving. It is thus conventional. For example, to say "I promise" involves a psychological state and a publicly available mental state that can be borrowed from a community of usages and customs: most communities recognize the mental state of placing one-self under an obligation and saying so as acceptable and meaningful. When someone says "I promise," it is understood at face value that the person's psychological state matches the publicly available mental state. The person borrows such a publicly available mental state and makes it his own by taking responsibility for the words he uses as expressing what listeners will take them to express. At that moment the speaker implicitly acknowledges that there is no discrepancy between the sentence he uses and the intention that presently gives it life by borrowing from the publicly available linguistic means. The sentence meaning matches the speaker's meaning.

Usually we consider that linguistic conventions, in their literal sense, express conventional intentional states, so that they represent one moment in the execution of a speech act. There can be, however, a discrepancy between the linguistic expressions and the conventional intentional state, if the person does not know what the publicly available mental state involves: when a child says "I promise," it does not have the same weight as when an adult says this. Similarly, there can be a discrepancy between the psychological moment of intending and the conventional moment of what people understand as the intention if the person saying "I promise" knowingly has no intention of following through on the content of the promise. This person, we say, is lying, seducing, or manipulating.

For people who speak the same language and have been socialized in the same linguistic community, there is most of the time an implicit matching of the psychological state when using the words "I promise" and the conventional mental state expressed. When asked why I place myself under an obligation, I can say meaningfully, as Searle reminds us, that I speak English. The fact remains, though, that such a conflation between psychological state and conventional mental state does not originate from the pragmatic use of language only but also from a shared background. Borrowing these claims when speaking makes the speaker a partner in the dialogue that takes place in a community by imposing rules for asserting, giving orders, making promises, and so on. The commitment of speakers, however, does not derive from those accepted usages only—from the mere fact that they speak—but from the conviction of the person that these usages serve the good of the community.

There has been and still is a rather animated debate regarding the cognitive privilege, or absence thereof, people have toward their own mental states. Although it seems uncontroversial to say that there is a difference between a first-person perspective—what I feel—and a third-person perspective—what others infer I feel—such a distinction loses much of its relevance in interpreting texts. Interpreters deal primarily with texts that have been written as the manifestation of an author's intention. It is thus only indirectly and, as it were, as a supplement to the text that interpreters have recourse to the first-person perspective, to what the author really felt. Authors, like interpreters, make claims, and their work is the articulation of these claims. Authors are certainly entitled to revisit their work, to criticize specific interpretations and to comment on the true intent of their work. And this information can be highly valuable to interpreters. For example, in the case of the different versions of Heidegger's text "The Origin of the Work of Art," it is very useful to interpreters to know the chronology of those versions not just for philological purposes but for understanding what those texts mean (what Heidegger could have meant).

When authors comment on their texts, however, they, like anybody else, have to use the available text as the basis for their revisiting, criticism, and comments. The best they can do is to add something and supplement the original articulation of their claims, but they cannot erase that first manifestation of their intention. Interpreters can thus speak of a Heidegger I and Heidegger II, even if the author himself adamantly denies any radical break. The claim to intelligibility authors make gives interpreters assurance that what is written in the work, which is the manifestation of publicly available mental states, matches what the author intended, the private psychological state of the person before or during the writing process. As a consequence, the historical writer does not have an authoritative status when it comes to the meaning of a work. And interpreters can sometimes understand better than writers themselves what they meant, for example, when the larger horizon of those particular writers, the influences they received, the impact they had, or the novelty of their writing is available.

The implicit claim made by the author thus makes irrelevant the somewhat common talk of an irremediable loss of, for example, what Sophocles really meant. Given the stages presented here, Sophocles meant what he wrote because he chose the articulation of his intentions. If we want to understand what he meant, there is no better candidate than what he wrote. That does not mean, of course, that any interpreter can recover what was meant. Loss can happen, and does so rather often. The fact is, however, that a loss does not have to take place on the basis of a principle stating that there is a necessary discrepancy between an author's psychological state and the publicly available mental states manifested by the work. If there is loss, it is due not to necessity but to empirical factors. Loss can be due to the difference in background between the manifestation of the author's intention in the work and the interpreter's cultural horizon against which the author's intention has to be made intelligible. For example, the interpreter's background might not allow for a clear grasp of what a Greek citizen of the fifth century BC thought of the gods, their powers, and their role in daily life.

Building on the distinction between psychological states and publicly available mental states and the fact that by their claims authors commit themselves to the matching of their psychological states and the publicly available mental states articulated in their work, an additional distinction can be made between the historical writer and the author (Foucault [2002] makes such a distinction). The historical writer is the specific persona of a given human being. The author is what interpretation takes as the cause of the text to be interpreted. The writer has psychological states and the author is the principle of unity between the publicly available mental states manifested in a work. The claims made by writers make it the case that writers present themselves as authors, that is to say, not as flesh-and-blood writing individuals but as the unity holding a work together. By writing or performing any publicly recognizable act, a writer takes the clothes of a public player, so that this public player is what the writer as a real person projects for being understood by interpreters.

Such a distinction between historical writer and author has essentially taken two different forms among commentators. An implied author can be seen as what the actual author produces, as Wayne Booth (1961) argues, or as a postulate originating from the readers for guaranteeing the coherence of what they read (Nehamas 1981, 1987; Iser 1976; Eco 1979). This latter view, which is sometimes called hypothetical intentionalism (Caroll 2000, 2002), finds strong support in cases where the distance in time between historical writers and their audience has grown so large that it becomes more and more difficult, because of empirical differences in contexts, to believe that what, for example, we interpret in twenty-first-century North America is what Sophocles claimed to mean in the Greece of the fifth century BC. When the past is remote to a point that a shared community of customs and habits and especially a commonality of language no longer exist, the author becomes more and more what interpretation reconstructs as the principle of unity behind a work, a postulated author.

If, however, the author is just what readers posit, as the notion of implied author indicates, interpretation is turned into something like the best story available at the present moment. Such a manner of speaking might be the best way to qualify an interpretation and might empirically fit the net results of most interpretations belonging to the past—we have come to identify their shortcomings and their mistakes. Yet there remains a fundamental difference between evaluating an interpretation as the best story available and an interpreter presenting his interpretation as the best story available. The former is a retrospective qualification made on the basis of some evidence that the interpretation did not or could not fully grasp the original. This is the descriptive, or third-person, perspective, which takes interpretation as an event. The latter (presenting an interpretation as the best story available) does not fit the pragmatic aspect of the act of interpretation through which interpreters make a commitment that what is said is true and that they are truthful. This is the first-person perspective, which takes interpretation as an act. To conflate these two perspectives is to commit the future-perfect fallacy.

We can find such a fallacy in Fish's claim that readers do not decode poems but make them (1980, 327). What he means is that individual readers are part of communities of interpretation and share the values, goals, and methods of those communities, so that they will see in a text what the strategies current in their communities allow them to see. The authority of an interpretation is thus neither in the text nor in an individual reader but in the community.

> Members of the same community will necessarily agree because they will see (and by seeing, make) everything in relation to that community's assumed purposes and goals; and conversely, members of different communities will disagree because from each of their respective positions the other "simply" cannot see what is obviously and inescapably there: This, then, is the explanation for the stability of interpretation among different readers (they belong to the same community). It also explains why there are disagreements and why they can be debated in a principled way: not because of a stability in texts but because of a stability in the makeup of interpretive communities and therefore in the opposing positions they make possible. (Fish 1980, 15)

Although I agree that such a description fits the situations of conflict of interpretation, the claim that readers do not decode poems but make them is pragmatically contradictory. The pragmatic contradiction appears more clearly when we reformulate this view in first-person statements: (1) "I offer an interpretation of a particular text" and (2) "I produce the meaning of that text through my reading." These two statements are made from two different, mutually exclusive perspectives. The perspective manifested by the first statement is the perspective an interpreter has at the moment an interpretation is performed and involves some validity claims, that what I say is intelligible, that it is true, that I am truthful, and that it is right, in the sense of appropriate to offer this particular interpretation at this time and place. The second statement can itself be seen from two vantage points.

2a. "I make of the text whatever I want, whether it is a newspaper article, a label on a soup can, or *Richard III*." By making statement 2a, however, I would implicitly deny that I interpret the text. I, thus, take Fish's statement about readers making poems to be about good-faith interpretations, different from simply enjoying a poem, finding inspiration in it, or musing about it. Statement 2a can thus be discarded. From a second vantage point, the statement can alternatively be seen as a qualification of what I do when I interpret:

2b. "I manifest the values, goals, and strategies current in my community." Now, the knowledge I have of the values, goals, and strategies of my community can be of two sorts. I could just say,

2b1. "This is how things are done around here," without further justification; or I can say,

2b2. "I have to start from where I am, in my community, its values, goals, and strategies, but I claim that, to the best of my knowledge, they are the best." If I hold 2b1, I in fact acknowledge that I am not, strictly speaking, interpreting this particular text but rather adapting it to the taste of my community, thereby violating the four validity claims at the core of the act of interpretation. If I hold 2b2, I in fact acknowledge that I do not know and do not believe that my reading is just what my community allows me to do, so that I implicitly deny that I make the poem by interpreting it.

In his pragmatically self-contradictory statement, Fish conflates the first-person perspective of the interpreter presenting an interpretation (where interpretation is an act) with a third-person perspective of those who observe the process of interpretation and can see the influences bearing on what a particular interpreter did (where interpretation is an event). At the time I claim to interpret a text, either I am not aware of the influences bearing on my interpretation or, if I am, I must make them clear through disclaimers or claim that they contribute to a better interpretation.

The characterization of interpreting texts as making them (Fish) or as a fusion of horizons (Gadamer) or, in a weaker form, as the best story available, might empirically fit the net results of most interpretations belonging to the past—we have come to identify their shortcomings and their mistakes and now know that interpreters projected their values and concerns into the text so that what we have is a construction by interpreters or a plausible story. Still, such a qualification does not fit the pragmatic aspect of the act of interpretation through which people make a commitment that what is said is true, that they are truthful, and so on. For example, most people would agree that the history of science is replete with refuted theories, skewed data, and flawed methods. Still, most of us would consider irresponsible a ballistics expert testifying in a court of law who would state, "Although I do not have any evidence to the contrary and although all empirical tests have been positive, I cannot affirm that the gun of the defendant fired the bullet I examined, since the science behind those tests is likely to be falsified, just as many past theories turned out to be wrong." Either the expert knows or has some evidence to suspect that there is a flaw in the science or method he used—in which case he is just honest—or he has no evidence and no feel for such a problem, in which case he just refuses his responsibility as an expert and in fact denies that he is an expert. In the same way, if we teach courses of literature or philosophy, we owe our students who take those classes a stronger justification than just telling them, "These are the stories we can tell about those works of the past, given what we know." To speak of a plausible story in the absence of any evidence that something has been missed by the interpreter is to speak in the future perfect: "I now qualify what I say—it is only plausible—because several years from now, 'it will have been demonstrated' that I had prejudices or was mistaken."

Hypothetical intentionalists face another problem. For instance, in his desire to keep the postulated author linked to the historical writer, Alexander Nehamas (1981) added the requirement that the author as hypothesis be historically plausible. Although the view defended here might in the end lead, as an empirical result of interpretation, to Nehamas's position, the problem with such a view is that it does not explain how one interpretation—the author as a hypothesis or a postulate—can be validated by another interpretation—the historical plausibility of the postulate. The narrative of justification that is in principle initiated by the claims interpreters make engages them in a conversation not only with other interpreters but also with the original writer, to the extent that the goal of interpretation is to understand what was meant.

As a result, even in cases of interpreting texts of a remote past, the claim interpreters make entails that what interpreters reconstruct as the author was what the historical writer claimed to be his public persona, with all the gamut of possible qualifications and disclaimers to which interpreters usually have recourse. Although not identical with the historical writer, the author is not just implied but claimed to be what in actuality caused the text. As Caroll puts it, "the hypothetical intentionalists's protocols yield hypotheses about authorial intentions, but they are plausible hypotheses about actual intentions, not hypotheses about plausible possible intentions" (2000, 83).

Even if we can say of most interpretive processes that this was the best story that could be told at the time—which satisfies Nehamas's threshold for a valid interpretation—the claims interpreters make regarding an interpretation of a specific object do not allow them to qualify such an interpretation as being a story they have concocted, unless of course they have evidence that some elements of the puzzle are missing and that they had to extrapolate or make educated guesses and so forth.

In the absence of evidence to the contrary, interpreters, by presenting their work as a valid interpretation, have to claim a higher status for their interpretation than a fusion of horizons (Gadamer), a construct (Fish), or even a historically plausible postulate (Nehamas). In the absence of evidence to the contrary, interpreters, when interpreting *The Republic*, for example, should say, "This is what Plato meant." The "should" comes from the claim that is implicit in the act of interpretation: to tell the truth and be truthful. Even if the interpretation later turns out to be false on the basis of a new perspective, the claim of telling the truth has not been violated by the interpreter. Claiming to tell the truth does not amount to actually telling the truth. The other claim to be truthful protects the interpreter against any empirical falsification. Of course, most of the time, interpreters do not have available all the evidence they would need to have to redeem a strong claim such as, "This is what Plato meant." Interpreters are not arrogant enough or foolish enough to use the formula, "Here is what *The Republic* means." They qualify their aim, perspective, and method: for example, "This is what Plato meant in this passage, if we reformulate it in the terminology and themes of contemporary American analytic philosophy" (or a specific feminist or deconstructionist interpretive framework). And interpreters do not always have to state those qualifications themselves. Usually publishers alert readers to the type of perspectives or methods to be expected.

These distinctions between, on the one hand, psychological states and publicly available mental states and, on the other, historical writer and author, ultimately depend on language for reconciliation. If a claim to interpret what a writer meant has any sense—and interpretation by its very purpose is bound to recover what was meant—it is on the basis of a medium in which the two claims of the interpreter to recover an intention and of the writer to articulate an intention can be made compatible: language.

Language and Intention

Since a text is written in a specific language and manifests an intention, how does an intention use language for manifesting itself? Without entering into a discussion about the relationship between thinking and language, it is safe to say that language is primarily what allows a private psychological state—whatever that may be—to gain a public status. Only when a psychological state has been expressed, articulated, or communicated in some way can the claim of a person be recognized. Although language is not the only means to express, articulate, or communicate, it is beyond doubt the most sophisticated means. Since we are dealing with written documents or texts, language is the only means of communication involved.

If language can articulate the intentional states of historical writers and allows an interpreter to decipher what the writer meant, then it fulfills a complicated function of articulating an intentional state, providing such an intentional state with its public expression, and referring to an outside world. What is commonly called reference is a rather multifaceted process through which a word, as it is commonly said, presents or names a thing. Obviously the name or the word must be uttered by someone (it must be intended) and recognized by someone else (it is supposed to be understood). To mean something, speakers must not only anticipate how they will be understood but also share a language or an idiom with the hearer. Anyone who has learned foreign languages is keenly aware that mastering the grammar and vocabulary (how words are to be put together and what their meaning is) is not sufficient for using words and sentences in appropriate contexts. To perform appropriate speech acts in a foreign language, a familiarity with the pragmatic site of usage of such a language is needed.

Thus the linguistic function has at least two components: a semiotic component and a pragmatic component. The semiotic component names the capacity of words to designate within the system of the language ("cat" is not "bat" is not "rat" at the phonological level, and "cat" is not "mouse" is not "cow" at the semantic level). This is what is usually called the meaning of the words. The pragmatic component names the capacity of words to refer to real entities in the real world, that is to say, the capacity for words to be used. The distinction between the semiotic and the pragmatic is obviously only a methodological distinction, since a language can only be spoken and thus work if it locks onto the world as it is lived by the community speaking that language. For it is precisely the world as it is that guarantees that the language spoken in that world fits that world, is a vernacular and not a dead language.

The distinction between semiotic and pragmatic components seems clear, but its consequences are less obvious. One of them is that any word can be stipulated as designating any entity and thus as having any meaning, in the sense of designation. Saussure spoke of the arbitrariness of a sign, in the sense that there is no natural link or motivation between a word such as *chat* in French and the animal so called. English users say "cat" and German users "Katze." The arbitrariness obtains between the semiotic component and the pragmatic component. What is not arbitrary is the link between what is signified and what is signifying within the semiotic component, what Saussure called the signified and the signifier. For example, "Watergate" is the name of a hotel in Washington that became the name of a scandal that led to the resignation of Richard Nixon. The headquarters of the Democrats in the Watergate hotel had been broken into, and Nixon was accused of covering up the break-in. The signifier is the sounds /watergate/ as different from /waterfall/ or /floodgate/. As a proper noun, the signified is what is meant, in our case /name for a hotel/ as different from /Marriot/ or /Hilton/, although in this case the noun can also be analyzed as "door for water." What is arbitrary is the link between (1) the phonetic complex /Watergate/ (signifier) and what it signifies (name for a hotel as well as door for water; signified) and (2) what is designated, the hotel in reality.

Once the word "Watergate" became accepted as designating a scandal, it became part of the system at the semiotic level and could even be analyzed in morphemes, "-gate" becoming a suffix for scandal, so that the word "Irangate" could be used, at the pragmatic level, for designating the scandal involving Ronald Reagan, whose aides oversaw the unlawful shipping of weapons to rebel forces in San Salvador. Then all the scandals that followed received the suffix "-gate," from filegate to Monicagate. Although the example of "Monicagate" illustrates that any sound can be stipulated as designating pragmatically any entity, clearly the word "Monicagate" is not arbitrary at the semiotic level, since it is made out of the suffix "-gate," which has been seen as a suffix for indicating scandal. The example also indicates that the meaning of a word is not just the designation nor the signification within the system. To say, like Peter Strawson (2001, 231–34) or Wittgenstein (1953, 20), that the meaning is the use of a word is to overlook the necessary mediation of a linguistic system with its constraints. At the opposite end of the spectrum, to claim, like Heidegger (1959a, 16) or Derrida (1972, 16), that language speaks is to overlook the pragmatic aspect of language, where words have to be put to use in order to designate.

Although I cannot analyze here the extent to which language shapes reality or reality influences the way a language is spoken, the interaction between words and things is relevant, since such an interaction is at play in what a text says and what an interpreter tries to understand. Saussure can help us understand how the interaction between words and things is manifested within a language. He uses the word value for the redeemable aspect a term has in the system, given how that term is used by real speakers in a real world.

Saussure is at the origin of a distinction that has become canonic in linguistics and most of the philosophy of language: langue (language as a system) and parole (language as speech). Langue is the system that is reconstructed by linguists as that which allows for the producing and understanding of speech acts. This specification is important, for, if language is only the system for producing speech acts, it represents either an innate faculty, in the manner of a linguistic instinct (Humboldt 1963; Chomsky 2001; Pinker 1994) or a social faculty, which the members of a given linguistic community happen to share naturally. If, however, language is also for Saussure an explanatory principle, in the sense of a system of regularities that can be observed among speakers of a natural language, speech always comes first and there is an interaction between language and speech. This interaction causes language as a system to play a role that is both descriptive and prescriptive. As description, langue is what a linguist reconstructs by examining the regularities of speech acts; it is descriptive of a given status of the language spoken by a given community. Langue is also what is transmitted from parents to children through a process of education and socialization; it is a mental faculty, which is passed on but also taught through classes, dictionaries, and grammars and which stabilizes the use of the language in a given community, thereby playing a more or less prescriptive role within a community.

What Saussure calls "value" allows the interaction between langue as system and parole as concrete speech act. The value of a word or a grammatical sign is the place this term occupies in relation to the other terms in the system. Saussure gives the example of the French word *mouton* (sheep), which does not have the same value as the English word "sheep." In contrast to *mouton*, which means both the dressed meat and the animal grazing in the pasture, "sheep" stands in relation to "mutton," the former designating the animal and the latter the dressed meat (Saussure 1985, 160). As commonly stated, *mouton* can be used in both senses. "A form does not have a *meaning*, but a *value*: this is the cardinal point. A form *has a value* and consequently it entails the existence of other *values*" (Saussure 2002, 28). As students of a foreign language know too well, the value of terms is what is most elusive in the mastery of a language.

The value of a word—its place in the system—is precisely where the system, as an abstraction, locks onto the pragmatic situation of the speakers, so that the linguistic system and the pragmatic situation can affect one another. The differences in the system explain the problems and difficulties of translations: languages are not nomenclatures, so that to each word of French, for example, there would correspond an equivalent in English. At the same time, though, people can communicate about real entities and real events in the world, even when they do not completely understand each other's language. The possibility of communication already indicates that the pragmatic situation is not subordinated to a particular worldview articulated by a specific language, as Benjamin Whorf claims, speaking of the Apache, "Such languages, which do not paint the separate-object picture of the universe to the same degree as do English and its sister tongues, point toward possible new types of logic and possible new cosmic pictures" (1956, 240–41). A change in the pragmatic situation, if significant enough, will cause a change in the value of terms, just as a change in the value of terms, if accepted by enough speakers, can have an impact on the pragmatic sphere of a whole community.

For example, an increased sensitivity in the United States to what were perceived as gender prejudices has been strong enough to change the value of the term "he" in the system of American English: it has become increasingly the case that "he" designates only the male pronoun. The gender-neutral term—traditionally "he"—is replaced with "he or she," "s/he," an alternation within a text between "he" and "she" (as used in this book), an absence (the plural pronoun "they" being used instead), or a unilateral replacement of "he" by "she." Conversely, it also appears that a change in the system of a language can have an effect on how the world is seen and lived. Now that we have terms that are more sensitive to women and minorities, when watching movies from the 1940s and 1950s, we can realize how detrimental to women and minorities it was to be named, qualified, or characterized by terms that appear now to have derogatory and discriminatory connotations. It seems that being more sensitive to the connotations of some words, at the linguistic level, makes us more perceptive of what is detrimental to some groups of people, at the pragmatic level.

The fact that there is an interaction between language as a system and the world as it is lived indicates that neither language as it is structured in its system (in its phonetic, syntactic, or semantic rules) nor the world as it is articulated is fixed. Rather language and world are constantly evolving, causing more or less significant rearrangements of the system of language and the world as it is lived. Put another way, the interaction between words and things is somehow captured by a language as a system that, because it is in part a reconstruction based on how speakers speak of the world, provides speakers with words already endowed with specific potential for being used. Since language as a system captures the values of terms used by speakers, and since the value of a term is where the world inscribes itself in language, language is directly linked to a set of intentional states, in the sense that it encompasses terms with how they are supposed to be used by real speakers in the real world.

The fact that language includes such potential for being used can be easily downplayed, if not ignored, because we do not pay much attention to the fact that language precedes our usage of it, confident as we are that we say what we mean. The basis of our confidence is a situation in synchrony: when speaker and listener or interpreter and author share the same linguistic system, the fact that language is linked to a set of intentional states is precisely why we can communicate. In synchrony, langue as a system guarantees in principle an isomorphism between what the text says and what the interpreter reads. In synchrony the terms used by a speaker have the same value for the other members of the linguistic community. It is precisely this identity that permits language to be both a system for the intelligibility of speech acts and a system for the production of speech acts. In the synchrony within a given linguistic community, the upbringing of children—the process of socialization, education, and cultural productions—makes way for a smooth passage back and forth between langue and parole. Such a dialectic permits speakers to understand and produce successful speech acts and to be expert witnesses of the langue of their language—the reference that linguists use for analyzing language. In synchrony within a given linguistic community, these two capacities are not differentiated and need not be. The system of langue has been integrated and is part of the background knowledge that makes speakers skillful in their own language.

The situation is not always in synchrony, however. Often the interpreter does not share the same linguistic community as the author of the text to be interpreted, for example, in the case of a translation or the interpretation of a text in the same language, but from the distant past. Here, the value of terms is not immediately shared. Since it is the value that allows the interaction between langue and parole, either in producing a successful speech act or in understanding such a speech act correctly, if the value is not shared naturally in a synchrony, it will have to be reconstructed. To translate or interpret a text that is written either in a foreign language or in the language of the interpreter, but belonging to the distant past, the interpreter not only will have to master the grammar and the vocabulary of the idiom in which the text has been written but also and especially will have to determine the value of words in that idiom. In other words, to determine the value of a set of words, the interpreter will have to figure out their place in a system that is not identical to his own. The sharing of a culture is at stake in terms of understanding customs and social habits. Only arduous labor and time spent examining a sufficient number of speech acts will allow a translator or an interpreter to reconstruct the system of langue of the text under study. Such a person might even become a competent speaker in this foreign language, like those specialists in Latin antiquity, capable of conversing in Cicero's or Tacitus's Latin, or those perfect bilinguals who have made a foreign language their second native language.

Discourse and Intention

If language as a system is directly correlated to a set of intentional states, the way an intention locks onto linguistic signs for enlivening them and making them carry that intention cannot be simply equated with the fact that "I decide to use available linguistic signs for meaning what I mean." The system, as a reconstruction of previous uses, precedes me, and I need familiarity with the system to express myself. Thus, when I speak, the "I" that has the intention and says "I" and the "I" that functions as a personal pronoun in the syntax of the sentence are indeed related but do not belong to the same category. The first one is a real flesh-and-blood person, and the second is a linguistic instance that plays out in the syntactic field of the English sentence. To the extent that such a sentence is uttered, a real person is linked to the words and is represented as a linguistic instance. At the same time, because of the pragmatic aspect of the utterance (someone performed an act in the world by uttering words), claims enter into play and the real person becomes a discursive instance that binds the real person to abide by the rules of the discourse: to be intelligible, to tell the truth, to be truthful, and to be right.

When uttered, "I" as a linguistic instance at the grammatical level syntactically represents the person who uttered "I" and inscribes that real person within a discourse, transforming the linguistic instance into a discursive instance. In an utterance, there is thus, in addition to the real person and words of a language, a third realm that underlies the real person and words of the language: a discourse. When I say "I," the real person I am claims to speak under the guise of a linguistic instance: I am and mean what the linguistic instance "I" says. But the linguistic instance, strictly speaking, cannot say anything, because it is merely a pronoun caught in the syntax of specific sentences. The "I" only speaks when it is also a discursive instance, when used, not only in a sentence but in a discourse.

Here is not the place to attempt to define what discourse is and what the different genres of discourse are (politics, literary criticism, law, advertising, etc.). It suffices for my present purpose to say that discourse constitutes an entity usually larger than a sentence where the syntactic terms and markers clearly represent a real person meaning something, so that at least the following can be assessed: who is speaking, to whom, about what, for what purpose, and in what genre. If I read on a wall, "Grass is green," it is difficult for me, although not impossible if I want to speculate, to identify the genre of discourse that this sentence embodies. Given what I know about history, reading "Ich bin ein Berliner" is enough for me to identify the political nature of the discourse: a statement by John Kennedy, speaking after the erection of a barbed-wire border between East and West Berlin in 1961 and making it clear that the United States would not abandon West Berlin. Similarly, reading the sentence "Everything 30% off" on the window of a store is enough for me to identify the genre of advertising discourse and its components.

Not only language as a system precedes me but also discourses, with their rules and stakes. The rules of a discourse are what allow words to be concatenated in sentences and thus linguistic instances to become discursive instances. When I intend to say something, not only do I need the means to articulate what I intend, but I also need available to me what is intendable, so to speak: a range of possible and acceptable intentional states. Of course, most of the time, I am already familiar with these intentional states because I grew up in a community where they were part of my background and have been cemented in the language I speak. When asked, "Why do you feel committed to do what you promised to do?" I have to answer, "Because I said 'I promise,' and that is what 'to promise' means in English." But as a child, I had to learn what a promise is and how to make promises. Although there remains a family kinship between different types of promises, the intentional state of making a promise also varies depending on whether I speak to my five-year-old child or to a judge, during a casual supper with friends or during a business meeting. The fact that language is a system and that the values of the terms in the system are points of interaction between words and things clearly eliminates the thesis that I know what a promise is just by learning the meaning of the word "promise." Rather, I had to learn how to borrow available intentional states. When I intend, I need to be represented as an instance of discourse and thereby to borrow available intentional states from my community.

Interpretation, the task of which consists in retrieving what was meant, cannot thus confine itself to what is merely written (at the expense of losing the real person who initiated the whole process), or to what real persons meant by using the words they used (at the expense of losing what is involved in what is said). Interpretation has to consider the background of possible and available intentional states from which specific persons borrowed to say what they said.

In most conversations, we do not need to consider the background, because it is shared. We can just focus on what our counterparts meant, given what they said. The situation is radically different when an interpreter talks to a person from another culture speaking English or to a native of another culture in her native language. In such a situation, she has to pay attention to three parameters to follow and continue the conversation: (1) the real person who is speaking and who obviously means something, (2) what is said in terms of how the person's intention is linguistically articulated or how the real person is represented as a linguistic instance, and (3) what intentional states the person manifests as having, given the background from which she speaks and the discourse in which she speaks (or how the linguistic instance is in turn represented as a discursive instance, with its rules and stakes).

What represents an intention is its linguistic articulation, and what makes the linguistic articulation a stand-in for the intention is the discourse to which that linguistic articulation belongs. The linguistic articulation provides an intention with its public manifestation, and the discursive articulation provides the speaker with his social manifestation. The speaker can act as a professional, a partner in the discussion. Discourse is the milieu in which claims come to life. Although the discourse de-realizes the flesh-and-blood person who speaks by transforming him into a discursive instance, the real person gains his social status in this de-realization: the person makes himself intelligible and takes a stance regarding truth, truthfulness, and rightness. What puts the rules of discourse in motion and what links those rules to the practice of people are the claims implicitly made. Claims initiate a narrative, to the extent that they commit the speaking person, if prompted, to continue to speak in a certain way by making a case for what is said (claim to be intelligible), justifying the basis on which it is said (claim to truth), showing that no hidden agenda pervades what is said (claim to be truthful) and that it is appropriate (claim to rightness). Claims initiate a narrative, in the sense that they link the rules of discourse to the practice of the speaking people. They give life to a discourse by putting it into motion, so that the linguistic instance, provided by the language as a system, becomes a discursive instance, speaking in accordance with the rules of specific discourses. This discursive instance is in turn the real person speaking and acting in the real world.

Conversation and Intention

The different claims implicitly made with any speech act regulate the discussion, to the extent that speakers apply the rules of discourse under their responsibility, since they are committed to intelligibility, truth, truthfulness, and rightness. The first three, however, cannot prevent the fact that the conversation can be submitted to the rules of one discourse only. Although in principle I agree with Barnes (1988) that the descriptions of interpreters are defeasible, I also agree with Hogan (1996) that in practice this is very difficult. Interpreters can stipulate the object of interpretation any way they want, so that it becomes rather difficult to falsify what an interpreter does given what that interpreter set out to do. If someone offers a Freudian psychoanalytic reading of the Gospels or a feminist critique of René Descartes, given the rules of those particular discourses—Freudian psychoanalysis and feminist critique—it is quite hard, if not impossible, to prove those interpretations, or parts of them, false. We usually speak of relevance rather than truth in those cases and accept as a fact that the validity of interpretation is relative to the object of interpretation stipulated. When interpreters recognize those limits of interpretation, they usually throw up their hands and acknowledge a pluralism in interpretation

(Thom 2000; Hogan 1996). Because interpreters can emphasize different aspects of the same work, a multiplicity of equally legitimate interpretations can result. In Krausz's terms, "The multiplist stresses that the interpretations are opposed in the significant sense that each interpreter—admittedly with different interests—assigns salience to different features of the same interpretandum" (2002a, 129).

Against such a view, I claim that there is a means to regulate the passage from one discourse to another, so that a Freudian psychoanalytic discourse or a feminist discourse can be forced to explain itself outside its own specific discourse. The claim to rightness plays this unique role by forcing speakers to acknowledge a wider framework than the discourse in which they speak and thus indirectly gives room for a conversation not limited to the rules of any single discourse. Although it is a discursive device, the claim to rightness transcends the boundaries of specific discourses.

It is indeed unavoidable for normal people to pass from one discourse to another, from being a professional lawyer or mechanic, and proficient in that particular discourse, to being a friend, a parent, or a citizen. The claims they make to tell the truth, to be truthful and intelligible only affect speakers as discursive instances. Those claims are interpretive. And although those claims are crucial for regulating the conversation because they bind speakers to abide by the rules of the discourse, they are not enough to regulate the passage from one discourse to another. It is possible to be an excellent professional in one's own discipline with its discourse and still be considered a flawed individual or a failure as a person. Because the narrative of justification can still be controlled by the rules of one specific discourse, the three claims are not enough to guard the conversation from being hijacked by special interests and they are not enough to protect any discourse from being infiltrated or even overtaken by power. For example, the difficulty of defending the environment in a capitalist system is that the rules of the economic discourse, which has become prominent, have a natural propensity to extend their purview to anything, the environment included. And defending the environment in economic terms can come very close to sacrificing the environment to economic interests, for example, by maintaining pollution or developing land to the highest threshold of tolerance possible.

What regulates the passage from discourse to discourse and what can thus prohibit the cannibalization of other discourses by a single one is the claim to rightness. By implicitly claiming that what they say is right, not only do speakers accept being bound by the rules of their discourse, but

they also accept that abiding by these rules is right. They thereby implicitly not only make claims but commit themselves to the good of the community in which this particular discourse is used. The claim to rightness thus
transcends the individual discursive boundaries.

Although a CEO is also bound as a person by the claims she makes to
be intelligible, to tell the truth, and to be truthful, it is still possible for her
to argue in strictly economic terms that the interests of the stockholders
she represents justify cutting thirty thousand workers from the payroll of a
given company. The claim to rightness, in contrast, makes it difficult for
the CEO to refuse to be dragged into another discourse, such as the social
welfare of the community. Implicitly, the CEO as a professional also claims
that what she does and says is right, that what is said is not confined to
the rules of one economic discourse but also contributes to the well-being
of the community as a whole. When asked whether it is right to do so,
the same CEO has to provide another line of argument, now linked to
the question of rightness: that cutting thirty thousand jobs is good for the
workers as well, because the stocks of the company—and workers own
some shares of those stocks—will increase in value. The claim to rightness
therefore commits the speaker in a larger array of discourses and, to that
extent, renders the discursive instance more like a real person accountable
to a living environment. By the same token, the implicit claim to rightness
also renders the speaker more vulnerable to criticism, to the extent that the
speaker has to argue in different discourses, not just within her own discipline. Although it does not represent an absolute guarantee that power will
not take over the conversation, the claim to rightness gives a wider range of
defense against such sidestepping or perverting of the conversation by providing another line of argument: not only regarding truth, truthfulness,
and intelligibility but also regarding rightness.

The claim to rightness thus provides some substance to the procedural
progress that the three other claims guarantee. The claim to rightness adds
to the procedural progress that it is for the good of the community. By
implicitly claiming that what I say is right, I have to abide by the rules of
the discourse from which I borrow, but I cannot justify the validity of what
I say by those rules alone. To justify the validity of what I say, I implicitly
have to make this rather extraordinary claim that it is right for me to say it,
which means that it is good for all. I link the well-being of my community
to what I say. And even more, not only my community but any community of the future and of the past. By not qualifying what I say as valid only
for this or that group of people, I am forced to make such an extraordinary
claim: I become liable and accountable to all. Of course, I can limit and

qualify what I say, "It is good for our economy" or "It is in our national interest." The direct effect of such a qualification is to decrease the convincing power of the argument. At the onset I accept that I do not address those who will not benefit from what I suggest. The smaller the qualification, the greater the convincing power. And with greater convincing power comes greater liability and accountability.

The three claims—to be intelligible, to tell the truth, and to be truthful—can initiate a narrative through which the interpreter will have to justify the validity of what he did. But an interpreter can satisfy these three claims while only offering a rendering of the original intention as it is intelligible to the present audience. What the claim to rightness adds—and the claim to rightness is also implicit in any act of interpretation—is that the validity of the interpretation has to be justified for any audience. The effect of the claim to rightness is to expose the interpreter to a broader audience, liable and accountable to a wider range of questions, objections, and criticisms, both looking forward (for future audiences not yet materialized) and backward (for past audiences toward which the interpreter in principle could justify his interpretation as being better).

The fact that the claim to rightness initiates in principle a narrative that transcends the boundaries of discourses also means that the interpreter has to be ready to respond to questions and objections that have not yet been formulated (coming from future audiences, which have not yet spoken, and from past audiences, which can no longer speak). This kind of narrative is thus not only a narrative of justification but also a narrative that establishes and maintains a conversation that is unlimited toward the past and toward the future. Such a narrative thus does more than justify; it also establishes a community. By claiming that their interpretation is right, interpreters make actual a community with a future audience. Thus, interpreters accept the falsifiability of what they did and thereby commit themselves to the perfecting of what they did. By the same claim to rightness, interpreters also make actual a community with past audiences in the sense that in principle they could show why their interpretation is better than interpretations of the past (they could not just say, "It is better for me or for us, twenty-first-century readers"). And, maybe most important, they establish a community with the original writer.

Such a community is not to be thought of as a virtual living dialogue between, for example, a twenty-first-century American interpreter and seventh-century Homer. Homer only matters to interpretation as the anchoring of publicly available mental states in a given historical background and the principle of unity behind those publicly available mental states.

Whether Homer really existed or whether his name is only an abbreviation for the names of several reciters in the course of time only matters if this changes how the publicly available intentional states recorded as Homer's are to be put together (if it affects the date of composition, the identity of the body of texts, the coherence or the structure of the works attributed to Homer). Since what matters for interpretation is not psychological but publicly available, the living dialogue that can take place within the community established by the claim to rightness can only be a dialogue with the author of the text, not with the historical writer. And since the author is an abstraction generated by both the claim of the historical writer to be intelligible, to tell the truth, and so on, and the claim of the interpreter to do the same, what is living in the dialogue is not so much persons but rather the community itself. Through interpretation, Homer has been made a member of our community. In this new community, Homer (or whoever hides behind his name) can again—even if it is by proxy—make claims, since we try to understand the work under the claims made in it. He can make claims, because it is he (under the public persona he took when composing) whom we try to understand. And the interpreter can address Homer (under his public persona) without disclaimers such as, "The interpreter only touches upon what is intelligible to present audiences, so that the original meaning is lost forever, because we cannot know what it feels like to be a seventh-century Greek author."

It is in this sense that the claim to rightness commits interpreters to the good of the community. The community in question cannot just be the interpreters' present community, since they have made themselves in principle liable and accountable beyond their own empirical community. By the narrative they in principle have accepted to tell if prompted, a new community has come to life, a community where future partners of communication are accepted and anticipated, a community where past writers and interpreters have become partners to whom present interpreters accept being accountable. In such a narrative of justification, past authors and future audiences have become contemporaries who can put interpreters to the question and ask them what good is served by the interpretation they offer.

The question in interpretation is thus not to choose between monism and pluralism or intentionalism, constructivism, or anti-intentionalism. Very often theoreticians fail to make three types of distinctions: (1) between the levels of meaning in a text, (2) between interpretation as act and event, and (3) between a psychological and a publicly available mental intention.

The failure to distinguish the levels of meaning leads theoreticians to privilege one of them—author's intention, textual or verbal meaning, read-

ers' imputation—without realizing that each of those levels can be a legitimate choice, if it is justified. The reason it can be a legitimate choice is
because these levels of meaning are what interpretation encounters: a text
has been put together by someone in order to be a text (first level); a text
has the meaning of the sentences it is composed of, which themselves have
the meaning of the words composing them, so that a reader knowing the
language in which the text is written at least understands what the text literally says (second level); a text expresses intentional states, but these intentional states have to be reconstructed by readers on the basis of what they
take the sentences to express; in a way readers colonize a text with their own
intentional states, to the extent that they have to figure out not only what the
words and sentences mean but also what the text represents (third level).

A second failure to make a distinction between interpretation as act and
as event leads most theoreticians to confuse what interpreters do when they
attempt to interpret a text—interpretation as act—and what theoreticians
describe them to be doing—interpretation as event. Gadamer is the best
example of a theoretician who takes interpretation exclusively as event and
declares the absurdity of a single right interpretation of a text. At the
moment an interpreter offers a new interpretation, she does not have the
knowledge of all the parameters of her own situation. However, what she
does is to perform an act as a person in a particular community through
which she makes claims about her interpretation: that what she says in her
interpretation is true, that she is truthful and did not just repeat what was
said before or steal from others, and that her interpretation fits the pragmatic circumstances (it is appropriate, not injurious, libelous, and the like).
Because her interpretation is an act she performed, she is engaged, if
prompted, in a narrative of justification about her decisions, choices,
methodology, and so on.

Once we accept that interpretation is also an act, we have the means to
set a framework in which we avoid relativism, despite the fact that we
acknowledge several levels of meaning as legitimate candidates for what a
text means. In such a framework, one of the key elements of the justification process is the author's intention.

Most theoreticians do not make the third distinction, between a psychological and publicly available mental intention. The justification of an
interpretation can only start if there is an agreement on what the boundaries of the text are, and this agreement can only arise if there is a recognition of an intention behind such a text. To speak of agreement does not
amount to speaking about the substance of the agreement—scholars disagree on which books truly belong to the Bible—but about the procedures

to reach a possible agreement. The author's intention, first of all, is not a privately psychological moment that few people could retrieve but can only be a mental moment that is publicly available. In addition, such a moment matters to interpretation not in its content but in its function within the discussion process. Even as a public moment, scholars do not agree on what Thomas Jefferson meant in the Declaration of Independence by "All men are created equal." They argue that because he was a slave owner he could not really have meant all people or that he had conflicted feelings about slavery and could anticipate such a future time of equality for all people. We can leave the content of the intention up for discussion, but only if we accept that such an intention is what allows us to have our discussion about its content.

The intention that I rehabilitate is thus the author's intention in its publicly available form, but not as content—which is itself an object of interpretation—only as a function: agreeing that there is an author's intention stabilizes the discussion about particular interpretations. The author's intention is thus a category of interpretation. Because I distinguish between different levels of meaning in a text that can be legitimate objects of interpretation—the author's intention being one of these levels—I do not defend intentionalism, whether actual or hypothetical, but am not anti-intentionalist either. Since interpretation is both act and event, what matters in interpretation is the process of its justification. And a key condition for a rational discussion of interpretations is the recognition of the author's intention, even if the interpreter decides to downplay such an intention or to ignore it in order to focus on the cultural unconscious of an epoch.

3

The Author's Intention

The Practice of Translation

The activity of translation can illustrate what the author's intention is and is not. The author's intention has been conceptualized quite differently by various theorists. Those who reject it as relevant in interpretation usually focus on a substantial understanding of what an author is, as Krausz does: "The very idea of an author seems to suggest a kind of fixity or stability of voice from which the work is supposed to have been issued" (1992, 152), a fixity or stability he cannot accept. It is precisely that stability of voice or that authority speaking over and above the text, guiding the interpretation of what the text says that Roland Barthes relentlessly fought. The death of the author he eventually pronounced was the death of that other voice, tagged to the text as its manual of explanation or as "the subject with the book as predicate" (2002, 5). "The Author is thought to nourish the book, which is to say that he exists before it, thinks, suffers, lives for it, is in the same relation of antecedence to his work as a father to his child" (5).

Offering an alternative, Barthes proposes what he calls the scriptor, which is what a reader configures when reading, so that the scriptor is a mixed creature, half writer and half reader, for whom "the hand, cut off from any voice, borne by a pure gesture of inscription (and not of expression), traces a field without origin—or which, at least, has no other origin than language itself, language which ceaselessly calls into question all origins" (5–6). In Barthes's view and the view of the *nouvelle critique* he initiated, the unity of a text comes not from the author but from the reader.

Because a text is made of language and not of thoughts, "a text's unity lies not in its origin but in its destination" (2002, 7), so that "the birth of the reader must be at the cost of the death of the Author" (7). Barthes has offered some compelling cases of interpretation to illustrate and defend his views. In *S/Z* (1970), for example, he examines the different cultural codes that are at play in Balzac's novel *Sarrasine* (1970), codes that allowed Balzac to write.

Foucault (2002) clarifies almost in sociological terms Barthes's views and shows how the notion of author belongs to a particular period. When one considers discourses, as Foucault advocates, according to their mode of existence, then one can see that "the modes of circulation, valorization, attribution, and appropriation of discourses vary with each culture and are modified within each" (2002, 21). In such a perspective, the author appears as a function within discourses: "The author does not precede the works; he is a certain functional principle by which, in our culture, one limits, excludes, and chooses; in short, by which one impedes the free circulation, the free manipulation, the free composition, decomposition, and recomposition of fiction" (21).

Barthes's and Foucault's unmasking of the author as authority has been refreshing in literary criticism, especially in French-speaking countries, where biographism had been the law of the land in academic studies for decades. After them a new generation of critics felt liberated and literary studies could claim to be more than philology or history. As often in the work of pioneers, Barthes had to overstate his case by overlooking or neglecting other aspects of what authorship can be. Eugen Simion, for example, had an easy task in showing how those who proclaim the death of the author, such as Barthes and Paul Valéry, still make use of the life of the author in their literary critique (1996). Another weakness of Barthes comes from his appeal to the notion of performative, as used in what he calls Oxford philosophy (2002, 5). He does not realize that he cannot just keep the performance without the intention. As Peter Lamarque notes, "Far from being the destruction of a 'voice of origin' the successful performative relies crucially on the disposition and authority of the speaker" (2002, 89).

In phenomenology too we find an attempt to consider the work of art as a self-enclosed entity from which the author is barred. Wolfgang Kayser, for example, argues that "the poet is not immanent to a literary text; as if his work would only be understandable when we know exactly the poet. The poet is not included in the proper object of literary criticism [*Literaturwissenschaft*]" (1992, 17). For him, "A poem lives and arises not as a reflection from anything else, but as a linguistic structure closed in itself" (5).

Two alternatives have been offered to a substantial authoritarian author: a constructed author and a real, although not authoritarian, author. Booth has a notion of an implied author as a creation by the real writer of a version of himself who speaks in the text and is, thus, the true "meaner," the real writer being irrelevant for the interpretation of the text. Another version of constructed author has been a construction made by readers. Levinson, among many others, defends such a view. "We are in the last analysis entitled and empowered to rationally reconstruct an author as meaning, in a work, something different from what he or she did, in private and in truth, mean, as long as we have put ourselves in the best position for receiving the utterance of this particular, historically and culturally embedded, author" (1992, 251). Some other critics have attempted to rehabilitate the author, although not in the version defeated by Barthes and Foucault. The author is not a projection by writers as in Booth or by readers as in Levinson. It is a mild construction based on the text and limited by the text. Juhl defends such a position: "We presume that the author holds the beliefs which his work expresses unless and until strong evidence to the contrary is produced" (1980, 187).

The difficulty of these two positions, hypothetical intentionalism and actual intentionalism, lies in the status of what is construed, a projection in one case and a "real" author in the other. But the real author has been construed, so that her reality contains some virtuality, and the projected, posited, hypothetical, or constructed author is about a real writer, and thereby submitted to the historical test of a real writing person. The challenge interpretation theory faces about what the author is lies in the discursive manifestation of such an author: a real person takes on a public persona when writing, while at the same time the discursive existence becomes the manifestation of the real person. The writing involves the writer and engages her responsibility in some way. But the writer does not preexist the writing as a writer. This challenge can be summed up by Nicholas Wolterstorff's remark,

> To speak is not, as such, to express one's inner self but to take up a normative stance in the public domain. The myth dies hard that to read a text for authorial discourse is to enter the dark world of the author's psyche. It's nothing of the sort. It is to read to discover what assertings, what promisings, what requestings, what commandings,

are rightly to be ascribed to the author on the ground of her having set down the words that she did in the situation in which she set them down. Whatever be the dark demons and bright angels of the author's inner self that led her to take up this stance in public, it is that stance itself that we hope by reading to recover, not the dark demons and bright angels. (1995, 93)

To take the challenge of finding out what an author is and what its function is in interpretation, I examine the case of translation, which is a case of interpretation, reformulating an original text into another linguistic medium, thereby presenting or representing or reconceptualizing this object in another linguistic medium. Translation, thus, follows the general model of translatability that Iser (2000) considers paramount to interpretation. Two interconnected questions arise: Do translations follow either monism or pluralism, and if so to what extent? What is the goal of a translator when rendering a text in another linguistic medium, and what decisions are made to reach that goal?

The first, more theoretical question involves two notions central to any discussion of authorial intention: the verbal meaning of that which is to be interpreted and the author of that which is to be interpreted, although some brands of pluralism dismiss these. Not surprisingly, the most sophisticated version of these two notions has been presented by monists. The renowned actual intentionalist Hirsch, for example, defends the self-identity of the verbal meaning of a text, and the hypothetical intentionalist Nehamas defends the thesis of a postulated author. The second, more practical question can be explored by putting these two notions to the empirical test of translation studies by comparing several translations of a brief passage from Homer's *Odyssey* in different languages—English, French, and German—and from different centuries.

Translation studies, which have flourished in the past forty years (Jakobson 1959; Mounin 1963; Steiner 1975; Lefevere 1975, 1982, 1992; Bassnett 1991, 1993), have shed new light on questions central to interpretation theory. By empirically addressing the question of the meaning that is translated or the intention that is rendered in a set of signs (a semiotic vector) other than the original, translation studies allow us to examine concretely what is at stake in the traditional models used in interpretation theory: monism (or singularism) and pluralism (or multiplism). Monism holds that there is only one correct interpretation of a text, which is usually measured against the author's intention, while pluralism maintains that a text is susceptible to multiple interpretations, none of them better from an absolute point of view. This second model gives up the idea of a unique, accurate interpretation and usually the idea of interpretive progress over time.

A quite similar polarization can be found in translation theory. George Steiner (1975) draws a distinction between two models of translation, which he calls universalist and monadic. The universalist position (akin to monism) posits the existence of a deep linguistic structure common to all human beings. Differences in natural languages are merely superficial and contingent and conceal the deep structures that can be discovered. The deep structures are precisely what make a translation possible. If an original can be understood as such, a faithful translation is possible, without any loss. André Lefevere qualifies this model as the production of a translation dictated by the norm of the original (1992, 18). The history of different translations of a text in the same language thus reflects the progress of an enterprise that attempts to grasp better and better the underlying sense of the original text.

The monadic position (akin to pluralism), in contrast to the universalist or monist position, considers that each language has its own specific semantics, syntax, phonetics, and so on. What English can articulate cannot therefore be fully translated into Chinese. This position leads to the thesis that translation, in a strict sense, is impossible. If the original is only accessible through its translation, a free translation is the only possibility that will give a target audience an approximate rendering of the original text. Lefevere qualifies this model as one that aims at satisfying the ideological and "poetological" expectations of the target audience (1992, 18). The text that has been translated is considered an original from the point of view of the translation, which is the point of view of what holds as a translation in a given target audience.

As Lefevere has convincingly shown with the translations of poem 64 by Catullus, translations offer a compromise of what would be two extreme positions. Lefevere offers seven strategies used by translators to make Catullus's poem a living text for English-speaking audiences (1975). His enterprise illustrates the fascinating but puzzling preface Walter Benjamin (1968) wrote to his own German translation of Baudelaire's "Les tableaux parisiens": a translation superimposes the expectations of the audience on the original and thus adapts the original, which, retrospectively, is posited as an original from the point of view of its transposition. "Thus translation, ironically, transplants the original into a more definitive linguistic realm since it can no longer be displaced by a secondary rendering. The original can only be raised there anew and at other points of time" (75). Regarding the meaning of the text to be translated, Benjamin notes that "the language of the translation can—in fact, must—let itself go, so that it gives voice to the *intentio* of the original not as reproduction but as harmony, as a supplement to the language in which it expresses itself, as its own kind of *intentio*" (79). The original is translated not directly in accordance with the author's intention, but indirectly through the translator's intention, because the translator reconstructs the author's intention. This dual intention, the intention to give voice (second intention) to a previous intention (first intention) results from Benjamin's view that the translator obeys two masters, the original author and the contemporary audience.

Benjamin's text has been the subject of several commentaries, for example, those of Steiner (1975), Paul de Man (1986), and Derrida (1987), all of whom question the status of an original text. The original both legitimates translating and justifies the new texts translators offer. In the first case, the original motivates a translator to offer another text claiming to be its faithful rendering in another language. In the second case, because the original is no longer accessible to the contemporary public, it needs to be adjusted, transformed, or made understandable, and this need justifies in principle the different choices made by translators.

Translation thus offers a special kind of interpretation that serves nicely as an empirical test in the debate between the two theses of monism and pluralism. Since translations are supposed to render an original, they seem to be more strictly bound to the original than an interpretation might be. And they claim almost by definition to follow the monist model: if we read a translation, common sense tells us that it is claimed to be a faithful rendering of the original. If, therefore, a strict monism does not appear to be the rigid model followed by several translators of the same text in the course of centuries, we might say that a fortiori this model is not likely to hold true in the general theory of interpretation. If, on the other hand, pluralism has not been the strict model manifested by translations, a minori it might tell us that a strict pluralism without qualification is also problematic in the general theory of interpretation. As a result, a study of translations might shed some light on what is at stake in interpretation and help either corroborate or qualify these two models of monism and pluralism.

I discuss monism for two reasons. First, the very notion of translation suggests that there is an original that is supposed to be carried over into another language. Monism, therefore, seems more likely to be the norm in the process of translating. The second reason is more strategic. Since monism—with its bold claim that there is only one right translation or interpretation—can be falsified more easily, it will suffice to examine the history of translations of the same text to find out whether there is any evidence controverting its claim.

Two notions that have been proposed as devices for supporting a defense of monism are verbal meaning, that which its author intends (Hirsch 1967), and a postulated author (Nehamas 1987).

Theoretical Background
The Verbal Meaning of a Text

In his groundbreaking book *Validity in Interpretation*, Hirsch shows how and why the author's intention is the best norm for establishing the validity of an interpretation. There are many authors who defend what is apparently the same view, such as Juhl (1980), William Irwin (1999), Carroll (1992, 2002), and Steven Knapp and Walter Michaels (1992). However, Hirsch remains for me the theorist who most clearly and convincingly presents and defends the thesis. Since he was also the author of this theory, it is only justice to focus on his views.

Hirsch tries to establish a theoretical framework for the validation of interpretation. I examine only one of the distinctions Hirsch makes in support of his thesis: that between the verbal meaning of a text and the significance an audience grants it. This distinction has a long history in hermeneutics and interpretation theory. To interpret involves first an act of reading (deciphering, decoding) and second an act of relating what is understood to some other thing. There result two levels of meaning that have received different names among interpreters: literal versus allegorical meaning (Gregory the Great 1971), grammatical versus psychological interpretation (Schleiermacher 1977), understanding versus application (Gadamer 1998), explanatory versus elaborative interpretation (Novitz 2002), meaning interpretation versus relational interpretation (Gracia 2000).

In Hirsch's version of these levels of meaning, the verbal meaning is what the signs of the text represent. Since signs have been put into a sequence by an agent, Hirsch argues, what a text means is what the author meant by the use of a particular sign sequence. "Verbal meaning is whatever someone has willed to convey by a particular sequence of linguistic signs and which can be conveyed (shared) by means of those linguistic signs" (1967, 31).

Verbal meaning thus has two sides: one is semiotic, the other mental (or, one is the sentence meaning, the other the speaker's meaning). To the extent that it is the meaning conveyed by signs, the verbal meaning remains constant and can be reproduced in the course of time. It can be understood by different readers. To the extent that it is the act of meaning something, the verbal meaning is also a matter of consciousness. It is the intentional act of the speaker who meant something. This twofold characteristic of the verbal meaning can account for a plurality of interpretive acts, for interpreting is also an intentional act that aims at the verbal meaning of the text. An unlimited number of intentional interpretive acts can aim at the same verbal meaning in the same way that an unlimited number of perceptual acts can aim at the same object of perception. It does not follow, Hirsch contends, that the verbal meaning changes in any of these intentional acts, just as the object of perception does not change by being perceived by several observers. The verbal meaning expresses the author's intention, so that the sequence of signs is only the manifestation of that intention. And it is precisely this intention that is the object of interpretation. Since the intention took the form of a sequence of signs, these signs are vicarious and provisional. The sequence of signs has been established by an agent who chose such a sequence for expressing what was intended. The intentional act of interpretation is thus directed to a verbal meaning as the expression of an intentional act, the one by the author that manifested itself in a sequence of signs. To interpret, therefore, should be "a recognition of the author's meaning," that is, of the verbal meaning as intended by the author (Hirsch 1967, 26).

This is Husserl's canonic position in the first of his *Logical Investigations* (1913), a work Hirsch quotes in support of his position. The semiotic character is instrumental in reproducing the meaning in its identity but does not belong to the meaning, which is essentially mental. Since, however, there is only meaning once this meaning can be reproduced, an author starts to mean when the mental content entertained is no longer psychological but has reached a level of public availability. "Although textual meaning is determined by the psychic acts of an author and realized by those of a reader, textual meaning itself must not be identified with the author's or reader's psychic acts as such" (Hirsch 1967, 216–17). In other words, it is only when an author can reproduce for himself, even silently, the original mental act that we have, strictly speaking, a meaning. Neither Husserl nor Hirsch wonders whether language has a productive role in the reproduction of meaning. They are both content to acknowledge that meaning can be repeated and that language offers the means to express such a reproducible meaning.

Since the meaning of a sequence of words is the meaning conveyed by an author who used this sequence of words, the task of the interpreter who wants to find out what is meant, and not only how significant a text is, consists in reproducing the mental act that gave life to particular signs. That act, however, is not private but public. The verbal meaning, as expression of the author's intention, is a type that is both willed and shared. Because it is a type, readers can have access to it, since the text is the tokening of a type. Furthermore, because it is willed, readers can connect the type to its originator, the author. Since the type is also shared, what readers understand and what the author meant are mutually compatible: the author can only mean what others can understand. "If verbal meaning is a willed type that can be conveyed through linguistic signs, it follows that the possibility of conveying the willed type depends on the interpreter's prior experience of the willed type. . . . The willed type must be a shared type in order for communication to occur . . . the willed type has to fall within known conventions in order to be shared" (Hirsch 1967, 66–67). When the interpreter succeeds in reenacting the publicly available mental acts the author performed, he can claim to have accessed the meaning intended, which is, in fact, the verbal meaning of the text.

Although people can do many different things with texts (such as enjoying reading them, applying them, or consuming them) without the need for a clear criterion for their own use of the text, if someone claims validity for an interpretation—which goes beyond her own enjoyment or consumption—the criterion for assessing the validity of that particular interpretation is precisely the mental act that gave life to the signs now available in the text: the author's meaning. For it is only what the author means that offers a constraining norm against which an interpretation can be evaluated. There is thus a difference between a plausible interpretation and a correct interpretation. Plausible means capable of being confirmed by the text. In this sense, it is possible to have several plausible interpretations whether they are compatible among themselves or not. But this does not entail that they are all correct, if correct, as Hirsch understands the term, means in adequacy with the author's intention.

Hirsch is careful in his argumentation and painstakingly differentiates the verbal meaning from what it is not. He mentions two pitfalls: biographism and a form of immediate empathy. The biographical approach has to be rejected given that the verbal meaning is not the experience that the author had of this verbal meaning. The experience of meaning is private: it is what a person experiences. Strictly speaking, however, it is not a sense. Although the aim of interpretation is to recognize the author's intention, such an intention is only accessible through the very means the author used for expressing such a sense: the sequence of words. As for the second pitfall, given that the verbal meaning of a text is a sequence of words, there is no way to grasp immediately, through empathy, the author's intention. Any interpretation has to go through and decipher signs. An act of understanding, of appropriating signs and their meaning, is thus required before the interpretation. It is precisely this understanding that builds the sense of a text. "There is no immediacy in understanding either a contemporary or a predecessor, and there is no certainty. In all cases, what we understand is a construction" (Hirsch 1967, 43). An interpretation thus refers to the construction of the sense accomplished in the primary act of understanding.

Given that the intention, although logically prior to the verbal meaning, cannot be grasped independently of the verbal meaning, what serves as the telos of interpretation is thus broader than the psychological sphere of the author. It must include what Hirsch, after Husserl, calls the horizon of meaning. The horizon of meaning is what the author could have known or could have meant, regardless of whether he actually knew or meant it. The verbal meaning, as expressing the author's intention, remains a construct by readers, with the constraints delineated above. This element nuances the strict distinction Carroll makes between actual intentionalist and hypothetical intentionalist. Although Hirsch aims at the actual intention, this intention, he believes, has to be recovered through a construction, and what is recovered is not what was in the head of the author but what belonged to the milieu of the author.

Unlike the verbal meaning of a text, the significance of a text covers "a relationship between that meaning and a person, or a conception, or a situation, or indeed anything imaginable" (Hirsch 1967, 8). Significance is thus essentially relational: "Significance is always 'meaning-to,' never 'meaning-in.' Significance always entails a relationship between what is in a man's verbal meaning and what is outside it" (63). In place of significance, Hirsch also uses the terms meaningfulness and present relevance (1976, 80, 85). Whereas the verbal meaning is the object of interpretation, significance is the object of criticism. Through criticism of the significance of a text, the critic can discover and make explicit the relationship between the verbal meaning and what is outside—whether it is the world, the subject matter, or the author's past. When readers enjoy a novel because they recognize some scenarios of their own lives or see how easily they could fall into the drama described or realize how useful it is for them for dealing with the loss of a loved one, they do not, strictly speaking, interpret the novel but rather apply the novel to their own situations. They focus on the significance of the text; whether the author meant what they see in the text does not change the fact that they see the novel that way. Interpreters, Hirsch argues with merit, often confuse the two tasks of finding out what was meant and what is meaningful to us. For Gadamer, as we saw, all interpretations are applications.

While the semiotic and mental character of the verbal meaning guarantees its self-identity and thus constancy, the significance of a verbal meaning can change through time. These changes in the significance are caused by transformations in the cultural milieu. Even an author can see his own work differently at different times. What is different, however, is only the significance that the text has for its author, which has no bearing on the self-identity of the verbal meaning. Similarly, when readers "agree about what the text means to them," they agree on how they take the verbal meaning (Hirsch 1967, 214). The object of agreement, however, is not the verbal meaning but the significance they confer upon this verbal meaning. The object of agreement is the relationship that the verbal meaning has with their cultural milieu or their historical background.

Not only is the significance different from the verbal meaning, it is also subservient to the verbal meaning, which has to be understood first. This understanding of the verbal meaning will allow readers to explain this meaning and come to an agreement about it. There would be no object of agreement or disagreement without a self-identical verbal meaning. "To fuse meaning and significance, or interpretation and criticism, by the conception of an autonomous, living, changing meaning does not really free the reader from the shackles of historicism; it simply destroys the basis both for any agreement among readers and for any objective study whatever" (Hirsch 1967, 214).

The recognition by Hirsch that the verbal meaning is not directly given—rather, it must be constructed—might be an indication that the distinction between verbal meaning and significance cannot be as strict and clear as Hirsch would like it to be. (For one of many critiques of Hirsch's distinction, see Juhl 1980, 32–44.) The fact that "meaning is an affair of consciousness not of words" (Hirsch 1967, 4) has a bearing on both the text and the interpretation of that text: on the side of the text, "A word sequence means nothing in particular until somebody either means something by it or understands something from it" (4), and on the side of interpretation, "The text does not exist even as a sequence of words until it is construed; until then, it is merely a sequence of signs. . . . Even on this primitive level, signs can be variously construed, and until they are construed the text 'says' nothing at all" (Hirsch 1967, 13–14). The meaning of the text is in the text, deposited there by the author, but the discovery is made through another act of consciousness by an interpreter who makes the sequence of words alive again. One of the motivations for Hirsch's emphasis on the author's intention is to rebut the view of the primacy of language: "What has been denied here is that linguistic signs can somehow speak their own meaning—a mystical idea that has never been persuasively defended" (23). While we can be sympathetic to Hirsch in his rebuttal, we can only wonder whether the role of interpreter he admits in the construction of the verbal meaning does not threaten any stability such a meaning can have. When he acknowledges that meaning requires understanding by someone, he grants a power to interpreters that might very well rival the power he wants for the author.

The reason for such an ambivalence in Hirsch is due to his conception of intention, which is both mental and verbal. Interpreters who want to retrieve the author's intention can understand such an intention either as extraneous to its linguistic formulation, having a self-identity before being articulated in words, or as being what is articulated, in which case the author's intention is logically different from its expression but does not exist independently of its expression. In the first case, the author's intention corresponds to a mental moment already identifiable before its verbal expression, and interpreters will try to reconstruct this mental moment when an author construed a meaning that she later expressed. In the second case, there is authorial intention only when it is articulated in signs, and although the author's intention is logically different from its expression, it cannot be identified independently of its expression. Interpreters will put the emphasis on what the author wrote and use the author's intention as a guide for construing the meaning of the text as expression.

This ambiguity in the status of the author's intention has significant consequences for the status of the verbal meaning. If the author's intention is a presemiotic moment, thus formed before its verbal expression, a thought is already articulated outside any semiotic vector, so that the signs only convey the expression. The signs give thought their "linguistic flesh," as Husserl says in *Logical Investigations* (1913). There would thus be an isomorphism between the intention as the act of meaning and the verbal meaning as the expression of the intention. The meaning intended by the author and the meaning of the text are one and the same thing. "On purely practical grounds . . . it is preferable to agree that the meaning of a text is the author's meaning" (Hirsch 1967, 25). Or again, "No example of an author's ignorance with respect to his meaning could legitimately show that his intended meaning and the meaning of his text are two different things" (22). On the basis of such an isomorphism, interpreters can retrace the exact path of the author's creation. By putting himself in the place of the author, reconstructing the author's horizon, the interpreter can first decipher the signs left by the author, thus construing the understanding of the verbal meaning, and then make this understanding explicit in an interpretation that will be measured for its accuracy against the author's intention in a process that Husserl (1991) calls empathy. Again the goal of empathy is not to recover the psychological idiosyncrasies of the author's persona but to reproduce and to reenact the mental acts that the author had to perform to become the author he became.

There are two advantages in such a Husserlian view. First, there is in principle no difference between understanding a contemporary and an author of a remote past. The only differences are empirical, in the sense that, in the case of the present, it is empirically easier to gather information and clues about the author's horizon. Second, while interpretation can content itself in taking as its object what the words and expressions mean, it can do more: by using the words and expressions as expressions of mental acts, the interpreter can redo the mental acts the author himself performed. Literally, the interpreter can re-create the work. Again, there are empirical constraints that will usually thwart the full success of such an attempt, but in principle such a re-creation is feasible.

By contrast, if the author's intention is what the author articulated in the text to be interpreted, the verbal meaning is the crystallization of the author's intention, and it is only through this expression that the intention can be grasped. The interpreter now has the initiative. The verbal meaning is no longer so much what, in the construction made by the interpreter, represents the author's will, but rather what an interpreter construes as what the author meant. Interpreters thus have, in this second option, more latitude, since they are no longer obedient to the direct authorial will and they can see what the author did not mean but could have meant as part of the verbal meaning, given the background in which he evolved.

Hirsch is unclear about his position and hesitant in his formulations. One example of such hesitation concerns the strict duality between intention as autonomous moment of thought and the semiotic inscription as expression. Sometimes this duality is reformulated as a duality within the use of signs; Hirsch claims that there is both a semiotic and mental moment already involved in the use of signs. This could suggest that the intention is not really an autonomous moment before the semiotic articulation itself. His critical remarks against biographism and the empathic grasp of meaning reinforce this suggestion, which leads one to think that, in Hirsch's view, the author does not have any cognitive privilege regarding what she meant, once she has said it. The author, like anyone else, has to decipher her intention in the signs she used.

Another example of Hirsch's hesitation concerns the status of the construction that interpreters do when they interpret. Most of the time Hirsch uses the term in a weak sense: interpreters have to use their acumen and make educated guesses when retracing the tracks of the author's intention (1967, 43). At times, however, he grants interpreters a stronger power of construction: "The nature of a text is to have no meaning except that which an interpreter wills into existence. We, not our texts, are the makers of the meanings we understand, a text being only an occasion for meaning, in itself an ambiguous form devoid of the consciousness where meaning abides" (1976, 76). He qualifies interpreters as he usually qualifies authors: they are "makers of meaning," and he says of a text in relation to interpretation what he usually says of it in relation to an author: it is an "occasion for meaning" and "devoid of consciousness" when standing alone. Hirsch came to recognize that his "earlier definition of meaning was too narrow and normative only in that it restricted meaning to those constructions where the interpreter is governed by his conception of the author's will. The enlarged definition now comprises constructions where authorial will is partly or totally disregarded" (1976, 79).

All these hesitations leave the verbal meaning somewhat ambivalent. It is at times a mere expression of authorial intent, at times a semiotic articulation by an author giving form to an intention that would not be fully what it is without it, and at times a construction by interpretation. If there is such an ambiguity in the verbal meaning, can the verbal meaning be strictly separated from and grasped independently of its significance for an interpreter?

The Postulated Author

In his articles "The Postulated Author: Critical Monism as a Regulative Idea" (1981) and "Writer, Text, Work, Author" (1987), Nehamas defends a fruitful position by drawing a distinction between the writer as a historical person and the author as an instance unifying the text. Through such a distinction, Nehamas claims to remain faithful to the ideal of monism that there is only one correct interpretation. He believes that his position offers a more coherent defense of monism than Hirsch's does. He starts by embracing a fallibilist position—no reading of a text is sheltered from being questioned—and a constructivist position—meaning does not lie in the text independently of the interpretation but requires a construction. Regarding the fallibilist position, Nehamas says that the fact that a text does not have an unrevisable interpretation does not entail that what a text means changes along with the mind that interprets it. Regarding the constructivist position, Nehamas considers the meaning of a text to be what is specified by the ideal interpretation of that text, which would account for all of the text's features. This is what he calls a regulative idea: "The critical monism which I advocate is a regulative idea and identifies the meaning of a text with whatever is specified by that text's ideal interpretation" (1981, 144). Although a construction is involved, it does not amount to a fabrication (144). The fact that a text is susceptible to multiple interpretations does not entail that different results necessarily have to be reached or that these results are equally plausible (142). The interpretation of a text aims at accounting "for all the text's features, though we can never reach it since it is unlikely that we can even understand what it is to speak of 'all the features' of anything" (144). This ideal interpretation, Nehamas recognizes, is a mere hypothesis and is itself submitted to changes depending on the results of new interpretations that could reveal previously unnoticed features of a text. New interpretations may force us to rearrange the canons of interpretations. The ideal is thus itself a construction based on already existing interpretations.

The function of an ideal interpretation is to allow us to posit a standard that serves as a yardstick by which different interpretations can be measured. The idea is thus regulative to the extent that it governs—regulates—interpretations and permits different interpretations to be submitted to common criteria for establishing their validity, the main criterion being what the author meant. By using criteria of validity and taking part in a regulated discussion of possibly different interpretations, the enterprise of interpreting texts becomes a rational project: the various interpretations can be judged, evaluated, and justified.

Following Hirsch, Nehamas identifies this ideal interpretation with the author's intention. The text has to be interpreted as the production by an author. Parting company with Hirsch, however, Nehamas establishes two distinctions: between the author and the writer and between the interpreted meaning and the original meaning. According to the first distinction, the writer is a historical person, the efficient cause at the origin of the materiality of the text, while the author is the postulated agent "whose actions account for the text's features" (1981, 145). The author "is a character, a hypothesis which is accepted provisionally, guides interpretation, and is in turn modified in its light" (145). It is not, as the writer, the efficient cause of the text, but its formal cause (145). Although it "has no depth," the hypothetical or postulated author is submitted to a constraint: it must be historically plausible. "The principle is that a text does not mean what its writer could not, historically, have meant by it" (145). For example, Nehamas suggests that particular lexical meanings cannot be attributed to an author if these words received these particular meanings after the death of the writer. "The author actually means what the writer could have meant, even if the writer never did. In producing texts, writers are immersed in a system with an independent life of its own. Many of its institutional or linguistic features, many of its values or connections to other systems, are beyond the most unconscious grasp of any writer. . . . The author, who is the joint product of writer and text, of critic and interpretation, who is not a person but a character, is everything the work shows it to be and what it is can in turn determine what the text shows" (1987, 285).

Nehamas quotes William Faulkner, who aspires to be such a minimal efficient cause: "It is my aim and every effort bent, that the sum and history of my life, which in the same sentence is my obit and epitaph too, shall be then both: He wrote the books and he died" (quoted in Nehamas 1987, 289). Although the author is postulated, the author is more than an implied author in the sense of a unifying principle at the basis of the text. The author is not just a category of interpretation, but also a property of the text. Nehamas sees that author as transcendental, because historical plausibility entails that such an author transcends a specific text and must account for all the works by the same writer.

The second distinction between the meaning to be interpreted and the original meaning allows Nehamas to liberate interpretations from the shackles of the original intention. In other words, the ideal interpretation is not submitted to the meaning as this was intended for its original audience or, for that matter, by its original writer: "What a text means is what it could mean to its writer. But this is not what it did mean to the writer and to the text's original audience, nor need they have been able to understand it given only the articulated knowledge of human affairs which they then had. The meaning of a text, like the significance of an action, may take forever to become manifest. . . . Each text is inexhaustible: its context is the world" (1981, 149).

An obvious consequence of such a view is that writers "are not in a position of interpretive authority over their writings, even if these are, by law, their property" (Nehamas 1987, 272), so that "what a writer takes a text to mean is relevant, but not telling evidence in literary criticism" (1981, 147). The writer might not even be aware of what he meant.

Theoretical Import of Translation

Homer's Odyssey

To test the two theses at the center of monism—that it is possible, through the verbal meaning, to recover the writer's intention and that the author as a regulative principle of any interpretation is ultimately constrained by the person and the historical background of the writer—I studied translations of a short passage taken from the *Odyssey* by Homer, verses 187–93 and 344–52 (or verses 213–20 and 391–401, depending on the manuscript used) of Song 13. Without any intent to be exhaustive, and only for the sake of illustration, I examined twenty-five English translations, thirteen French, and twelve German. These translations stretch from the sixteenth to the twentieth century. In these different translations of the same text, I tried to discover whether an agreement exists among the translators that the verbal meaning of the text (understood as the author's intention) is the ultimate criterion of the validity of a translation, as Hirsch believes it should be, or whether the translators make use of the postulated author that Nehamas sees as the regulative idea of any interpretation.

This passage in the *Odyssey* describes the arrival of Ulysses in his homeland. While asleep, he is brought back to Ithaca by the Pheaceans. He wakes up, unaware that he is home. The text says, in A. T. Murray's translation (1931),

> . . . Odysseus awoke out of his sleep in his native land. Yet he knew it not after his long absence, for about him the goddess had shed a mist, even Pallas Athene, daughter of Zeus, that she might render him unknown, and tell him all things, so that his wife might not know him, nor his townsfolk, nor his friends, until the wooers had paid the full price of all their transgressions. (verses 187–93)

[Athena:] "But come, I will shew thee the land of Ithaca, that thou mayest be sure. This is the harbour of Phorcys, the old man of the sea, and here at the head of the harbour is the long-leafed olive tree, and near it is the pleasant, shadowy cave, sacred to the nymphs that are called Naiads. This, thou must know, is the vaulted cave in which thou wast wont to offer to the nymphs many hecatombs that bring fulfilment; and yonder is Mount Neriton, clothed with its forests."

So spake the goddess, and scattered the mist, and the land appeared. (verses 344, 352)

In the translations I consulted, and in an interpretation offered by Hermann Kleinknecht (1958), two elements, which seem closely related, are at the center of the strategy followed by translators. These two elements can be explained to the extent that they correspond to two difficulties of reading. The first difficulty deals with Athena's intention when she casts a mist all around: does she want to hide the native land from Ulysses' eyes, or does she want to hide Ulysses from his townspeople's eyes? The second difficulty is about the relationship or absence of relationship between the verb *muthesaito* of verse 191—which Murray translates "she might tell him all things"—and Athena's act of dissipating the mist in verse 352. Does Athena's *muthos* consist in the act of dissipating the mist, and hence unveiling the native land to Ulysses, or is there absolutely no link between what Athena says in verse 191 and what she does in verse 352?

The first difficulty concerns Athena's goal when she casts a mist all around. The text says, in order to make him or her or it (*min*) *agnoston*. *Min* and *agnoston* can be masculine, feminine, or neuter. They can thus be related to the earth (*gaiè*, feminine) as well as to Ulysses (*Odysseus*, masculine). Moreover, *agnoston* can be an adjective with an active sense (unaware of) or a passive sense (unrecognized). Thus, grammatically, Athena can pursue four different intentions by casting a mist all around: (1) she can try to make the land unrecognizable to Ulysses; (2) she can try to make Ulysses unaware of his own native land, the mist preventing him from recognizing the familiar landscape (this second reading yields the same propositional content as the first one, but through a different parsing); (3) she can try to make Ulysses unrecognizable to his townspeople's eyes; and (4) she can make the land unaware, which is an absurdity, although grammatically possible. We thus have three different plausible grammatical parsings that result in two logical possibilities, since one and two have the same content and four is absurd: the mist can be understood either as preventing Ulysses from recognizing the place or as preventing Ulysses' townspeople from recognizing him.

One of the reasons for the presence of such ambiguities or inconsistencies is probably the type of composition of the text. Most likely composed orally in the eighth or seventh century BC, the *Odyssey* was probably put in writing later. Homer, or whoever composed the book, was the inheritor of a series of oral compositions in which bards improvised around known story lines and had recourse to what Bernard Knox describes as "an intricate system of metrical alternatives for the recurring names of heroes, gods and objects. . . . There was a way to fit the names into the line in any of the usual grammatical forms they would assume" (1996, 14–16). For example, Ulysses can be characterized as much-enduring, a man of many schemes, godlike, great hearted; ships can be hollow, swift, black, well oared, or well benched. The bard chooses one epithet that fits the metrics of the verse he started. The story, then, is slightly different each time it is told.

By the time Homer's story was put in writing, some formulations had acquired a canonic status and the writer had to assemble several episodes that would be recited separately for different occasions. "Gradually a complete text would be assembled, to be refined in detail and extended by insertions, the longer sections welded into unity by connecting links. It was inevitable in such a process, with writing a newly acquired skill and writing materials, papyrus or leather, not convenient for cross-reference, that the final version should contain inconsistencies" (Knox 1996, 21). As an example, Knox mentions the impossibility of figuring out the ground plan of Ulysses' palace, where rooms have openings and exits that change in the course of the story. Our passage might also be a casualty of how the written copy was assembled. Be that as it may, translators have to make decisions about the meaning of the passage they want to convey.

Instead of choosing among those options, a translator might try to render those ambiguities in the target language, so that the richness of the original would be preserved. Although this option appears sound at first glance, most translators abhor it, following an almost cardinal, yet implicit, rule of translation: "In case of ambiguity, choose one option." This again illustrates Benjamin's talk of translation as an intention superimposed on the original. The first, obvious reason why translators do not render an ambiguous text by an ambiguous translation is the practical impossibility of doing it in all cases. Languages have different structures and obey different systems, so that it would be impossible, or at least excruciatingly difficult, to come up with expressions in English that could preserve the two meanings of *min* and *agnoston* (masculine and feminine in the first case, passive and active in the second case). Another reason, probably even more important than the first, is the need for coherence and consistency. The options chosen have to be compatible with the line of the story. Even if *min* and *agnoston* are grammatically ambiguous, it is not clear that the Greek audience entertained the different meanings at the same time. They most likely did what we do when hearing something grammatically ambiguous: we choose one parsing. Our choice is governed by what preceded and what follows. Translators do not hesitate to switch around parts of sentences to make a given passage intelligible and coherent with the way they understand the story. By choosing a path of coherence and consistency, they select and eliminate options.

The second difficulty in the passage concerns the verb *muthesaito*, which stems from *mutheo* or *mutheomai*, "to utter or perform a *muthos*"—*muthos* designating a type of word. The question bears on the type of word that Athena addresses to Ulysses. This word can offer some remarkable features depending on whether or not it is linked to the act of dissipating the mist. At the time she casts the mist, verse 189, the text says that one of the goals of this act is to utter a *muthos* to Ulysses. In verse 344, Athena dissipates the mist, thereby showing and naming the familiar surroundings that Ulysses did not recognize. Is there a relationship between Athena's *muthos* and the act of dissipating the mist?

When combining the two difficulties of the reading, the role of the mist, on the one hand, and the link between the *muthos* and the act of dissipating the mist, on the other, we have then four options for translators: (1) the mist hides the land and the *muthos* consists in dissipating the mist, (2) the mist hides the land and the *muthos* is not linked to the dissipating of the mist, (3) the mist hides Ulysses and the *muthos* consists in dissipating the mist, and (4) the mist hides Ulysses and the *muthos* is not linked to the dissipating of the mist. The majority of translations chose option 4, one chose option 1, a very few chose option 2, and none chose option 3. (All the translations of the texts in French and German that follow are my own.)

The Mist Conceals the Land and Muthos Is Revelatory

If one thinks that the goal of the mist is to make the place unrecognizable to Ulysses, a direct link can be established between *muthos*—which is promised when the mist is cast—and the act of dissipating the mist in verse 344. *Muthos* is then Athena's word, which makes the surroundings appear in all their truth. If there is such a direct link between the mist, which manifests Athena's desire to reveal everything to Ulysses, and Athena's revelation, which consists in simply dissipating the mist, then *muthos* is a revealing word that exerts an effect on reality. It is a magical act, analogous to the use Athena later makes of her stick to transform Ulysses. The significant difference, however, is that, in the passage I examine, the magical stick would be her very word, her *muthos*.

Such an option is offered and defended by Kleinknecht in his detailed analysis "Platonisches im Homer. Eine Interpretation von Odyssee XIII 187-354" (1958). His analysis of a relatively short passage, which thus does not offer a translation of the entirety of the *Odyssey*, contains several references to Walter Otto's views on *muthos* in the Greek world in general and in Homer in particular. Kleinknecht's analysis even appears as an application of Otto's views (Otto 1951, 1955, 1962). Otto himself quotes the passage I examine, without any detailed analysis, as an illustration of his thesis about the unity of gods and humans in Greek thought: "[Greek religion] did not render the divinity human; Greek religion saw the essence of the human as divine" (1984, 264). Following the views of Otto and Kleinknecht, Johannes Lohmann quotes the same passage and follows the same interpretation (1960, 175).

In Homer, there are several terms to designate a word: *muthos*, *logos*, *epos*. According to Otto, whereas *epos* designates the word as what is phonetically pronounced, there is a characteristic difference between the other two terms, *logos* and *muthos*. Both can name the word, the sentence, or the story told (1962, 358). In Homer, *muthos* appears more frequently than *logos* for naming short or long speeches. "*Logos* designates the word seen from the subjective side of the one who thinks or speaks, the word as what is thought or envisaged" (1951, 55). *Logos* designates something that is thought or desired. There can thus be a difference between what is said in a *logos* and what is really the case. This is the difference between what is thought and what is. *Logos* can deceive. In contrast, *muthos* is the thing itself that is under discussion. "It is the 'word' as an immediate testimony to what was, what is and what will be. It is the manifestation of being in the sense of what has been venerable for a long time, where there is no difference between word and being" (1951, 59; 1955, 71). *Muthos* seems to name a true story that shows how things are in themselves, reaching for the true being of a thing to the extent that this thing is unveiled in the words spoken about it. *Muthos* is "the 'word' which reports on what is real or which establishes something that must become real through this very utterance of the word"

(1962, 358). Between the thing as it is wrapped up in the *muthos* and the thing as it is, no difference obtains. The thing is as the *muthos* unveils it. Moreover, such a word must have an effect (*Kraft*) in the realm of things. "[Such a word] must be that word which does not merely designate the thing, but *is* the thing itself" (Otto 1951, 67). As authoritative word, *muthos* pertains to the past: what is true is what really happened. The more remote and significant this past is, the more sacred and different it is from what is said in the present. Thus, one sees why *muthos* shifts toward the nontemporal legend, the fable. *Muthos* can become myth.

In Kleinknecht's interpretation of our passage, the way Athena is going "to tell all things" to Ulysses (this is how Murray translates *muthesaito*) is rather peculiar. She is not going to let him know by words only. Since Ulysses cannot recognize his homeland due to the mist Athena has cast, she will "tell him all things" just by dissipating this mist so that the land appears to Ulysses as it is in truth, as his native land. This is the power of *muthos*, the *Kraft* of which Otto speaks (1951, 66) and which Murray's translation renders as, "Athena: But come, I will shew thee the land of Ithaca, that you mayest be sure" (verse 344); "So spake the goddess, and scattered the mist, and the land appeared" (verse 352).

Such an interpretation is only possible if one thinks that the mist makes the surroundings unrecognizable to Ulysses and that the verb *muthesaito* of verse 191 is put in a direct relationship with the act of dissipating the mist of verse 352. "Without a doubt: Athena first intently surrounded the earth in a mist so as, through her 'word,' to be able to 'tell' Ulysses in detail what the situation is" (Kleinknecht 1958, 73). For Kleinknecht, *ekasta muthesaito* means that Athena wants to let Ulysses see things one by one.

Here are some arguments and counterarguments in favor of the first reading—the mist makes the land unrecognizable to Ulysses:

1. After mentioning Ulysses' long absence, the text immediately introduces Athena's intervention with *gar*, for. The act of casting a mist around is presented as an explanation of the fact that Ulysses does not recognize his homeland. Counterargument: Some translators, however, such as R. D. Dawe (1993, 512), regard this passage as interpolated.

2. Some verses further down, the text says, "Therefore all things seemed strange to their lord" (verse 194). The strangeness of the surroundings would be caused by the mist. Counterargument: It would be possible, however, to account for the strange appearance with Ulysses' long absence.

3. In verse 344, when Athena reveals the surroundings to Ulysses by dissipating the mist, she says that she wants to convince him. This suggests

that when she cast the mist she meant to prevent Ulysses from recognizing his homeland.

4. There is a good reason for Athena to prevent Ulysses temporarily from recognizing his surroundings. She wanted to temper his ardor to rush to his palace to meet his wife and son. Such intemperate behavior would have led him to a certain death at the hands of the suitors. This is precisely what Ulysses thanks Athena for later on, after she informs him of the situation in his palace: "Lo now, of a surety I was like to have perished in my halls by the evil fate of Agamemnon, son of Atreus, hadst not thou, goddess, duly told me all [ekasta eeipes]" (verses 383–85).

5. Kleinknecht's reading was recommended by Aristophanes in his edition of the Homeric text around 200 BC. He proposed to change the text in the following way: ophra min (for gaian) auto (for Odyssei), "in order to make the earth unrecognized to him." This is also the version recommended by Wilamowitz. And Knox understands the passage in this way: "Odysseus meanwhile . . . wakes to find a landscape he does not recognize—Athena has covered it in mist" (1996, 46).

If the act of dissipating the mist accompanies, or even constitutes such a word, Kleinknecht must explain the sequence of Athena's acts: dissipating the mist and thus unveiling the familiar surroundings to Ulysses and speaking by offering an explanation. As Dawe formulates the problem, "It seems absurd that Athene should first point out the harbour, the cave and the mountain, *and then* dispel the mist" (1993, 520). In addition, if this were the sequence, Athena's words would be reduced to a mere explanation, in the sense that she would first dissipate the mist and then speak. Kleinknecht is aware of the difficulty. Like Dawe, he acknowledges that Athena's words would be completely superfluous after showing Ulysses the place. "Why would there be a further need for words of a goddess when anybody can already see what the situation is really like?" (1958, 71). The words are the revelation, the *muthos* is the dispelling of the clouds. He continues, "No: in the goddess' mouth the word is not an explanation and a subsequent representation of what already lies before the eyes. The word is what properly is" (71).

According to Kleinknecht, the word that *muthos* is has accompanied as well as caused the dawn of the truth. He reminds us that Ulysses, when meeting Athena, asks her to save him (*sao d'eme*, verse 230). Athena saves him, according to Kleinknecht, "to the extent that she lets him be what he is. . . . And to the extent that she helps him . . . *ta phainomena sozon* [to save what appears]: through her word she makes it the case that what appeared to Ulysses be fully what it is: Ithaca" (1958, 73). Knowledge through *muthos* is, properly speaking, a divine knowledge. Thus *muthos* stands in a particular relationship to the gods, and probably for this reason it is truer than *logos*, truer in the sense of more disclosing. For Kleinknecht, such a conception of revelation is an indication that there are already platonic elements in Homer.

Kleinknecht's analysis of *muthos* as a revelation is based on two interpretive decisions: the mist is understood as dissimulating the native land to Ulysses' eyes, and the act of performing a *muthos* is directly linked to the act of dissipating the mist, which takes place sixty-one verses farther down. There are, however, other options.

The Mist Conceals Ulysses and Muthos *Is a Mere Explanation*

Twenty out of the twenty-five English translations, ten out of the twelve German translations, and eight out of the thirteen French translations propose a reading opposite to the one by Kleinknecht. These translations understand by and large that the clouds conceal Ulysses' identity from his fellow people, not the surroundings from Ulysses' eyes. And they see no direct link between the *muthos*, which is supposed to follow the act of casting a mist around Ulysses, and the act of dissipating this mist to reveal the familiar surroundings. However, some ambiguities remain in many of these translations. These are two arguments and their counterarguments regarding this reading:

1. Speaking in favor of the reading is the fact that, already in Song 7, Athena uses this subterfuge where she casts a mist around Ulysses to protect his entrance into the Pheacean city. This subterfuge of shrouding someone in a mist seems to mean only that Athena makes that person invisible. Counterargument: The fact is that, in the passage I analyze, Athena will dissipate the mist long before Ulysses meets any townspeople or his wife. Moreover, Athena tells Ulysses in verse 344 that she is going to show him his native land, and thus to dissipate the mist to convince him. This makes it hard to maintain that the mist aims at protecting Ulysses' identity.

2. The text says farther down, after the mist has been cast, "so that his wife might not know him, nor his townsfolk, nor his friends" (verse 192), which makes it plausible that Athena disguised him. Counterargument: In verse 429, however, Athena turns Ulysses into a beggar by touching him with her magical stick, a transformation that she undoes in Song 16, verse 172. Why use a second artifice to conceal Ulysses from the eyes of people if

the mist already fulfilled such a role? Some translators, however, such as Victor Bérard, in French, consider verses 192–93 interpolated.

Most translations that unequivocally state that the mist conceals Ulysses make a connection between the mist and Athena's intention to hide him from other people's eyes. It started in English translations with George Chapman: ". . . Minerva threw / A cloud about him . . . / . . . lest upon his shore / He should make known his face. . . ." (1956, first published in 1598–1616). This was taken over by Alexander Pope: Athena "diffused around a veil of thickened air / . . . to keep unseen / His royal person . . ." (1848, first published in 1626). Other translators followed suit, using similar expressions: "that she might make him unknown" (Buckley 1851), "render him unknown" (Palmer 1921, first published in 1884; Murray 1931, first published in 1919), "make him / unrecognized" (Merrill 2002), "that he might not yet be known" (Bryant 1871), "to conceal him" (Cotterill 1911), "to make him unperceived to mortal sense" (Mackail 1932), "Athena had shrouded the King in a mist" (Rees 1977, first published in 1960), "to keep him safe from recognition" (Hammond 2000).

In German, Simon Schaidenreisser started a similar trend in 1537: "The goddess Minerva had put around him a thick mist so that neither his fellow countrymen nor his friends could recognize him [*die göttin Minerva mitt ainem dicken näbel umbgeben hat, auff das in weder seine Burger noch freünd möchten kennen*]" (1911, first published in 1537). Johann Heinrich Voss continues this line: "A goddess shrouded him around with a dark night . . . in order to make him unknowable [*eine Göttin umhüllt ihn / Rings mit dunkler Nacht . . . / Ihn unkennbar zu machen*]" (1980, first published in 1781). Analogous formulations are quite common: "to make him unrecognizable [*unkenntlich*]" (Donner 1858; Schröder 1948; Hampe 1979), "until she had made him unrecognizable [*unerkennbar*]" (von Scheffer 1938), "she wanted that no one recognize him [*Sie wollte, / Dass ihn niemand erkenne*]" (Schwitzke 1960), "so that she [the goddess] make him invisible to the eye [*unsichtbar . . . den Augen*]" (Jünger 1979), "she wanted to withdraw the hero from alien gaze [*sie wollte den helden fremden Blicken entziehen*]" (Ebener 1983).

In French too we find analogous formulations: "And the Goddess . . . casts a divine mist around Ulysses so that he remains unknown" (*Minerve . . . répand un divin nuage autour d'Ulysse pour qu'il reste inconnu*, Bareste 1842), (*afin qu'il demeurât inconnu*, Personneaux undated), (*restât inconnu*, Leconte de Lisle 1923), (*reste ignoré* , Dugas Montbel 1870). "Pallas Athena who wanted to make him unrecognizable [*qui voulait le rendre méconnais-*

sable]" (Dufour and Raison 1965), ". . . so that he remained invisible [*qu'il demeurât invisible*]"(Jaccottet 1982).

A few translations connect the mist directly with the *muthos*: "and round about him there / . . . Athena . . . spread a mist amid the air, / that all things she might tell him while yet unknown" (Morris 1904); " . . . that ere yet agnized / By others, he might wisdom learn from her" (Cowper 1910); "to the end that she might expound to him all things" (Butcher and Lang 1937); "desiring first to tell him herself all things necessary and to shroud his likeness from all eyes" (Shewring 1980). A translator can also leave the ambiguity by making a transition between the fact that Ulysses does not recognize his land and the cloud shed by Athena: "Moreover, Pallas Athena . . . poured a grey mist all around him, hiding him from common sight—for she had things to tell him" (Fitzgerald 1961).

Other translators also understand the cloud as hiding Ulysses but allow for some ambiguities. Athena cast a mist overall, which means, we can assume, over the land and Ulysses:

- "Moreover . . . Minerva had made it a foggy day, so that people might not know of his having come, and she might tell him everything" (Butler 1900)
- "For Athena . . . had covered the place with mist that she might tell him everything first and disguise him" (Rouse 1937)
- "For the Goddess . . . had thrown a mist over the place to give herself time to make plans with Odysseus and disguise him . . ." (Rieu 1946)
- "Pallas Athena had spread a haze all around. The Goddess wanted to explain things to him / And to disguise him . . ." (Lombardo 2000)
- "For the goddess . . . poured a mist overall, so she could make him unrecognizable and explain all the details to him" (Lattimore 1965)
- "For the goddess . . . showered mist over all, so under cover she might change his appearance head to foot as she told him every peril . . ." (Fagles 1996)
- "For the goddess . . . poured mist around, to make the man himself unrecognizable, and so that she could tell him everything" (Dawe 1993)

Sometimes the translator is more explicit in the connection between absence and cloud: "Not that he knew his whereabouts. Partly he had been absent for so long, but in part it was because Pallas Athena had thickened the air about him to keep him unknown while she made him wise to things" (Lawrence 1991, first published in 1932). We find the same choice in German: "in order in part to inform him of all conditions, in part to make sure that his fellow countrymen . . . not recognize him [*um ihn von allen Fällen / Zu unterrichten theils, theils aber zu verfiellen, dass ihn die Bürger nicht . . . ihn / . . . erkennen sollten*]" (Sedlezki 1784), as well as in French: "such was the length of his absence and such is the thickness of the cloud that Minerva put around him: she wants him, while remaining unknown, to have the time to learn from her mouth everything that concerns him [*telle a été la longueur de son absence et telle est l'épaisseur du nuage dont Minerve l'environne: elle veut que, demeurant inconnu, il ait le temps d'apprendre de sa bouche tout ce qui l'intéresse*]" (Bitaubé 1883).

A translator can also grant the cloud a dual function, keeping Ulysses from being recognized and preventing Ulysses from recognizing the land, as in the following cases: ". . . he did not know just where he was because Athena had enveloped him in a mist. She shielded him from prying eyes" (Mandelbaum 1990). A French translator does the same, although the mist is around the land: "for Minerva put a mist around it [the land], so that he himself remained unknown and that she informs him of all things [*car Minerve l'a enveloppée de brouillard, pour qu'il demeure lui-même inconnu, et qu'elle l'informe de toutes choses*]" (Giguet 1880).

In addition, there are some inconsistencies. Chapman understands the clouds to hide Ulysses, but he seems to have changed his mind later on when Athena dissipates the cloud: "This sayd, she cleer'd the clowd / that first deceyv'd his eyes . . ." (1956), suggesting that the cloud was also keeping Ulysses from seeing the land. In German Schaidenreisser (1911) understands the clouds as hiding Ulysses, but when Athena makes the mist disappear, he understands that she actually disappears in the air: "and with these words the Goddess disappeared in the air [*und mit diesen worten verschwand die Göttin in den luft*]."

Understanding the function of the mist as concealing Ulysses affects the way Athena's *muthos* is to be understood. For, if one thinks that Athena intended to conceal Ulysses from his townspeople's eyes through the mist, the *muthos* that is supposed to follow this act of concealment does not seem to have any particular link to the later act of dissipating the mist that makes the surroundings recognizable. The *muthos* that is promised after the act of concealment seems to be rather an explanation Athena provides about what Ulysses can expect and the plan Athena will concoct with him for avenging the suitors. Here are two arguments speaking in favor of a *muthos* as a mere explanation:

1. Immediately afterward the text says, "so that his wife might not know him, nor his townsfolk, nor his friends, until the wooers had paid the full

price of all their transgressions" (verses 192–94). The expression *ekasta eeipes* (hadst not thou told me all) in verse 385, by which Ulysses thanks Athena, would be the perfect equivalent of the expression *ekasta muthesaito* in verse 192, Athena's *muthos* being nothing else than an epos. Bérard (1972), however, considers verses 192–94 to be interpolated.

2. Against Otto and Kleinknecht, it is rather obvious that *muthos* in the *Odyssey* does not necessarily and certainly not constantly have the sense of revelation. *Phato muthon* (verse 37) can very well be translated as "he uttered those words." Similarly, when Athena says of Ulysses that he is the best in calculations and *muthoisin* (verse 298), one can understand that he reaches excellence in the art of speaking and telling stories. There is even mention of a deceptive *muthos* in verses 294–95 when Athena tells Ulysses, ". . . not even in thine own land, it seems, wast thou to cease from guile and deceitful tales [*muthon klopion*], which thou lovest from the bottom of thine heart."

As a consequence, and as an implicit refutation of Kleinknecht's and Otto's views, these translations maintain Athena's word, her *muthos*, within a dialogue; that is, Athena's *muthos* is the explanation she will provide of the situation in Ulysses' palace and of a plan of action appropriate to the circumstances. When Athena later dissipates the mist she had cast around Ulysses, this act of dissipating the mist is only, for these translators, one argument used by Athena for convincing Ulysses of her good faith. In other words, the act of dissipating the mist does not represent Athena's *muthos*— in which case *muthos* would be a divine revelation of the truth of things, as in Kleinknecht—but the attestation of her good faith, showing that her *muthos*—the information she has provided and the counsel she has given—is credible and trustworthy. Through her words, thus, Athena acts upon Ulysses and upon his capacity to be convinced rather than upon the things around Ulysses, as Kleinknecht and Otto claim.

This second option thus leads the relationship between Athena and Ulysses on a psychological path. They converse almost like two equals: over and against Ulysses as a master in the art of the *muthos* (verse 298), Athena only proposes her own *muthos*, on the horizontal plane of a dialogue. There is, however, an evolution in the way *muthos* has been translated in the course of time. While older translations attempt to preserve a somewhat mysterious aspect of Athena's intervention, the more recent translations have opted for a full psychologization of the dialogue between Athena and Ulysses.

In the early English translations, *muthesaito* is translated as a simple act of saying, but associated with several terms or various expressions that betoken a divine plan. Chapman (1956) translates *muthesaito* as utter all: "Athena threw a cloud about him, to make strange the more / His safe arrival . . . and utter all / that might prevent th'event that was to fall—which she prepar'd so well . . ." He understands Athena's role as an orator or a preacher who aims at acting upon the man so that he sees what the situation is really like: "Come then, I'll shew thee why / I call this Isle thy Ithaca. To ground / Thy credit on my words . . ."

Alexander Pope's 1726 translation (reissued 1848) also disseminates *muthesaito* in paraphrases: "Besides Minerva, to secure her care, / Diffused around a veil of thickened air: / For so the gods ordain'd, to keep unseen / His royal person from his friends and queen." Athena wants "to secure her care," because this is what "the gods ordain'd." In Pope too, as in Chapman, Athena's word takes effect through oratorical and rhetorical means: "Now lift thy longing eyes, while I restore / The pleasing prospect of thy native shore."

English translations of the nineteenth and twentieth centuries continue in that direction, reinforcing the rhetorical aspect of *muthos*, while at the same time psychologizing the relationship between Athena and Ulysses: they discuss and take part in a dialogue that aims at convincing Ulysses. This option gives a new orientation to the divine plan Athena has concocted by reinforcing the dialogical character of *muthos* and bringing Athena down to the human level. To utter a *muthos* is nothing else, for English translations, than an act of

- telling (Buckley 1851; Bryant 1871; Palmer 1921; Butler 1900; Morris 1904; Murray 1931, first published in 1919; Rouse 1937; Fitzgerald 1961; Shewring 1980; Dawe 1993; Fagles 1996; Hammond 2000)
- making plans (Rieu 1946; Rees 1977)
- informing (Mackail 1932)
- expounding (Butcher and Lang 1937)
- explaining (Lattimore 1965; Lombardo 2000)

In this psychologization of the debate between Athena and Ulysses, Athena speaks as an orator, providing proofs and evidence

- to be believed (Buckley 1851; Bryant 1871; Palmer 1921; Butler 1900; Lattimore 1965; Lombardo 2000)
- to convince Ulysses (Lawrence 1991; Rieu 1946; Rees 1977)
- so that Ulysses has some assurance (Cotteril 1911; Murray 1931; Butcher and Lang 1937; Mandelbaum 1990; Hammond 2000)
- that Ulysses ceases to doubt (Mackail 1932)

Some accents of a superior and mysterious power remain, especially in English. Here is how William Bryant translates the passage in 1871: ". . . But now / Attend and I will show thee Ithaca / By certain tokens; mark them and believe." Similarly in Lawrence (1991), Athena "made him wise to things" and in Cowper (1910) Ulysses "might wisdom learn from her." A similar trend is found in one German translator. In a free translation by Schwitzke (1960), Athena asks whether she has to open Ulysses' eyes.

We find the same type of words in German as in English. *Muthesaito* is translated variously as
- to impart knowledge (*unterrichten*; Sedlezki 1784; Ebener 1983)
- to discuss (*besprechen*; Voss 1980; Schwitzke 1960; Jünger 1979)
- to deliberate and give counsel (*beraten*; Hampe 1979)
- to show or to point out (*weisen*; von Scheffer 1938)
- to explain (*bedeuten*; Donner 1858)
- to say (*sagen*; Schröder 1948)

Voss, at the end of the eighteenth century, seems to have imposed the psychological trend. The act of dissipating the mist will then be a mere piece of evidence supporting her credibility: she purports
- to alleviate Ulysses' doubts (Schaidenreisser 1911; Sedlezki 1784)
- to be believed (Voss 1980; Donner 1858; Jünger 1979; Hampe 1979)
- to be trusted (von Scheffer 1938; Schröder 1948; Ebener 1983)

In French we find translations such as
- to inform (*informer*; Bareste 1842; Dugas Montbel 1870; Personneaux undated; Giguet 1880; Leconte de Lisle 1923; Dufour and Raison 1965)
- to explain (*expliquer*; Jaccottet 1982)

The act of dissipating the cloud is a mere explanation: "Now I will show you the sites of your Ithaka and your doubts will vanish [*Maintenant je vais te montrer les sites de ton Ithaque et tes doutes s'effaceront*]" (Giguet 1880). In this second option, *muthesaito* is a mere word addressed by a goddess who tries to convince a human being in a dialogue between two minds. The divine aspect of revelation is almost absent, except in the early translations, where some sense of mystery remains.

The Mist Hides the Land and Muthos Is Explanatory

There is still a third option for solving the difficulties in the text: the function of the mist and the link between Athena's *muthos* and the act of dissipating the mist. This option is found in only five of the thirteen French translations and one of the twelve German translations I have examined. These translations explicitly state, as in the first option, that the mist is intended to conceal the land from Ulysses' eyes and not to conceal Ulysses himself, but they do not state any link between uttering a *muthos* and dissipating the clouds.

These translators take it that the mist is supposed to calm Ulysses, who might rush to his palace if he knew he was in Ithaca, and give Athena time to debrief him on the situation in the island. Here are the French translations:

- "For the goddess . . . had cast a mist over it [the land] so that he did not recognize his Ithaca; she desired to inform him herself of everything [*car la déesse . . . avait répandu sur elle [la terre de sa patrie] un nuage, afin qu'il ne reconnût point son Ithaque; elle désirait elle-même l'instruire de tout*]" (Hachette 1855).
- "For a goddess . . . had spread a mist around him so that he could not by himself recognize the place and that he learn everything from her [*Une déesse en effet . . . avait autour de lui répandu un brouillard, afin qu'il ne pût pas lui-même reconnaître les lieux et qu'il apprît tout d'elle*]" (Meunier 1961).
- "For Pallas Athena had cast a cloud around him . . . so that he would not recognize anything from his surroundings and learn everything from her [*Car Pallas Athena . . . avait autour de lui versé une nuée, afin que de ces lieux, il ne reconnût rien et qu'il apprît tout d'elle*]" (Bérard 1972).
- "Moreover since she had put a mist on his eyes, he did not recognize Ithaca [*De plus comme elle luy avait mis un nuage sur les yeux, il ne reconnoissoit point Ithaque*]" (Barbin 1682).
- "And the Goddess Minerva wrapped him immediately with a thick cloud so that he could not recognize it [*Et la déesse Minerve l'enveloppa sur-le-champ d'un épais nuage, afin qu'il ne pût la reconnaître*]." Although grammatically *l'enveloppa* can mean shrouded Ulysses [*l'* for *le*] or shrouded the land [*l'* for la: *la terre*], the passage definitely means shrouded Ulysses, as confirmed later on when Athena dissipates "the cloud that she had put around him" (Dacier 1815).

One German translator has analogous formulations: "he could not obviously recognize it [the land]; for he was away for so long and the goddess . . . cast a mist over it [the land] until she revealed everything to him and made him unrecognizable [*er konnte es freilich / Gar nicht erkennen; denn lange ja war er schon fort und die Göttin . . . übergoss es mit Nebel / Bis sie ihm alles verriete und unerkennbar ihn mache*]" (Weiher 1990).

All those translators think that the *muthos*, which is supposed to follow the act of casting the mist, does not consist in dissipating the mist, as in the first option. Athena's *muthos* is a mere act of explanation, as in the second option. The oldest translation, published by Barbin in 1682, does not really translate the verb *muthesaito*: Athena "has arranged Ulysses' return [*avait ménagé son retour*]" and "has put a mist on his eyes [*elle lui avait mis un nuage sur les yeux*]." Although *muthesaito* is not exactly translated, we can feel an aura of mystery or religious awe in the formulations: in order to have him recognize his homeland "she dissipated the illusion with which Ulysses' eyes were held spellbound [*elle dissipa l'illusion dont les yeux d'Ulysse estoient charmez*]." Athena, however, first and foremost acts upon Ulysses, on his senses, and not on the things around him. This is sufficient to show the difference that exists between the option chosen by that translation and the option of a *muthos* acting upon things as in the one found in Kleinknecht. Moreover, even if the translation of the seventeenth century preserves some magical aspect to Athena's intervention—the use of a spell causing an illusion—this way of presenting Athena's intervention represents a psychologization of the relationship between the goddess and Ulysses. She behaves more like a magician playing with Ulysses' senses than like a divinity revealing the true being of things.

In the other translations, Athena's *muthos* is increasingly understood in a psychological and dialogical framework; *muthesaito* is rendered as
- "to learn from her mouth [*apprendre de sa bouche*]" (Bitaubé 1883)
- "learned everything from her [*apprît tout d'elle*]" (Meunier 1961; Bérard 1972)
- "to warn [*avertir*]" (Dacier 1815)
- "to inform [*instruire*]" (Hachette 1855)

Bérard summarizes the way the act of dissipating the mist is seen, again as a mere evidence for Athena's credibility: "look up with me, perhaps you will believe me [*regarde avec moi, tu me croiras peut-être*]" (Bérard 1972).

In the same psychological vein, Weiher (1990) translates *muthesaito* as *verraten*: to deliver information, to transfer information unseen, as a spy. After dissipating the mist, Athena, in that same translation, says, *uberzeuge dich selbe* (convince yourself).

The results of this comparison are mixed. The three options clearly indicate a significant variation among translators. Even within one option, an evolution through time takes place in the way the relationship between Ulysses and Athena is depicted. We clearly have a multiplicity of interpretations according to the particular aspects translators decided to emphasize. This multiplicity, however, is limited: only three options are chosen by the translators, and there is a historical convergence among these options (the psychologization of the dialogue between Athena and Ulysses), so that similarities among translations significantly outweigh differences.

If we appeal to the model of monism or pluralism, we will have to acknowledge that the two models apply, although not in the same respect and not to the same extent. When we look at the translations from a historical point of view, in a third-person perspective, pluralism can account for how translations evolve in the course of time or across linguistic communities. Considered pragmatically, however, from a first-person perspective, at the moment the translations were performed, the similarities between translations and the arguments supporting the coherence of each of the three options indicate that translators aimed at rendering the original text and attempted to model the translation on the original. In short, although a strict pluralism can be excluded as a model followed by translators, monism alone does not account for the diversity that seems intrinsic to the task of translation.

Theoretical Repercussions

Along with Hirsch and Nehamas, one could respond that these translations and interpretations, even if essentially plausible, are not necessarily correct. The factual multiplicity of interpretations of the same passage does not prove the legitimacy in principle of such a multiplicity. This counterargument, however, which follows Hirsch and Nehamas, suffers from two weaknesses. First, within Hirsch's and Nehamas's framework, the principles that guarantee the legitimacy and correctness of an interpretation are in part interpretive: to take the author's intention as a norm of interpretation is, according to Hirsch (as is any choice of a norm), "a free social and ethical act" (1967, 260). This particular ethical act of choosing the author's intention as a norm entails "interpretive guesses" (170). According to Nehamas, the ideal interpretation, which would account for all the characteristics of the work to be rendered, is a hypothesis. There is nothing noninterpretive that could definitely anchor the correctness or validity of an interpretation. The second weakness comes from the fact that the diversity in translation follows a rational pattern of coherence, consistency, and even adequacy to the original text. Since the different options are equally rational (which is not the same as equally justified), the fact of diversity cannot be explained away by some principles, let alone by principles based on educated guesses (Hirsch) or hypotheses (Nehamas).

Hirsch and Verbal Meaning

My comparison shows that the strict distinction Hirsch makes between verbal meaning and significance—the former being supposed to yield the author's intention, the latter involving meaning for a community, and so forth—is not tenable as such and would necessitate a greater conceptual sophistication. In the passage of the *Odyssey* I examine, it is precisely the verbal meaning that resists understanding. What is the verbal meaning of *muthesaito* or *agnoston*? If there is already an opacity at the level of the verbal meaning, how can the interpreter appropriate the author's intention? This is even more confusing in the case of the *Odyssey*, where the writer might very well be a team of writers or a series of successive reciters.

The general distinction between the verbal meaning of a text and the significance it has for an audience is both legitimate and relevant: in general it corresponds to a real difference between what the text says and the way it can be used or understood. The contention lies in the two theses at the basis of such a distinction. Hirsch's first thesis is that recourse to the author's intention is the only criterion for establishing the validity of an interpretation, to the extent that this intention guarantees the stability of the verbal meaning. Only what the author means can offer a compelling norm through which an interpretation can be measured. The second thesis is that the verbal meaning can be grasped independently of the significance it has for interpreters. These two theses are merely two sides of the same view. If there is a verbal meaning that can be grasped as it is in itself, it is because it has an identity in itself that can only stem from the intention of the one who used those signs.

The difficulty is to find strict criteria for deciding what belongs to the verbal meaning and to the significance of this verbal meaning, without this distinction being itself the result of an interpretation. Two elements in Hirsch's thought indicate that, despite his efforts, he is unable to maintain the purity of the distinction. In fact, he seems implicitly to acknowledge that the two notions of verbal meaning and significance define themselves in contrast to each other, which makes them somewhat unstable and susceptible to interpretation. These two elements are the fact that interpretation relies on an understanding and his appeal to a distinction Saussure makes between langue (language) and parole (speech).

Interpretation is a "commentary that is primarily about meaning" (Hirsch 1967, 143). If interpretation is a commentary, a moment of understanding must have preceded it. This understanding is defined as "a perception or construction of the author's verbal meaning" (143). Such an understanding, which is "a silent and private phenomenon" (8), presupposes a mastery of language that includes "the convention systems and the shared meaning associations" (134). If understanding constructs the meaning, then, strictly speaking, interpretation directly bears not on meaning but on the understanding of meaning. The specific task of interpretation is thus not to construct meaning but to explain, to evaluate, and to validate the meaning that understanding has clarified. "The systematic side of interpretation begins where the process of understanding ends. Understanding achieves a construction of meaning; the job of validation is to evaluate the disparate constructions which understanding has brought forward" (170). Given, however, that meaning is not conveyed directly in a form of intuition, but requires a construction, meaning becomes the object of an interpretive task: "It is perfectly true that the complex process of construing a text always involves interpretive guesses . . . validations of sort" (170). If the understanding of meaning already involves an embryo of interpretation—whereas in principle interpretation is supposed to arise from the understanding of meaning—how can the interpreter maintain a strict difference between verbal meaning and significance? Is it not implicitly acknowledged that verbal meaning is itself interpreted and that it is the relevance of this verbal meaning for the interpreter that allows the interpreter to identify it as such? In this case, verbal meaning is not the basis of interpretation but a result of interpretation.

To refine my criticism of the strict distinction between verbal meaning and significance, I draw upon Saussure, whom Hirsch himself invokes, but with another goal. Hirsch makes use of Saussure's distinction between langue and parole to undermine the thesis that a text is "a fragment of language" and that its meaning comes not from an intention but from language. Against such a thesis, Hirsch rightly notes that a text consists of sentences, the sentence being on the side of speech and not language as a system. As speech the sentence is an utterance, an act—oral or in writing. Since an act requires an agent, the latter can only be a speaker in the case of a sentence or an author in the case of a text. This undermines, Hirsch contends, the thesis that the author of a text is language itself—that it is language as a system that speaks.

Remarkably, Hirsch does not appeal to Saussure when he discusses the notion of verbal meaning, though the distinction between language as system and speech as act seems at first glance to lend itself to such a discussion. Similarly, the definition of understanding that lies at the basis of interpretation as a silent act, which presupposes the sharing of a system of linguistic conventions, seems to appeal implicitly to Saussure's notion of langue as system. Since Hirsch uses Saussure's theory in other instances, and since he mentions Saussure among the seven thinkers to whom he owes his major ideas, reexamining the distinction between verbal meaning and significance in Saussurean terms seems pertinent and legitimate.

Language is a linguistic system that we interpreters share within the linguistic community to which we belong. It is thus tempting to believe—as I think Hirsch does—that verbal meaning is understood in the sense that it is constructed in immanence, so to speak, because it is regulated by language as a system that author and interpreter share. Strictly speaking, then, meaning is not given, but construed, since one has to master language and its conventions for deciphering meaning. Besides the fact that this scenario does not envisage the case where author and interpreter speak a different language and thus act in a different system—as with the translation or the interpretation of a text written in a foreign language—Hirsch seems to overlook some basic distinctions in Saussure.

For instance, he does not take into account what Saussure says about the value of terms. Whereas Hirsch seems to put the verbal meaning on the side of langue—it is sufficient to master langue to be able to decipher, and thus understand, the verbal meaning—Saussure states that there is no verbal meaning independent of the value of the signs in the system; the value is precisely this crossing point and moment of exchange between langue and parole. The value, one could say, is the meaning of the terms of a language for their speakers, the same "for" used by Hirsch when he defines significance.

Hirsch overlooks Saussure's nuances, in particular the value of terms, because he only considers a situation in synchrony. Hirsch seems to reason in the following way: what allows a speaker to speak and be understood is the fact that speaker and listener share the same linguistic system; they can in principle understand the verbal meaning of what is said, even if there can be a disagreement on what this verbal meaning means to them, which is the significance of what is said. Applying this schema to interpretation, Hirsch thinks that langue as system guarantees in principle an isomorphism between what the text says and what the interpreter reads. For it is true that, in synchrony, the terms used by a speaker have the same value for the other members of the linguistic community, and it is precisely this identity that permits language to be both a system for the intelligibility of speech acts and a system for the production of speech acts. In the synchrony within a given linguistic community, the upbringing of children—the process of socialization, education, and cultural productions—allows for a smooth passage back and forth between langue and parole. Such a dialectic permits speakers to understand and produce successful speech acts and to be expert witnesses of the langue of their language as native speakers. In synchrony within a given linguistic community, these two capacities of producing speech acts and being an expert witness are not differentiated and need not be. The system of langue has been integrated and is part of the background knowledge that makes speakers skillful in their own language.

When we look more closely at what is involved in this mastery of one's native language, it appears that the verbal meaning is already a product. The verbal meaning results not only from mastering signs but also from internalizing the value of those signs in a system. It is by this internalization of signs and their value that language allows (1) someone to be a speaker (addressor), (2) someone to receive the message (addressee), (3) something nonlinguistic to be referred to (referent), and (4) something to be communicated (communication). What blurs the fact that even a verbal meaning is a product and what gives the impression of an immediacy between verbal meaning and understanding is the synchrony of the situation of both speaker and interpreter. They happen to share the same linguistic system and thus to feed on the same values for words and expressions.

When the situation is not in synchrony, however, the value of terms is not immediately shared. This happens when the interpreter does not share the same linguistic community as the author of the text to be interpreted, whether in the case of a translation or the interpretation of a text in the same language but from the distant past. Now the value of terms is crucial. Since it is the value that allows the interaction between langue and parole, either in producing a successful speech act or in understanding such a speech act correctly, if the value is not shared naturally in synchrony, it will have to be reconstructed. To translate a text or to interpret either a text that is written in a foreign language or a text written in the language of the interpreter that belongs to the distant past, the interpreter must not only master the grammar and the vocabulary of the idiom in which the text has been written but also learn to determine the value of words in that idiom. In other words, to determine the value of a set of words, the interpreter will have to figure out their place in a system not identical to his own. Speaking a foreign language is such an exercise in mastering the values of terms and expressions, which amounts to sharing a culture and acquiring a feel for habits and customs. It is only after examining a sufficient number of speech acts in the foreign language that a translator or an interpreter of texts from the past will be able to reconstruct the system of langue that governed the community of the historical author.

In the situations where the place of terms in a system has to be reconstructed on the basis of a description or investigation, the point of departure that the translator or interpreter has to take can only be what a word, a sentence, or a text means to the interpreter. And this goes directly against Hirsch's views, since it is the other way around for him: the significance comes from the verbal meaning. In the case of translators or interpreters of texts from a distant past, they have to start where they are, which is not where the author was. It is from their own cultural horizon and their own language that translators or interpreters can determine the extent to which this or that speech act manifested by this or that work—for example Athena's *muthos*—is different from or is similar to what they can articulate in their own language. Against Hirsch's claims, what a translator or an interpreter recovers in a situation other than synchrony is not what the author intended, but, strictly speaking, (1) the verbal meaning of the signs the author left (2) such that this verbal meaning can be reconstructed (3) in accordance with the significance this verbal meaning now has for the translator or the interpreter who has a particular audience in mind.

The case of translation and interpretation of a text from a remote past does not undermine Hirsch's distinction between verbal meaning and significance. What this case shows is that the verbal meaning is what is reconstructed and posited through the significance a text had, so that the distinction between verbal meaning and significance is not fixed, but a methodological device used by interpreters. As such a device, which originates from the community of the present translator and interpreter, the verbal meaning cannot be the criterion for assessing the validity of an interpretation. At best it is what methodologically regulates what interpreters do, in the sense that the verbal meaning is what they try to render.

As a methodological device, however, the verbal meaning is a category of interpretation and not an intrinsic feature of the text. We can agree with Juhl that "textual features are evidence of what a work means in virtue of being evidence of what the author meant" (1980, 149), but what the author meant is not necessarily, as Juhl claims, what an actual historical author had in mind. My comparison indeed defends a form of intentionalism, but one in which the author has no ontology. Is it then a hypothetical author, so that this comparison leads to hypothetical intentionalism? Not quite.

The Author as a Regulative Idea

In my comparison of different translations, is there a place for Nehamas's postulated author, this hypothesis of an ideal interpretation transcending centuries? The translations show that there is indeed an ideal interpretation, but this ideal does not transcend centuries and linguistic communities, as Nehamas wished. When diachronically comparing translations of the twentieth or twenty-first century with those of Pope and Chapman, or when comparing English translations with French translations, the transcendental regulative idea of a perfect and complete interpretation does not account for the divergences and convergences found between translations. What is questionable in Nehamas's views is his use of historical plausibility as a criterion for guaranteeing the brand of monism he defends, as well as his method for determining what is historically plausible and what is not.

Regarding the historical plausibility of the author, Nehamas seems to think that, if the author as interpretive hypothesis is himself interpretive in nature, there is no ultimate instance in the conflict of interpretations and one has to accept that an interpretation is just a fabrication. Although I fully share Nehamas's desire to discriminate between interpretation and fabrication, it seems that the price he pays for the stability of meaning sometimes exceeds the benefit. I do not see how the historical plausibility of the author could be anything else than an attempt to confirm an interpretation (of the author's intention) by another interpretation (of the historical data surrounding the writer). Verifying an interpretation by another interpretation can only be relevant within the consensus that obtains in a community. In this case, despite what he would like, Nehamas would have to accept that the ideal author is itself produced by the community for whom the interpretation or translation is made. As with Hirsch, Nehamas's thesis assumes a situation of synchrony, and so must be amended to account for diachrony.

In synchrony, Nehamas's thesis holds true in the case of interpretation, because the interpreter shares the same cultural background as the one against which the text arose. In the case of translation, if several translators of the same text belong to the same linguistic community—for example, the translators of the *Odyssey* in the late twentieth or early twenty-first century—the regulative idea is what allows a community of interpreters or translators to discuss texts and agree or disagree on how to interpret them and to demonstrate the validity of their hermeneutic tools. Each of these interpreters must raise the claim to offer a better interpretation or to offer an original insight. Not making such a claim would result in disqualifying oneself from scholarly activity, not being understood in one's intellectual enterprise, not being published, and not being part of the intellectual dialogue. A postulated author can mean that a community of interpreters posits, as the guarantee that they investigate and discuss the same text, a unifying principle behind the text they examine. In this sense the author is of course different from the historical writer, but it is also a production by the interpreters. It is an ad hoc author. We can, therefore, accept that this author can change with time, as Nehamas recognizes.

When the situation of interpretation is not in synchrony, as with, for example, the various translations of the *Odyssey*, the regulative idea seems to be the principle that unifies the text to be interpreted or translated as it is posited by a specific community of interpreters or translators. This regulative idea is the guarantee that interpreters or translators, as a unified community, interpret and translate the same text. In this sense, the author is obviously different from the historical writer; it is also a production by interpreters—what Nehamas accepts—but not transcendental, as Nehamas wishes, in the sense that it does not hold across time. When trying to account for the three options regarding the role of the mist cast by Athena and the psychologization of her role, I do not find a posited author that transcends cultural and historical boundaries. The author posited at each time seems to respond to what a particular linguistic community expects and can find intelligible.

The reason there is such a possibility of discrepancy in how an author can be constructed lies in its impossible status. This impossible status is manifested by the following—in my view contradictory—statements by Nehamas: (1) "Being a construct, the author is not a historical person whose states of mind we can ever hope, or even want, to recapture," so that, when interpreting a text, "there is nothing there . . . for us to re-create" (1987, 286), and (2) "To interpret a text is to consider it as its author's production. Literary texts are produced by agents and must be understood as such. This seems to me to be self-evident" (1981, 145). If there is any plausibility involved in the author, as Nehamas wants, the author must be more than a construct. It has to be anchored, however loosely, in a real agent, the historical writer. The author must be a possible person with possible thoughts and experiences, and interpreting must mean somehow reenacting or at least accessing thoughts or intentional states, even if only hypothesized. The author, contrary to Nehamas, must be more than a character and have some depth.

The second element in Nehamas's theory that needs to be amended is the method he advocates for evaluating the historical plausibility of the meaning ascribed to a text, for discriminating what can and cannot belong to the meaning of a text. Nehamas himself acknowledges the difficulty: "In a sense there is something arbitrary about constructing a historically plausible figure as a text's author" (1981, 146). This task is highly interpretive, since an intention has to be ascribed through a postulate to an author who is himself nothing more than a heuristic hypothesis. How can a translator or an interpreter limit the arbitrariness of such a construction? Nehamas thinks that he can establish such a limit by stating that "meaning . . . depends on an author's intentions even if a writer is not aware of it" (145) but that these intentions of the author "depend on what the writer could have meant" (145). This historical plausibility reformulates Hirsch's notion of the author's horizon, itself borrowed from Husserl.

Nehamas gives two examples illustrating what is plausible and what is not. According to him, the Oedipal complex belongs to the meaning of Sophocles' tragedy, "even if we could not have realized it until this century" (1981, 146). Sophocles could have known this stage in the psychological development of the person. However, a theory of psychological development, such as that of Peter Dow Webster, who claims that the superego is formed at age five, cannot belong to the meaning of Kafka's *Metamorphosis*. Kafka, according to Nehamas, could not have known this highly problematic theory. It thus cannot be claimed, as Webster does, that in *Metamorphosis* the hours on the clock correspond to Gregor's age; that when Gregor realizes that he should have taken the five o'clock train to go to work, this means that a psychic change should have taken place at age five—in the present instance, the formation of the superego (Nehamas 1981, 146).

Do these examples given by Nehamas not show that, contrary to his claims, what the writer could have meant is in itself the product of an interpretation, so that, consequently, the regulative idea is itself a production springing from interpreters? In this case, there might be as many regulative ideals as there are interpreters or communities of interpreters. When Nehamas considers Webster's interpretation to be based on a "highly doubtful . . . theory of development" (1981, 146), while accepting Sigmund Freud's theory of the Oedipus complex, he makes his hermeneutic move and implicitly acknowledges that the historical plausibility is itself based on what is accepted—interpreted—as valid. Even if what is accepted is highly probable, such as the last historical evidence found, for example, that does not prove the transcendental aspect of the author, only its high degree of plausibility for a given interpreter or at best for a given community of interpreters.

The translations studied yield the same result: they attempt to recover a meaning as intended by an author who is posited as highly plausible for the interpreter or the community of interpreters. The option a translator chooses, even if the goal is to remain faithful to the text and the author, seems almost necessarily guided by, if not modeled on, the cultural horizon of the translator. Her goal is to render a word with its particular connotations—this is the ideal of monism—but in such a way that this rendering is intelligible to the audience the translator (or the publisher) has in mind—which opens the door to pluralism.

Validity and Community

Although pluralism is clearly not the model of translation, neither the verbal meaning of the text stemming from the author's intention, as Hirsch believes, nor the postulated author guiding the ideal interpretation that is indifferent to the passing of centuries, as Nehamas suggests, succeed in weeding out elements of pluralism in monism. Because continuity in history is itself a discursive matter and thus an interpretive production, the limit to arbitrariness in translation and interpretation is what a community posits and accepts as the norm of a translation or an interpretation. Are we thus bound to accept another form of relativism? Not quite. It is possible to keep a rational process of evaluation and validation and to speak of progress in interpretation, although with significant qualifications.

An interpretation or a translation has to make claims in order to be an interpretation or translation. It has to claim to render a meaning that is not the mere product of the interpreter or translator. Such a claim is a claim to tell the truth. The interpreter also claims to be truthful as an interpreter in the sense that he fulfils his responsibility to what is expected from him. For example, he claims that his translation is original, that he knows the original language, and that he does not have a hidden agenda or aim at propaganda. Finally, the interpreter is also accountable to the community at large to the extent that the interpretation is claimed to be right and to fit the pragmatic situation that exists at the time, whether the goal is to reinforce such a situation or challenge it. By making those claims, an interpreter or translator is part of the community of investigators and functions as a partner of good standing. All the translators examined here seem to fit that description of decent and serious scholars, even if they have a tendency to take their cues from their predecessors and to borrow from them, sometimes heavily.

On the basis of those claims, what is interpreted is what is claimed to be rendered: a text's meaning. At best, it is a postulated author's meaning. The verbal meaning and the author are thus categories of interpretation. Because they are produced by particular communities of investigators, they can change. What changes is thus not only the content of the verbal meaning or the postulated author, in which case the progress of interpretation would only depend on empirical information that is discovered or falsified. What can change is also the very nature of the claims interpreters make. To satisfy the claim to truth, English translators have recourse to a language close to Shakespeare's English, like Murray in 1919, or to common English or verses, or they may even sacrifice literality for meaningfulness, as Chapman does, not feeling bound by the wording of the original. Regarding the claim to truthfulness, translators can try to render the original impression the Greek audience could have or to adapt the text to a particular audience, without much concern for what was initially meant for a Greek audience. With respect to the claim to rightness, some translators do not hesitate to paraphrase some expressions or sentences—for example, those involving the expression *muthesaito*—whereas others show an almost religious respect for the sanctity of the literal meaning. It would thus be difficult to defeat the enterprise of most of those translators under the charge that they made mistakes or were not faithful.

In the absence of a transcendental postulated author, which would indeed serve as a criterion of validity over time and across linguistic communities, what we have left is only the claims that interpreters make when interpreting, which bind them to their respective communities. Although these claims are themselves interpretive—accuracy of translation for Aquinas and for a contemporary university scholar does not have the same extension—claims force interpreters into a discussion and, in this sense, submit them to scrutiny. And the broader the community of discussion, the stronger the scrutiny. By submitting the claim of a translator or interpreter to tighter scrutiny, the extension of the community in principle makes the justification and validation of an interpretation or translation stricter and more rigorous. Now we can tell the person who translated Hans Christian Andersen's fairy tales into English for the first time without knowing Danish and using the German translation instead, or Claude Roy, who translated Chinese poetry into French without proficiency in Chinese, that this is not serious work. But we can also acknowledge that, at that time, they were the best translators available and that they satisfied the demands of their audiences.

In the case of the translations of Homer, if we take those of the twentieth or twenty-first century, not only do we have a full array of intellectual tools at our disposal for understanding Homer's Greek as well as his worldview, we also have a tradition of reflection on what a translation is supposed to achieve. What we have, consequently, is the ability to compare, criticize, and evaluate several translations of Homer from different linguistic realms in terms of accuracy, philological competence, and literary achievement. It is in such a community that a translator must justify his work if he wants to offer a new translation of a text. And he will succeed if he manages to show that his translation is better.

Denying the existence of a transhistorical ideal as I do avoids the hermeneutic unfairness of judging the past in accordance with the present. When comparing our twentieth- or twenty-first-century translations with those of the seventeenth century, we judge and evaluate them according to our criteria, criteria that most likely were not current in the seventeenth century. We can only evaluate the translations of the past in an ad hoc procedure, considering them as contemporary and submitting them to criteria that are often alien to them. Since we cannot appeal to common criteria of accuracy, literacy, and scholarly achievement across centuries, we must remain aware of the interpretive character of our evaluation as better. When we consider older translations as contemporary, we both overlook our cultural and historical contingency and, consequently, are always sure to come out as the best.

The claim to validity is the basis for a rational evaluation. Not to submit to such a process of validation current in a community of interpreters would amount, for a particular interpreter, to not being recognized as an interpreter, not being published, and thus being excluded from the community. The conversation initiated and fostered by the claims interpreters or translators make allows them to evaluate rationally various interpretations or translations. This rationality is less substantial than formal. It does not yield content and cannot be an ultimate court of appeal for resolving conflicts between different options in translation and interpretation. In the twenty-first century we still have the same options for translating Homer's passage as before. To the extent that it is formal, the rational procedure can only regulate the very process of evaluation, not the evaluation itself. The immediate consequence is twofold. The process of evaluation will not be able to resolve a certain diversity or multiplicity of interpretation, which will have to be tolerated. Because it is the product of a community, the evaluative process will not be able to prevent the existence of periods of hermeneutic instability in a given community, where interpreters question some criteria of validity and propose other, heterogeneous criteria that cohabit with the old ones.

Just as the rationality of evaluation is less substantial than formal, the progress in question is essentially procedural. It does not so much deal with the interpretation itself, as if all interpreters of all times participated in the same universal project, as reside in the extension of the community of interpretation. If, as my comparison shows, the criteria of what makes a translation or interpretation better are relative to the community of the interpreter and are thereby objects of discussion, progress is less the intrinsic quality of the translation or interpretation, as Nehamas suggests, than the extension of the community that establishes and justifies those criteria.

An extension of the community makes the process of evaluation more rigorous, and thus better, because it forces each interpreter to situate and legitimate his own project within the broadened community. The intersubjective process through which errors and misunderstandings are weeded out can in principle lead to the broadening of the community of interpreters that establishes and agrees on the justification procedures. The progress in question therefore does not primarily lie in the substance or the materiality of what has been achieved but essentially in the extension of the community that justifies and validates this achievement, what Rorty, in another context, refers to as "the widest possible intersubjective agreement" (1998, 63). Although it always remains an open possibility and a risk, such a notion of procedural progress is not necessarily relative to a factual and historical situation. Thus, it is not simply a contingent historical progress, because the extension of the community imposes on each interpreter the burden of making intelligible and justifying her claims within this broader community. The justification and the legitimation are placed under greater scrutiny and are thus, we can reasonably—although not necessarily—expect, more rigorous. In such a framework, objectivity does not naively imply that a given translation is in adequacy with the original. Objectivity implies that the translation is claimed to be in adequacy with the original, and that means that such a translation is claimed to be free from biases and prejudices. This in turn means that, in the community making use of the concept of objectivity and believing in the validity of the criteria used for assessing objectivity, such a translation is the best that can be given at present. Objectivity, then, is intersubjective and linked to the communication or the conversation that obtains in the community.

The more comprehensive understanding that results from, for example, what an original means, is better not in the sense that this understanding comes closer to what the original meant, since most of the time there is no native perspective available on what an original truly meant. The understanding is better because the point of view regarding what the original means has expanded. Better is thus not primarily a qualification of the materiality of the claim by translators but a qualification of the procedure or the process through which the qualification has been made.

Our community of interpreters in the twenty-first century, for example, is an open community because of its history. Through technology and through the nature of contemporary studies, the exchanges between linguistic communities have become such that several linguistic communities increasingly form in synchrony one and the same community of experts and researchers. As a result, a good French translator is someone who can also consult translations of the same text in other languages. The extension of present studies also opens the community vertically, thereby encompassing historical communities of the past. When translating Homer in the twenty-first century, translations of the past cannot be ignored: the translator has to claim not only that the translation is better than the one made by contemporaries, but also that it is better than those of the past. And that means reciprocally to let ourselves be challenged by the choices made in those past translations.

A translator obeys two masters. The two voices of the author and the translator's audience can only resonate, as Benjamin said, in the harmony that a translator provides. The distinctions between verbal meaning and significance and actual writer and postulated author are very useful heuristic devices, but the differences expressed by these distinctions depend on what communities hold as harmony. On this point I agree with Fish (1980). However, what keeps pluralism from invading the process of translation— a point Fish ignores—is that it is a process, with claims involved, so that the voice of the translator, in order to be heard, remains accountable to the voice of the first master, the author. And even if we can only hear the voice of the translator, the first master's voice can still resonate in the claims translators make to speak in one voice, in harmony.

4

The Literal Meaning

The Hermeneutics of Gregory the Great

The first decision interpreters have to make when interpreting a text concerns the author's intention: what is conveyed by those sequences of letters? The second decision concerns the literal meaning. When we interpret a text written in our language, we understand the sense of the sentences through the sense of the words in it. This is usually called the literal meaning: the meaning in accordance with the letter, before any attempt to construe the representative content has been made. A text can be read from different perspectives, however, so that the literal meaning can be understood differently depending on the readers' backgrounds. I follow the method used in chapter 2 and examine the status of the literal meaning by turning to people who have offered theoretical views on the subject and others who empirically deal with the nitty-gritty task of interpreting texts. On the theoretical side I appeal to John Searle, who offers a general conceptual framework to explain how the literal meaning can be applied differently, while keeping its self-identity. Although the literal meaning is relative to a background, the literal meaning, Searle argues, does not change with the background.

On the empirical side I focus on Gregory the Great, father of the church and pope in the sixth century AD, who is the inheritor of a long tradition of biblical reflection on the different senses of the text and who offers a model for interpreting a text. He argues that the literal meaning is a construct originating from a specific background or framework: such a background, which for Gregory is Christian charity, not only is necessary for the literal meaning to be understood but also configures such a literal meaning so that it is a category of interpretation. Gregory powerfully summarizes his position on the priority and weakness of the literal meaning by writing that "the text grows with its reader" (1971, I.7.8:145).

Searle on Meaning and Background

In interpretation and translation theory, the literal meaning has usually served as a guiding principle. It is precisely on the basis of a literal meaning that interpreters and translators can agree or disagree on how to understand a sentence or a text. However, the literal meaning can cover two different moments: the mental act of intending to convey something and the semiotic means used for conveying that something, be it a word, a sentence, or even a text. Usually, the literal meaning covers both moments, what has been called speaker's meaning and sentence meaning. As a result, to understand a sentence or a text is to reconstruct what has been meant by the speaker who uttered that sentence or wrote that text. Similarly, to understand someone consists in deciphering what that person conveys.

Linguists and philosophers have tried to come up with examples manifesting what would happen if one of these components, either the speaker's meaning or the sentence meaning, were to fail. Noam Chomsky gives the example of "colorless green ideas sleep furiously" (1975, 145), which is grammatically correct, but meaningless, so that nothing can be meant by that sentence. Similarly, an example from Searle, "Bill cut the sun," might have components that are meaningful and might give the impression of being meaningful, but we do not know what is meant by someone uttering such a sentence unless we know against what background the sentence was uttered.

Interpretation theory has struggled to determine whether the intentional moment or the semiotic moment should receive priority. What complicates the situation is that a sentence can have a meaning independently of what was meant by its use or even if we know nothing about the person who used the sentence or wrote the text. The resulting question is thus a question about the status of the sentence itself: is it, then, just an expression of an intention, because the intention has a self-identity before being semiotically articulated in that particular sentence, or is the sentence itself the very configuration of an intention which could not fully exist as the intention it is without being articulated through the signs of that sentence?

Whether linguistic articulation or thought has priority is a crucial question for any theory of interpretation, at least any theory that has criteria for the validity of interpretations. If an intention can exist without linguistic or symbolic articulation, such an intention is a prime candidate for serving as a criterion for evaluating different interpretations: since an interpreter is supposed to decipher the signs used by an author for expressing a presemiotic thought, the best interpretation is the one that matches the author's intention. The prelinguistic thought, it is assumed, exists and has a self-identity before its semiotic articulation, so that it can function naturally as the telos of any interpretation and as the criterion by which an interpretation can be evaluated.

However, if the linguistic articulation of an intention is not just an expression but a configuration of an intention that, without that articulation, would not be publicly articulated and thus intelligible, then a linguistic sentence is not just an expression of something that has a self-identity before being expressed. The interpreter, who wants to understand what is meant, has thus to take into consideration both what the author meant and what the sentence means. He can only start by understanding the components of the sentence and the background against which such a sentence is uttered. The interpreter will then try to reconstruct, as best he can, the intention he believes is the most compatible with the sentence.

This is clearly the case with texts of the past, where authors are no longer around, but would also apply when an author is still alive. For even in the latter case, deciphering the signs of an expression does not lead directly to the intention, but at best to the configuration of such an intention. And the question remains whether the interpreter reconstructed this configuration correctly or whether the author configured her intention in the way the interpreter takes it to be. That is to say, since the sentence meaning is uncoupled from the speaker's meaning, the object of interpretation is no longer directly what the author meant, but what the author configured. A large array of possibilities are then open for understanding the link between the configuration and the author: besides the author's intention, an interpreter can focus on the unconscious of the author— Freudian or Lacanian—or the spirit of an epoch that permeated the author or the sociological milieu in Marxist literary theory of which the author is a product or the dispensation of being in Heidegger, where the author is a placeholder, or the *episteme* of a period of history in Foucault, which allows for a system of beliefs, values, or concepts from which authors borrow without being aware of the condition of possibility of their thoughts. There are, of course, other possibilities as well.

In the first case, where an intention preexists, the claim can be made that there is only one correct interpretation. In the second case, where the intention is configured by its expression, a plurality of interpretations is almost unavoidable, and any evaluation of these interpretations has to be made according to criteria outside the sentence or the text.

Searle's position offers the means to reconcile these two options. A student of Austin and a proponent of the speech-act theory, Searle has come to be known more recently as a champion of the importance of the context—what he calls the background—for understanding any speech act and even for having any intentional state. However, while recognizing the importance and necessity of a background, he holds that the background does not affect the self-identity of the literal meaning, that the literal meaning does not change with a change in the background. His views on the interaction between background and literal meaning can be summarized in four theses.

Thesis One

Meaning is first and foremost a mental act—someone means something—and only secondarily a feature of a sentence. And the sentence means what the utterer meant (the sentence meaning corresponds to the speaker's meaning). "Literal meaning is an expression of intentional content" (Searle 1992, 184). More explicitly, Searle states that "the literal meaning of a sentence is in a sense the notion of conventional and hence fungible intentionality: it is what enables the sentence to represent out there in public, so to speak" (1979, 131). If I say, "I promise," I mean that I am bound by a promise. This is what my sentence "I promise" means: what I mean. Obviously, if I want to be understood, the best way for me to convey that I place myself under an obligation is to use the available English sentence "I promise," because the community of speakers to which I belong take it that, when someone says, "I promise," she places herself under an obligation. As Armin Burkhardt puts it, "the illocutionary point [what makes my sentence a promise] is nothing else than the conventional intentions that one normally has when performing a certain act" (1990, 107). The "literal interpretation" (Searle 1992, 181) of my sentence "I promise" is thus the understanding of a meaning according to the "conventional intentionality" that anybody using that sentence would have.

Thesis Two

The literal meaning, in the sense of the meaning of a conventional intentional stance, can only be understood against a background of beliefs and abilities. "For a large number of cases the notion of the literal meaning of a sentence only has application relative to a set of background assumptions, and . . . these background assumptions are not all and could not all be realized in the semantic structure of the sentence" (Searle 1979, 120). The literal meaning of a sentence is thus not reducible to the sum of the meanings of the components and their combination. For example, "Cut the cake!" needs a background to be understood literally as a request to use a knife instead of a lawn mower and to cut an appropriate number of appropriately sized pieces instead of one piece of an odd shape from the middle of the cake. The literal meaning must be applied to a background in virtue of information that is not part of the literal meaning of the sentence but belongs to the background of speaker and listener. The assumptions necessary for making sense of a sentence, that is, for identifying its literal meaning, cannot be exhaustively specified, for there is no way to know when to stop in our specifications: "Use a knife for cutting the cake," "Use a knife that will allow you to cut several small pieces," "Use a knife that cuts soft surfaces," and on and on. Furthermore, each of these sentences used for specifying the assumptions requires in turn a set of assumptions, so that the specifying task is not only indefinite, it might be infinite as well.

Searle uses the notion of background in both a generic and a specific way. The generic use includes the "network," the "deep background," and the "local or cultural practice." If I have the desire to go to a restaurant, then, in order for this intentional state to arise, a network of other intentional states is involved, such as the belief that there are restaurants, that restaurants are places where one can eat, that the food there will be prepared, that I will have to pay for the meal, and so on. An intention "can only have the conditions of satisfaction that it does, and thus can only be the intention that it is, because it is located in a Network of other beliefs and desires" (Searle 1983, 141). Were we to try to specify the network, "we would soon find ourselves formulating a set of propositions which would look fishy if we added them to our list of beliefs in the Network; 'fishy' because they are in a sense too fundamental to qualify as beliefs, even as unconscious beliefs. Consider the following propositions: . . . the things people walk on are generally solid; . . . objects offer resistance to touch and pressure" (142).

Once we reach this level of propositions, which do not really qualify as beliefs, "we reach a bedrock of mental capacities that do not themselves consist in Intentional states (representations)" (Searle 1983, 143). This background is a set of nonrepresentational mental capacities making possible all representations. To have the intentional states that I do, I must have certain kinds of know-how: I must know how things are and how to do things. But the kinds of know-how in question are not, in these cases, forms of "knowing that" (143). This means that the skills and habits involved in knowing how to do things are not necessarily just an application of a propositional knowledge about things, about what to do with them, and about how to do things with them. This background includes a deep background that comprises the capacities that are common to all normal human beings on the basis of their biological makeup: the capacity to walk, to open the door of the restaurant, to sit, and to chew food; the motor skills to handle the silverware; and so forth. Some of these capacities or skills are more specific to a particular culture; for example, the use of a door, the attitude we have toward tables and napkins, and the kind of food we accept to eat. This is part of the local or cultural practices. The background, however, is not, as in Heidegger, a set of things referring to other things or a set of relationships between humans and things. "It is simply a set of skills, stances, preintentional assumptions and presuppositions, practices, and habits" (Searle 1983, 154).

Thesis Three

Although in need of a background, the literal meaning does not require an interpretation. It is directly understood, precisely because of the background of beliefs and abilities that speakers have. "The notion of the literal meaning of a sentence is not a context-free notion; it only has application relative to a set of preintentional Background assumptions and practices" (Searle 1983, 145). By application, Searle has in view the fact that the meaning of a sentence is what connects that sentence with our language and our beliefs about the world. Although it is true that the meaning is relative to some system of background assumptions, this relativity is not interpretive: it is not as if we had to understand the sentence first and then interpret it—relativize it—according to our background assumptions. We understand the literal meaning when we can apply it, given our background assumptions. To the extent that it is this intersection between language as it is used and the world as it works, the literal meaning guarantees the isomorphism between intention and convention. The literal meaning manifests, in linguistic means, the know-how that we have, given the cultural and biological background we happen to have.

Thesis Four

Despite the change of backgrounds that can occur—as in "Cut the cake," "Cut the grass," or "Cut the cloth"—there is only one literal meaning. "When I say that the literal meaning of a sentence only has application relative to the coordinate system of our background assumptions, I am not denying that sentences have literal meanings. Literal meaning, though relative, is still literal meaning" (Searle 1979, 132).

This is, in my view, the most important claim. Unfortunately, Searle does not explain why the literal meaning does not change in the different applications nor how the literal meaning can be identified. He defends his view regarding the relativity of the literal meaning and its self-identity through an analogy with movement, an analogy he considers obvious: "When one says that the notion of the movement of a body only has application relative to some coordinate system, one is not denying the existence of motion. Motion, though relative, is still motion" (132). Such an analogy is interesting to the extent that it might yield more than Searle intended. It could be replied to Searle that motion is a notion that science has defined and clarified. The parameters we use for measuring motion have been handed down by scientists. They decide and specify what they take as their coordinate system. And they decide because they are the experts, recognized by the community to have that authority. In the case of interpretations of sentences, though, there are no obviously agreed-upon experts in a linguistic community who can peremptorily decide what the coordinate system is.

The difference between the two cases turns around the stability of the background. In the case of motion, there are indeed several coordinate systems for apprehending an entity we see with our eyes on earth, an entity we infer to be far out in space, or an entity we mathematically project at a subatomic level. However, there are means available for reformulating the parameters from one system into another, so that these systems are somehow compatible and convertible. There is thus a stability in these systems. When we deal with the meaning of sentences or texts, there is no guaranteed stability among the different backgrounds against which a literal meaning can be understood. We do not have the means for converting one referring framework into another. We cannot even easily circumscribe and identify the different backgrounds susceptible to be used by interpreters.

In the absence of conversion tables between backgrounds, the relativity of the literal meaning to a background is of a different kind than the relativity of motion to a system of coordinates. While the latter is a relativity determined by the type of entities studied (whether these are bodies visible to the naked eye, bodies surmised in the depth of the universe, or subatomic particles, for example), the former is a relativity determined by interpreters and can thus be a radical relativity. To use an example mentioned by Steven Pinker, if a speeding driver argues with a police trooper that, from a cosmic perspective his car was not really moving, the trooper can nonarbitrarily justify his coordinate system of space/time on earth for issuing a ticket by appealing to the type of institution he represents on earth and the type of regulation it enforces. By contrast, there is no institution that can authoritatively decide which framework is valid and which one is not valid for interpreting texts. An interpreter cannot nonarbitrarily point to a system of reference, as a trooper can stamp his feet on the tarmac, and say, "This is the coordinate system."

The need for a background to be justified is precisely what Gregory the Great recognizes. He offers a solution to the problem of the identity of the literal meaning in the relativity of its applications.

Gregory's Hermeneutics of the Bible

Biblical interpretation is well suited for examining the interaction between literal meaning and background to the extent that any interpretation has legitimacy as biblical interpretation only if the Bible is in fact a document claimed to be authored by God. There is in the Bible, for it to be the Bible, a meaning that is claimed to originate from God. There is also, obviously, a human meaning in the letters (words and sentences) that have been used for manifesting God's word, since these words have been written in a particular language at a particular time. Explicitly or implicitly, the question for interpreters regarding meaning and intention has been twofold. On the one hand, there is the question regarding the level of intention—whether there are indeed two intentions, human and divine, or whether the human intention is itself just a moment in the divine intention. On the other hand, there is the question regarding the level of meaning—whether there are indeed two meanings, of the words and of the spirit, or whether the meaning of words is conveyed by the meaning of the spirit.

One common way to express this ambivalence of the Bible is to say that the human words are the flesh of the divine revelation, while the spirit is what speaks in these words. In this common view, letter and spirit are both heterogeneous and complementary to each other: the letter is carnal but directly intelligible, while the spirit is a mere breath but of divine inspiration. The biblical text is thus the result of two levels of meanings and intentions crossing over one another: the letter, which is an object of human convention and which means what the historical authors of the Bible meant, and the spirit, which is the divine inspiration and which carries the meaning of what God intends.

Wolterstorff offers a more modern way of formulating this dual level of meaning. Using Austin's distinction between locutionary acts and illocutionary acts, Wolterstorff defends the view that God can speak without using words, just as one can ask a question, make a statement, or give an order without using words, through other semiotic means or by proxy. God can make illocutionary acts without any locutionary acts. Thus, saying that God speaks does not necessarily mean that God has to make sentences: "Perhaps the attribution of speech to God by Jews, Christians, and Muslims, should be understood as the attribution to God of illocutionary actions, leaving it open how God performs those actions—maybe by bringing about the sounds or characters of some natural language, maybe not" (1995, 13).

Gregory the Great directly addresses these two levels of meaning by developing the art of allegorical reading in his numerous and lengthy writings on the Bible. The audacity of some of Gregory's interpretations caused his method of reading to be both the object of praise and the source of controversy. Such praise and controversy began in the Middle Ages and persist today. Gregory was seen, Thomas O'Loughlin writes, "as the most illustrious exegete after Augustine throughout the seventh and eighth centuries" (1998, 183). His *Morals on the Book of Job*, for example, was abundantly copied until the thirteenth century and translated into vernacular languages (Wasselynck 1964, 1965). A translation into Old German appeared as soon as the tenth century. A translation into Spanish was available in the eleventh century and a partial translation into Old French in the twelfth century. Gregory has been called "the magnificent doctor" (by Hincmar, who died in 879) as well as "the wisest pope" (by Bernon of Reichenau, who died in 1048; both quoted in de Lubac 1959, I, 2, 538–39). Alcuin calls him "the most lucid interpreter of the holy Scripture" (quoted in de Lubac, 1959, I, 2, 538–39). Later commentators, however, have not been as enthusiastic; some, such as Rosenmüller in the nineteenth century, deemed him "an uneducated man," even "a most superstitious man," responsible for the "barbarism of the Latin Church" (de Lubac devotes a section to the "barbarism of Saint Gregory" and lists some of his critics, I, 1, 53–77).

The *Homilies on Ezekiel* [1] and the *Morals on the Book of Job* [2] illuminate two related elements among the many that have troubled commentators. The first problem deals with the extent of the growth Gregory has in mind when he says that the divine text grows with the reader (*Diuina eloquia cum legente crescunt*). Does he mean only the subjective growth of the reader enriched by the text or does he also mean an objective growth of the text, that the text can change through the reading? The second problem concerns the order of the three different senses Gregory sees in the biblical text: literal, allegorical, and moral. Usually, Gregory considers the literal sense as the first, on the basis of which the allegorical sense yields a moral sense. However, sometimes Gregory changes the place of the allegorical sense from second to third (the moral sense yields the allegorical sense) or from second to first (the allegorical sense is at the foundation of the literal sense). I will begin with the second problem.

Gregory's Use of the Different Senses of the Bible

I do not claim to offer an account of Gregory's hermeneutics or the historical import of Gregory in the development of biblical interpretation in general (see Bori 1987; Wasselynck 1965). My interest lies exclusively in the status of the different senses in Gregory's method of reading, not in the results of Gregory's exegesis or the content of the different senses. Furthermore, the history of the exegesis of the fourfold sense of the Bible is complex, as indicated by the four volumes (1,820 pages) of Henri de Lubac's monumental and impressive *Exégèse médiévale* (1959), and has been and still is the object of discussion and controversies that cannot be discussed here. I focus only on what pertains to Gregory's understanding of the multiple senses of the Bible.

1. Unless otherwise noted, I use the English translation by Theodosia Gray (see Gregory 1971). References are given in the text and correspond to the book, homily, paragraph, and line(s) in Corpus Christianorum Series Latina 142 (Gregory 1971).

2. Unless otherwise noted, I use the English translation (see Gregory 1979). References are given in the text in Corpus Christianorum Series Latina 143 (Gregory 1979).

What seems to be an object of agreement is that Ambrose (who died in 397) already distinguishes three levels in the understanding of scripture: a somatic level, which corresponds to the literal or grammatical sense; a psychic level, which corresponds to the moral content of the text; and a pneumatic level, which corresponds to the mystical substance of the text (see McNally 1959, 53). But it is Augustine who offers the more sophisticated and clear categories of the four levels of meaning in the Bible: "In all sacred books one should note the things of eternity which are announced [*quae ibi aeterna intimentur*], the facts of history which are reported [*quae facta narrentur*], future events which are foretold [*quae futura praenuntientur*], moral precepts which are enjoined or recommended [*quae agenda praecipiantur vel admoneantur*]" (1894, 1.1.3 CSEL 28.1).

The facts of history correspond to the literal sense, to the extent that it is what the letters say: what is said at the level of the letters narrates the events that took place. The moral precepts will be known as the moral or tropological sense. The Bible teaches us how to act and how to live. In Gregory's formulation, on this point following Augustine, it is said, "As you find increase in divine speech you will yourself have progressed within it" (Gregory 1971, I.7.8:156–57). The future events will be known as the allegorical sense to the extent that this level of sense prefigures what is going to happen. The things of eternity will be known as the anagogical sense to the extent that the narrated events are the figure of eternal realities accessible through contemplation. Augustine's distinction will be summarized in the following hexameter by Augustine of Dacia, known by all medieval interpretation schools: *Littera gesta docet, quid credas allegoria. Moralis quid agas, quo tendas anagogia* (The letter teaches us what happened, allegory what to believe. The moral sense tells us what to do, the anagogical sense what to strive for; quoted in, among others, Nicholas of Lyra 1879a, col. 28D).

Although influenced by Augustine, as well as by Origen (de Lubac 1959, I, 1, 221–23), Gregory mostly distinguishes only three senses in the biblical text: first, the historical or literal sense; second, the allegorical or typical sense; and third, the moral or contemplative sense. Gregory is not always consistent in his use of the allegorical sense. Sometimes he qualifies as allegorical what is properly the typical sense, according to which events are the figure or the "type" of Christ and his church here on earth (see de Lubac 1993), and sometimes what is properly the anagogical sense, according to which what is narrated refers to the eternal realities accessible to contemplation. Furthermore, in some passages the allegorical sense also includes the moral sense. In general, however, he follows a clear order of exegesis: on the basis of the literal sense, the allegorical sense gives the moral sense. An *allegoriae intelligentia* is mentioned as leading to contemplation. "In one and the same sentence of the Scripture one finds his nourishment in history alone, another in the typical sense, another seeks through the type a contemplative understanding" (Gregory 1971, I.7.10:181–83; translation modified). Gregory likes to compare the reading of the different levels of meaning to the construction of a building: "For first, we lay the historical foundations; next, by pursuing the typical sense, we erect a fabric of the mind to be a stronghold of faith; and moreover as the last step, by the grace of moral instruction, we, as it were, cloth the edifice with an overcast of colouring" (1979, *Ad Leandrum*, 3:110–14).

Gregory seems to take over the metaphor Origen uses, where the letter corresponds to the body, the allegorical sense to the spirit, and the moral sense to the soul. De Lubac argues that this order of the senses is Christian to the extent that readers read under the guidance of their faith, which allows them to see the literal meaning as an allegory for a moral message (1959, I, 1, 203).

There are two variations of that *ordo exegeticus* worth examining: the allegorical sense can be the third or the first. Regarding the first variation, instead of the order literal, allegorical, moral, Gregory sometimes uses the order literal, moral, allegorical: "Maybe another seeks through history a moral lesson and, through an understanding of allegory, an object of contemplation" (Gregory 1971, I.7.10:206–8; translation modified). This sequence follows the linear order of reading the text: we first understand what the text says (literal sense); then we understand what it tells us, that is, how we can apply it (moral); and lastly we understand what is revealed through it (allegorical). That is the reason de Lubac qualifies it as pagan. Pier Cesare Bori somewhat disagrees with de Lubac and argues that the two orders can coexist, as in Origen or Gregory, due to the circularity of meaning (1987, 56–57).

In the second variation the allegorical sense becomes the first and thus replaces the literal sense in its foundational role. This is most clearly stated in *In I Regum*: "Because as far as the salvation of the believers is concerned faith comes before the works, we put forward the typological interpretation as a solid foundation; the whole construction of the work in its moral and historical interpretation will be based upon it or will follow it" (Gregory 1963b, *Prologus* 8).

Faced with this problem of the order of the senses, commentators either consider the passages containing the unusual order "some exceptions" (de Lubac 1959, I, 1, 187) or "caused by mere distraction" (de Vogüé 1989, 66). Some marvel at Gregory's ingenuity and creativity (de Vrégille 1967), while others are skeptical about his audacity. R. A. Markus, for example, in his presentation of Gregory's understanding of allegorical interpretation, argues that Gregory, compared to Augustine, "is doing . . . neither 'exegesis' nor even 'interpretation'"; exegesis concerns the truth of the matter in question, while interpretation is an "exposition of a truth related in some other way to the text in question" (1996, 20). The reason for this, according to Markus, is that "Gregory's allegorical exegesis proceeds from the signified to the signifier" (60). This explains in part what Markus characterizes as exegetical free-wheeling (50).

On the problem of the foundational sense, some commentators point to the fact that these unusual passages are most clearly formulated in *In I Regum* (Kessler 1995, 201–2) and either explain them away as caused by distraction or as possible evidence that *In I Regum* is not an authentic work by Gregory. Commentators generally agree that Gregory did not write *In I Regum* himself. The consensus, for a long time, was that his secretary, Claudius, drafted it. There has been a continual controversy on whether Gregory revised and made Claudius's work his own. Adalbert de Vogüé, who edited two volumes of this work and translated them into French, was confident that "the *Commentary of Kings* is . . . a fully Gregorian work, while bearing the mark of a collaboration" (1989, 60). He radically changed his views later on and became confident that the author was a twelfth-century monk of the abbey of Cava in Campania, named Peter Divinacello (1996, 319–31). Although already questioning Gregory's authorship at a time when de Vogüé was still championing it, Francis Clark moderated de Vogüé's reversal of opinion and maintained that, all things considered, the work has a core of Gregorian provenance: "There is in *In I Regum* a substantial core of genuinely Gregorian material, used by the medieval author as the framework on which to construct his own fabrication" (1998, 66). I stay away from the discussion about the authenticity of *In I Regum*, and the few references I make to it are made with a caveat.

Gregory's particular interpretive goal, together with the use he makes of the different senses of the Bible, can explain both his apparent inconsistencies and the divergent opinions about him. Gregory was essentially guided by an interest in predication: how to live and how to teach others to live a good Christian life (Rapisarda Lo Menzo 1986, 215–17). In this sense Gregory is not an exegete, not a specialist of the biblical text with a sophisticated method for approaching the written document in its materiality and historical significance. For him, the Bible is sacred reading, known later as *sacra pagina*, as opposed to *sacra doctrina*. The utility of the Bible for guiding life consists in the message of charity: "God speaks to us through the whole of scripture solely in order to attract us to the love of Him and our neighbor" (Gregory 1971, I.10.14:219–21; translation modified). Or, "There are two precepts of charity, to love God and to love one's neighbor. It is through both precepts that the words of the Holy Scripture vivify us" (Gregory 1971, I.7.16:340–42; translation modified).[3]

In his *Homilies on Ezekiel*, given as sermons in 593,[4] and his *Morals on the Book of Job*, given between 579 and 585 and revised as late as 595, Gregory presents himself as an interpreter or even a privileged reader, who was indeed highly regarded in his time. As Beryl Smalley reminds us, "The *Moralia in Job* originated in the monastic *collatio*, the daily conference where the abbot preached and the monks were allowed to ask questions suggested to them by their reading" (1952, 32). The *Homilies on Ezekiel* were also intended to fulfill a specific goal for a particular audience: as homilies they were preached by the pope to an audience in Rome (Markus 1996, 52–54; Banniard 1986, 477–79). Of interest to Gregory is the correlation between history and mystery.

Although Gregory distinguishes three senses in the Bible, when it comes to his practice of interpretation, he usually contents himself with a duality, be it a duality between carnal and spiritual sense, between literal and allegorical sense (scripture *in littera dividitur et allegoria*, Gregory 1971, II.3.18:427), between historical and typical sense, or between external and internal understanding. Commenting on Ezekiel and his vision of a scroll, Gregory writes, "For the Book of Holy Writ is written within by allegory, and without by history. Within through spiritual understanding, but without through the plain sense of the letter" (I.9.30:590–92). Similarly, paraphrasing the passage that speaks of "stretching out heaven as a curtain" (Psalms 103:2–3), Gregory asks rhetorically, "What is meant by the name of heaven if not Holy Writ? . . . This is stretched out as a curtain because shaped by the tongue of the flesh through His scribes it is unfold-

3. Among the many accounts of Gregory's use of charity, see Markus 1996, 17–19 and 58–60.

4. For a full description of Gregory's *Homilies on Ezekiel*, see Kessler 1995.

ed before our eyes by explanation through the words of learned men"
(I.9.30:601–6).[5]

Gregory sees the historical writer as the one who transmits the facts
(*per scribentis vocem*; Gregory 1979, *Praefatio*, I.2:24), and through such a
historical writer we have the words of history (*verba historiae*; 1971,
I.12.15:222) that provide the human meaning. The author (*auctor*) is the
Holy Spirit who inspired (*inspirator*) and dictated (*dictavit*) what was to be
written (*scribenda*; 1979, *Praefatio*, I.2:22–24). Special attention is thus
required to take into account the two layers of meaning and intentions
(human and divine), what Gregory calls discernment (*discretio*; 1971,
II.7.1:1).[6] This discernment allows the adjudication of what belongs to letter and spirit: "For, behold, we read Holy Writ: if we were to understand all
things literally we would have lost the virtue of discernment [*virtutem dis-
cretionis*]; if we reduce all things to spiritual allegory, we are likewise bound
by the stupidity of lack of discernment" (I.3.4:64–67).

Gregory's conviction is that what is narrated in the Bible evokes a superior reality, which our intellect can grasp through the light of the Holy
Spirit. "And it happens that you perceive the words of the Holy Writ to be
heavenly if, kindled through the grace of contemplation, you are suspended on heavenly things" (I.7.8:160–62). At this level, the narrative—Augustine's *narratio rerum factarum*—has become mystery.

Since Gregory refers to three senses, but most often uses only two, these
senses seem to mean different things and have different statuses. My focus
is the apparently unstable states of the literal and allegorical senses, leaving
aside the moral sense; there is both consistency in Gregory's method and
justification for it. I thus strongly disagree with Markus when he states of
Gregory that "little is to be gained by attempting to disentangle the oddly
haphazard vocabulary" (1997, 46).

---

5. In light of Gregory's texts, it appears that de Lubac makes an overstatement when
he claims that Gregory is "one of the main initiators and greatest masters of the
medieval doctrine of the fourfold sense" (1959, II, 1:189). Gregory clearly distinguishes
three and most often two senses, but not four. However, such an overstatement by de
Lubac does not warrant O'Loughlin's accusation that the four volumes of de Lubac's
Exégèse médiévale represent a "theological agenda" that is "based on the apologetic need
of Catholics" and that is "of very limited worth to the historian" (1998, 159–60).

6. On Gregory's use of *discretio* in general, see, among many others, Cabassut 1960,
3:1311–30; Dagens 1977, esp. 117–24; Dekkers 1984, 79–88; and Gillet 1975, 17–19. These commentators, however, do not focus on the role of *discretio* in the activity of reading the Bible.

The status of the allegorical sense, when part of a duality, is different from the status of the allegorical sense, when it is part of a triplicity. In the duality, it is a sense opposed to the literal, whereas when part of the triplicity, it is sometimes what mediates between the literal and moral meaning. I cannot examine here the role of allegory in the interpretation of the Bible or the differences between the allegorical sense and the typical sense.[7] I thus use allegory in a generic sense as the transformation of the literal sense into a spiritual sense. As mediation, then, the allegorical understanding is both a sense and a method of reading, as Gregory suggests in his letter to Leander (a letter de Lubac, alluding to Descartes, considers Gregory's "discourse of allegorical method"; 1959, II, 2:134). Gregory writes that his monk brothers demanded that he "not only unravel the words of the history in allegorical senses [*verba historiae per allegoriarum sensus*]"; they also asked that "I would go on to give the allegorical senses the turn of a moral exercise [*allegoriarum sensus protinus in exercitium moralitatis*]" (1979, *Ad Leandrum*, 1:48–49).

The fact that allegory is both a sense and a method of reading causes a split in the literal meaning: the literal meaning is a foundation (e.g., for the allegorical sense) but has to be read in a certain spirit through allegory, so that literal is what allegory posits as literal, in which case the literal sense comes after allegory. Literal is thus both the foundation for the allegorical sense and the result of the allegorical method of reading.

For Gregory, the literal meaning is what is conveyed by the *littera*, which in turn can mean two things. Within the *verbum* (or *sermo*)—word or expression—as opposed to *res*—thing—a distinction is made between the *littera*—letter—which pertains to the linguistic aspect, and the *sensus*, which is the meaning. Very often, however, *littera* means not just the letter but also the intention conveyed by the letter. Gregory speaks of an intention of the letter or a literal intention (*intentionem litterae*; 1979, V.23.7.14:6–7). Similarly, he speaks of the words of the literal intention (*verbis litterae*; 1971, II.10.2:24). Gregory makes use of three different senses of the term "literal" (*iuxta litteram*), depending on that with which it is contrasted. These uses were also common to many fathers of the church. "Literal" can mean nonfigurative, non-Christian, and the basis for the spiritual sense.

---

7. Regarding the role of allegory in the interpretation of the Bible, see Dahan 1999; regarding the difference between allegorical and typical senses, see de Lubac 1993.

Literal as Opposed to Figurative

Since there is already a meaning in the letters, *littera* most often refers not to the material linguistic sign but to the intention carried by the words of the text. *Littera* refers to things and constitutes the narrative of the biblical text. *Littera* thus means the story told, so that the literal meaning, as the intention carried by the words, is the historical meaning of what is said: a reference to what really happened. The literal sense is thus also called *historia*, and the two terms are interchangeable. This is the first meaning of the text (*prima significatio*). It is also the first exposition (*prima expositio*) for the commentator and the first understanding (*primus intellectus*) for the reader. Commenting on Gregory, O'Loughlin writes that "history is the direct reading of the text setting out the bare physical facts" (1998, 184). These equivalences between literal and historical will remain common in the Middle Ages: "literal or historical meaning [*sensus litteralis, vel historicus*]," wrote Nicholas of Lyra, among many others (1879a, col. 28C). As Hugh of Saint-Victor advises his reader, "I do not think that you can be perfectly adept in allegory if you do not take your support on history" (1880, col. 799C). In accordance with its Greek etymology, where the verb *historeo* means conducting a concrete search or study, *historia* first names the narrative of what the author could have seen (Hugh of Saint-Victor 1879, col. 12A). Scripture, according to most church fathers, essentially narrates facts that really took place, not myths or timeless facts. Divine revelation has taken shape historically and is thus a fact belonging to history. Gregory speaks of a historical truth [*veritate historiae*]; 1971, I.12.1:1) from which interpretation must take its departure.

In Gregory's first use, the literal meaning (in the sense of a literal intention) is sometimes opposed to the figurative meaning. This general and rather vague sense of "literal" is at the origin of an implicit agreement among the church fathers, which Gregory shares: the biblical text should not be interpreted simplistically or naively, because there are some passages of the Bible that are not to be understood according to the letter, but only figuratively. In Ezekiel, Gregory claims, a passage can be found that "does not seem to be tenable according to the letter" (1971, I.12.20:386; translation modified) or of which we know that it "is devoid of reason according to the history" (I.12.21:410-1) or "in which there is according to literal reason no historical meaning" (II.1.3:88–89). In such passages, the literal meaning in the sense of a literal intention does not make sense. This opposition between literal and figurative will also remain. Hugh of Saint-Victor uses the same formulation: "There are some passages in the divine text that cannot be read according to the letter" (1880, col. 801B).

Besides this first use of the term "literal"—as opposed to "figurative"—which has been sanctioned by common usage, the literal meaning can be the meaning of the Bible taken without the light provided by the New Testament and thus a non-Christian meaning. This is the second use of "literal."

Literal as Non-Christian

Clearly, as a text the Bible can be read in many different ways and with many different goals. Christians, however, do not read the Bible just as a document, as nonbelievers do, but as a revelation. The particular status of the biblical text—human manifestation through the letter and sacred text through the divine intention—consists in the fact that the words (*verba*) in the Bible referring to things (*res*) are not the whole of the Bible, for the things themselves have a meaning that results from God's work as creator and as one who intended some things to mean other things. The meaning of words, which is carried by the letter and is thus a literal meaning, is determined by human convention. As such, the words (*verba*) constitute a "language of the flesh [*carnis lingua*]" (Gregory 1971, I.9.30:605). By contrast, the meaning of the things (*res*), carrying the divine intention, is the spiritual meaning. Accordingly, Christian biblical interpreters agree that, besides the literal meaning, there is a spiritual sense in the Bible that we can uncover by paying special attention to the text under the guidance of the Spirit. "But in Holy Writ also those things which can be accepted according to the history are very frequently to be understood spiritually so that faith in the truth of history is retained and spiritual understanding is derived from the mysteries of allegory" (Gregory 1971, II.1.3:61–65). This opposition between literal and spiritual meaning is based on the warning of Saint Paul that "the letter kills, but the spirit gives life" (2 Corinthians 3:6).

Words in the Bible are thus necessary, but, like a Wittgensteinian ladder, they have a provisional necessity in the sense that they have to be passed through so that they cancel out once their task has been fulfilled. Such a fulfillment takes place when the things have been revealed to the reader, that is, when the spiritual sense has been grasped. Hugh of Saint-Victor later summarizes the problem concisely: "In the other writings the philosopher only knows the meaning of words [*verba*]; but in a sacred page, the meaning of the things is by far superior to the meaning of words. For the former has been established by use, while the latter has been dictated by nature. The former is human speech, the latter is God's word addressed to humans. The meaning of words is a matter of convention among men, while the meaning of things is natural. Such a meaning results from the creator's operation who wanted some things to be meant by others" (1879, col. 20D–21A).

The difficulty is to adjudicate what belongs to the letter and what belongs to the spirit. Gregory sees this difficulty in terms of a somewhat subtle interaction between the literal or historical meaning and the spiritual meaning. Divine authorship both motivates a spiritual interpretation—we try to understand what God tells us—and legitimates the point of departure for this spiritual interpretation. We interpret what is written, that is, the historical meaning, "because the words of prophesies for the most part narrate facts that took place in history, so that mystical realities are also thereby described, it is appropriate to explain spiritually these same facts that we presented" (Gregory 1971, I.12.20:382–85; translation modified).

In another passage, Gregory takes the fact that the preachers of the Old Testament spoke of heavenly mysteries in an obscure language, through the shadows of allegories, as justification for his allegorical interpretations (II.3.17:420–42). That means that the literal meaning is the foundation of the spiritual meaning, as our starting point, but the literal meaning itself needs some form of foundation to be intelligible. The literal meaning is only fully meaningful if the things (*res*), which are part of God's plan, are understood. We thus need a familiarity with the story told in the Bible. For if we do not have that background, not only would we not know how to interpret passages of the Bible, but we would not even know what these passages relate, report, or convey. We would only have grammatical functions and would not know what kind of divine realities such a literal meaning could possibly express. To be meaningful, the literal sense must be read against the background of the history of scripture.

A knowledge of *historia* is required for the letter of the text to function and be deciphered. This knowledge, however, is of a certain sort. *Historia* must be understood in the light of the New Testament. This use of the term "literal" in the sense of historical from the perspective of the New Testament is typically Christian. Sharply diverging from the faithful Jews (who are the second son of the church; Gregory 1971, 1.3.6:36), Christians think that God's revelation took a significant turn with the New Testament so that this second revelation provided new guidance for reading the Old Testament. The Spirit revealed in the New Testament retrospectively cast the

Old Testament as a preparation and prefiguration of the New Alliance. For Christians, borrowing de Lubac's terms, "everything [scripture] narrates really took place in history, but the narrative of what happened does not have its whole aim in itself; all of this must still be accomplished and must be really accomplished in us every day through the mystery of this spiritual intelligence" (de Lubac 1959, I, 1:308). Quoting Origen, de Lubac writes that "understanding the Bible 'spiritualiter' or understanding it 'evangelico sensu' is one and the same" (I, 1:310). As Gregory puts it, "We who came to faith through the grace of God, did not learn the Gospel through the Law [the old alliance of the Old Testament]; we learn the Law through the Holy Gospel" (1971, I.6.11:214–16; translation modified). In even more concise formulations, Gregory says, "The New Testament has manifested what the Old Testament indicated" (I.6.15:277–78; translation modified) or, "The New Testament is the explanation [*expositio*] of the Old Testament" (I.6.15:325; translation modified).

Commenting in his *Homilies on Ezekiel* on the fact that Ezekiel saw a wheel inside the wheel, Gregory sees this wheel inside the wheel as an allegory of the place of the New Testament within the Old Testament. The wheel inside the wheel—the New Testament reinterpreting the Old— shows allegorically that reading the Bible requires a conversion: interpreters have to turn their soul to the mystery of Christ. The allegorical interpretation that follows from such a conversion—seeing the Old Testament as allegories of the New—does provide a conversion of both the letter and the soul. Jesus and his revelation give the Old Testament its meaning. This conversion to Christ, permitted by the New Testament, in turn allows the conversion of the reader. Through the allegorical interpretation, the reader discovers a new understanding, the truth of the Word in the letter. "Allegory builds up faith [*fidem aedificat*]," says Gregory in his homilies on the gospels (1849, 2.40.1.1302AB). Allegory edifies faith in the sense that allegory says what is to be believed—*quid credas allegoria*, as Augustine of Dacia says—and what is to be believed is essentially the message of charity revealed by the New Testament.

The *littera* is thus predetermined by its background, to the extent that a correct interpretation cannot dispense with the knowledge of such a background. The *littera* is also overdetermined, to the extent that the background not only predetermines interpretations but also forbids other possible interpretations and narrows the possible choices to what the background allows. Such an overdetermination is best manifested by the canonic example of Jerusalem. The name "Jerusalem" is analyzed by Jerome in his *Commentary on Ezekiel*, and Nicholas of Lyra (thirteenth–fourteenth century), several centuries after Gregory, reexplains it as follows: "According to its literal meaning it [the word "Jerusalem"] means a given city which was before the capital of the Judea kingdom; it was founded by Melchisedec, then expanded and fortified by Solomon" (1879a, col. 28D). The literal meaning of any word is determined by what that word can designate in the corpus of the books of the Bible and in accordance with what those books say. Such designation in the case of Jerusalem would include, as manifested by Nicholas of Lyra's analysis, the capital of Judea, founded by Melchisedec, expanded and fortified by Solomon.

Hugh of Saint-Victor even gives the list of the books to read to understand the literal meaning: Genesis, Exodus, Joshua, Judges, Kings, and Paralipomena; in the New Testament, one has to read the four Gospels and the Acts of the Apostles. Hugh ends by saying, "Such are the eleven books which seem to me to concern particularly history, besides those that we properly call 'historiographic'" (1880, col. 801A). It is even possible to use the exegetical principle of the New Testament to level retrospectively a charge of adulteration of the letter against the interpretations of the Old Testament that did not see the foretelling of Christ's work. Nicholas of Lyra, for example, makes the following recommendation to those who have recourse to Hebrew manuscripts: "On this point one has to be very suspicious about the passages of the Old Testament which refer to Christ's divinity and its consequences. For the Jews have adulterated some of those passages in order to defend their mistake" (1879b, col. 29D–30B). In the commonsense notion of literal, the Old Testament could not refer to Christ.

It is certainly possible to focus exclusively on "the letter in the story [*in historia litteram*]" and to take "the words of history literally [*verba . . . historiae iuxta litteram*]" (Gregory 1979, *Ad Leandrum*, 4:163–64). Such a decision, however, would amount to ignoring the revelation offered by the New Testament, a revelation that manifested "the spirit through the meanings of the letter" (1971, I.3.4:69–70). Thus, by confining oneself to the Old Testament, as do faithful Jews, one embraces the old letter that was once the way God spoke to his people, but that, after the New Testament, turns out to be a meaning not enlightened by the Spirit of the New Alliance. Remaining in the revelation of the Old Testament, the people "ignoring the faith in the Trinity, only possessed the decalogue in the Law" (1971, II.4.9:299). Seen from the point of view of the New Testament, such a meaning is, thus, literal and, as such, "a letter that kills." In Gregory's terms, "All that happened, as we know, when the Jewish people understood the words of God only according to the letter which kills [*ad solam litteram quae occidit*], whereas the converted gentility penetrated the divine words through the spirit that vivifies [*per spiritum qui vivificat*]" (1979, III.11.16.25:33–36; translation modified).

Literal as the Foundation of the Spiritual Sense

Besides these two senses of literal—literal as opposed to figurative and literal as non-Christian—there is also a third, technical use. In Gregory, as well as in other church fathers, the literal meaning is one of the three senses of the biblical text Christian exegetes have to bring to the fore, the other senses usually being the allegorical or typical and the moral or contemplative.

As a component of the three senses, the literal meaning constitutes the basis for the others. When Gregory uses a duality of senses, the spiritual sense is sometimes used generically as covering the other, nonliteral senses (moral and allegorical). When coupled with the spiritual sense, the literal meaning is no longer part of an opposition, as in the second use of the term, where literal means non-Christian. There is now an interaction: the literal meaning is the foundation for the spiritual meaning and thus belongs to it. There are passages in which the exegetical principle of charity can even justify downplaying the literal meaning and engaging in allegorical interpretations, as Gregory candidly acknowledges in *Morals on the Book of Job*: "I shall be found often therein to put rather in the background the order of exposition, and to employ myself at greater length upon the wide field of contemplation and of moral instruction" (1979, *Ad Leandrum*, 2:90–92).

As the *Morals on the Book of Job* states it, "For first, we lay the historical foundations" (Gregory 1979, *Ad Leandrum*, 3:110–11). The act of laying the literal sense (*Primum quidem fundamenta historiae ponimus*) is part of a series of metaphors in Gregory's text linked to the construction of a building. The literal meaning is thus at the foundation of the edifice. The act of laying (*ponimus*) the literal meaning, however, also suggests that the literal meaning is put at the foundation, in which case the literal meaning is also the result of the act of laying a foundation.

This view that the literal meaning is put at the foundation is confirmed by another line of metaphors, also linked to building. In his commentary on the Song of Songs, Gregory writes, "Allegory is a kind of machine [*quandam machinam*] which allows the soul, separated from God by a great distance, to be lifted up to him" (1963a, 2:14–15).[8] Allegory is a machine that works by reading the text in a certain way. In these metaphors, it appears that the literal meaning (which is at the foundation of the building and thus—one might think—the first layer) itself turns out to be the object of a first act of building: the literal meaning has rather been engineered and placed at the foundation. Allegory as a method of reading is a machine of meaning.[9] Thus, while saying that the building has to be firmly set on the historical meaning, Gregory also says that the firm foundation of the historical and moral senses is provided by the allegorical sense. The literal meaning is thus what supports the building and what has been engineered for fulfilling such a function.

This dual place of the literal meaning explains the dual function of the allegorical reading, which can then be also the first sense as the method for reading. When Gregory conveys the link between literal and spiritual meaning through the metaphors of root and marrow, the precedence can be granted to the literal meaning, which works as a root in the heart of listeners (*in corda audientium iuxta litteram verbi radicem . . .*) and will produce the fruits of the spiritual meaning (*spiritales fructus*; 1971, II.1.1:36–37). Alternatively, the spiritual meaning is given precedence as a spiritual marrow hidden in the letter (*latens in littera spiritalis medulla*; II.10.2:26). This precedence of the allegorical meaning is explicitly stated in *In I Regum*: "We put forward the typological interpretation as a solid foundation [*typicam significationem uelut solidum fundamentum praemittimus*]; the construction of all the works in moral and historical interpretation is based upon it or follows it" (1963b, *Prologus* 88:54). This statement in *In I Regum* is more explicit than what we find in the *Homilies on Ezekiel* or the *Morals on Job*.

What is striking in this use of "literal"—literal as the basis for the spiritual meaning—as well as in the second sense—literal as opposed to Christian—is that they are both defined extrinsically. The latter use is defined negatively: "literal" means not guided by the spirit. And the former use is

---

8. Quoted in Zinn 1995, 170; Markus 1997, 47. Markus translates *machina* as pulley (1997, 50) because of the movement of the soul being lifted up toward God.

9. Although he does not make reference to Gregory, Yves Delègue uses a Gregorian formula in the title of his book *Les machines du sens: Fragments d'une sémiologie médiévale*, which presents texts by Hugh of Saint-Victor, Thomas Aquinas, and Nicholas of Lyra (1987).

defined retrospectively: "literal" means what the spiritual sense takes as its foundation. In both cases, to use a contemporary expression, "literal" is a category of interpretation in the sense that it is a qualification given to a certain meaning once an interpretation has already taken hold of the text. Gregory equates the literal meaning with a non-Christian meaning, in the second use of the term "literal," and takes the literal meaning as the foundation for the spiritual meaning, in the third use of the term literal." One solution is to distinguish, as the humanist Lefèvre does, two literal meanings: "For I believe that there is a twofold literal meaning: one, improperly so called, is the meaning of the blind and the shortsighted who understand divine realities in a wholly carnal manner and submit them to change; the other meaning, the true one, is the meaning for those who are enlightened by the Spirit" (quoted in de Lubac 1959, II, 2:413).

These equivalences (equated with non-Christian, in the first case, and equated with the historical meaning, in the second case, where the literal meaning is the foundation of the spiritual) are clearly interpretive decisions and, I submit, part of a hermeneutic judgment that Gregory sometimes characterizes as *discretio*: to strike a balance between the two extremes of understanding everything literally or allegorically.

Such a hermeneutic decision to allocate what pertains to the literal or the spiritual levels is not directly legitimated in the text of the Bible: neither the literal nor the spiritual meaning is simply extracted from the text. In addition, the virtue of *discretio* itself is not in the text, even if it was shaped by reading the Bible. At this point, it could be argued that the qualification of "literal" is nothing else than a retrospective qualification made from what is seen as the spiritual meaning. The spiritual meaning would then arise from the encounter of the biblical text and the background of those (Christians in Gregory's case) who read it "in that particular spirit." It would be an extra meaning, as O'Loughlin calls it, which accompanies what the text says. Since "the justification for the existence of this 'extra' lay not in the nature of the text as text," it is tempting to conclude with O'Loughlin that, for Gregory, the justification of the spiritual meaning lies "in the basic religious assumptions held by those engaged in reading the text" and that the need for "'additional meanings' arose out of the actual encounter of reading the text with their assumptions about what the text they were reading should mean" (1998, 157).

O'Loughlin seems to believe that, if the spiritual meaning is not in the text, then it can only be a product of the assumptions of the readers. I contend that, for Gregory, this is a false dichotomy. The discernment (*discretio*)

Gregory praises is precisely what allows us to find a middle way between a spiritual meaning given in its self-identity in the text—what he denies— and a spiritual meaning that is a mere projection of the readers' assumptions—what he rejects. Gregory solves the apparent contradiction between a foundational and an engineered literal meaning by introducing the role of the reader and her background.

Cooperation between Text and Reader

Gregory's hermeneutic position is difficult to assess given that he at times is quite traditional in his method of reading the Bible, but at other times makes startling statements, for example, regarding the literal meaning as both a foundation and a product, or regarding the place of allegorical understanding as both a sense, founded upon the literal meaning, and a method of reading. Gregory summarizes these controversial ideas in his famous statement that "the divine text grows with the reader [*divina eloquia cum legente crescunt*]" (1971, I, 7.8:145). Usually such a growth is understood as the subjective growth of the reader, to the extent that readers learn something when reading and learn in accordance with their abilities. There is also the possibility of an objective growth, the growth of the text itself. Most commentators understand such an objective growth of the biblical text as its capacity to respond to readers at whatever level readers approach the text, with naïveté or sophistication. Such a growth, however, is only metaphorical and amounts to the subjective growth of readers, only with an emphasis on the supple character of the text.

Gregory, however, is more audacious. Those who recognize that he means more than a metaphor fall into two camps: those who dismiss it and those who embrace it. Among those who dismiss the objective growth in a nonmetaphorical sense is Markus, who holds that "Gregory's sense of the inexhaustible riches of the scriptures encouraged him to roam at ease among its meanings. The meaning of a text was as much the creation of its reader as it was determined by the text," so that "his own homiletic practice illustrates the unlimited freedom from textual restraint to which he felt entitled of his exegesis" (1997, 44–45). As a consequence, Markus subscribes to Paul Meyvaert's view that Gregory's works represent "a grand exercise in the use of the imagination" (quoted in Markus 1997, 45).

Others wholeheartedly embrace the idea of the growth of the text in a nonmetaphorical sense. Bori, for example, shows that such an objective growth was already present in previous commentators, even if these commentators were not as explicit as Gregory: "Gregory the Great does not appear as responsible for a rupture [with the tradition], but as the clear end point of a coherent and substantially unified evolution" (1987, 71).

The problem with Markus's assessment is that Gregory is fairly explicit about what he means, and he is consistent. The principle of charity in interpretation—not in the sense of the Christian charity—which says that we should grant to an author at least as much intelligence and sophistication as we have, should lead us to be more charitable to Gregory than Markus is. Bori's view presents problems, however. The difficulty is twofold. First, he essentially offers an argument for the stronger objective growth based on its compatibility with previous authors who were not as explicit. But weaker versions do not explain the appearance of a stronger version. Second, and more troubling, Bori puts together statements by Gregory from different works, which reinforce each other, but without considering the context from which these passages are taken and without, for example, considering the fact that one of these works, *In I Regum*, is at best of Gregorian inspiration. He relies heavily on the statement from *In I Regum* on contemplation that characterizes it as "the power through which the scripture, had it not been composed, would be composed" (1963b, 3.171:3475–77).

We do not have to make such a radical choice between an objective growth produced by the imagination, as Markus believes, and the real organic growth of the text, so that the reader has precedence over the text of the Bible and can cause not only the meaning of the text to grow but also the materiality of the text, as Bori is inclined to believe. The activism of the reader is, in Gregory, somehow tempered by the motivation of such an activism: it is in order to be faithful to the spirit of what is said. As Grover Zinn points out, "The 'construct' results from a process which interprets the sacred text for the edification of Gregory's audience, listeners and readers" (1995, 172). Gregory justifies his hermeneutic engineering by showing the necessary cooperation that takes place between text and reader.

The primary goal of reading the Bible has, as for early Christian interpreters, always been more than an attempt to understand what is said. It is also supposed to be a contribution to God's glory. For one to witness God's presence, one first has to be touched by God's word. In such a framework, reading the Bible is thus one of the most efficient ways to access the divine intention and thereby to become a witness. Reading is thus essentially an exercise or training in order to let oneself be transformed by the reading so that one's own ways of thinking regarding the church, Christ, or the afterlife can be reevaluated and deepened. In this sense, there has always been a pragmatic aspect in the reading of the Bible as a moral exercise where one's own ethical framework or *habitus*, in the sense of a set way of life, is questioned. Gregory is clearly motivated by such a moral concern. He essentially writes for an audience composed of his monk brothers or future preachers. In the text on which he comments, it is for their sake that he accentuates a meaning that, lying beyond the letter, will help them or will enlighten them in their task of preaching. In his *Homilies on Ezekiel*, Gregory explains the interaction between biblical text and readers by borrowing Ezekiel's vision of the Chariot of Yahweh. Bori (1987) has offered an excellent reading of Gregory's allegorical reading, to which I in large part subscribe.

The chariot is made of four creatures that Gregory, after the church fathers, understands as the four evangelists as well as all perfect Christians. The four wheels are understood as an allegory for scripture, a metaphor Bori believes specific to Gregory (1987, 32). Gregory writes, "But what does a wheel signify, if not Holy Writ, which rolls from every direction to the mind of hearers, and is retained by no snag of error from the way of its preaching? It rolls from every direction because it proceeds straight and humble amid diversity and prosperity alike. For the circle of its precepts is now above, now below, those which are spoken spiritually to the more perfect, and accord with the letter for the feeble, and those which little children understand literally, learned men lift above through spiritual intelligence" (1971, HEz I.6.2:17–25).

The movement of the biblical word is infallible and unstoppable as it moves forward toward its proclamation. However, the power of the word depends on its adaptability to those addressed by it. The wheels rise or go down to the ground depending on the receptivity of the listeners or readers. The movement of the word is thus circular—forward and upward like a wheel—and not transitive—from one point to another on a straight line. It leads those who are able to understand the sense at this level to contemplation and, because it moves forward and upward, comes back to the humble, so that the spiritual sense gained by the learned can be shared. This sharing is precisely the purpose of preachers, as it was the evangelists' goal.

Reading the Bible is thus not only an intellectual act of appropriating the sense. It is also a commitment to proclamation: preachers who have gained a superior understanding must come back to enlighten others: "The living creatures move forward for the utility of neighbors" (Gregory 1971,

I.7.15:328–29; translation modified), in the sense that readers, who become better through their reading, become walking men. Gregory says, "There are some people who progress to a point where they know how to dispense appropriately the earthly goods they receive, how to apply themselves to the works of mercy, and assist those who are oppressed. These people are walking, given that they apply themselves to the utility of neighbor" (1971, I.7.15:309–11; translation modified).[10]

Ezekiel writes, "And when the living creatures went the wheels also went together by them: and when the living creatures were lifted up from the earth the wheels also were lifted up with them" (1:19). Here is Gregory's comment: "Because divine words grow with the reader [*quia divina eloquia cum legente crescunt*], for the deeper each understands them the deeper they penetrate into him . . . because if the minds of the readers have not attained the heights, divine words, as if in the depths, lie there not understood" (1971, I.7.8:145–49).

The wheel is the scripture and the living creatures, both the evangelists and all readers who are made perfect by the Gospels, are the authors of the scripture (I.2.18:348–51; see also I.6.11:203–4). In Gregory's understanding of Ezekiel's vision, there is harmony between the movement of the living creatures and the movement of the scripture, but there is no dependence. The text grows not only through its authors but also through its readers. The text grows with the one who reads it. Glossing the fact that the wheels followed the living creature, Gregory writes, "It is well said of these same wheels: 'and followed it.' For the reader's spirit, if he there seeks moral or historical understanding, the moral sense of the history follows him. If he seeks figurative knowledge, allusive speech is soon recognized. If contemplative, the wheels forthwith almost take wing and are suspended in the air because heavenly understanding of Holy Writ is laid bare in words. . . . The wheels follow the spirit because the words of Holy Writ, as has often been said already, grow through the intellect according to the perception of the reader" (I.7.9:171–80; translation modified).

Both a weaker and a stronger reading of Gregory's claim are possible. In the weaker reading, which is the most common among commentators, the growth of the text can be understood as a metaphor for the subjective growth of the reader when reading the Bible. The soul is enriched as it listens to the word of God, so that the text has reached its goal. In this sense

10. On Gregory's views on the role of the preacher and the ecclesiastical hierarchy, see Markus 1996, 54; 1997, 23–25; Dagens 1977, 312.

of being successful, the text grows as its meaning has been unfolded or has exerted its effect on readers. As such a subjective growth, the text adapts to the readers: simple people will rejoice in the story and advanced readers contemplate the deeper truths. They take from the text what their intelligence and interests allow them to take. That the text of the Bible follows the spirit of the readers only means in this reading such an adaptation of the scripture to the level of the readers. As Markus summarizes Gregory's statement, "The scriptures contain what the reader finds in them" (1997, 43).

While Gregory certainly has this understanding in mind, he also has a much more radical, nonmetaphorical view. In this stronger version, the text grows in the process of reading insofar as the text expands and unfolds; it gains its existence as biblical text when readers make use of it. Bori speaks of a simultaneous growth of the reader and the text (1987, 59–63). Gregory's insistence that the spirit of the readers leads the movement of the scripture indicates that there is a form of cooperation between text and readers that takes place. In my view this is the originality of Gregory.

Cooperation means more than an active participation in the text or the acceptance of bringing the text to life. Umberto Eco (1979) has used the expression cooperation in the weaker sense where the text sometimes asks for the involvement of readers, that they make guesses or complete parts of the plot. For Gregory it means a mutual enrichment. The text is "life or fire" (1971, II.10.1:14–18). The cooperation of the reader consists in letting the life or fire spring from the text by opening the mind to the possibility that the text can transform the reader. "Thus indeed the words are of the sacred Scripture. They are held cold in the story told by the letter. But if someone were to strike those words, with the intelligence focused and with the inspiration of God, fire would spring forth from their mysterious meanings, so that now the heart is inflamed spiritually while before it remained cold when hearing those words according to the letter" (II.2.7:166–69; translation modified).

Besides a fire that can kindle us, the text is also a way for us to measure our commitment as Christians. Commenting on Ezekiel's mention of a reed, Gregory understands the reed as the scripture: "This reed is said to be a measuring reed, for we measure through the Scripture every action of our life in order to see either how much we have progressed or how far we fall short of perfection" (1971, II.2.7:166–69; translation modified). Because it is a measuring device, the scripture tells us the extent of our commitment, and thereby challenges us, so that "the life of the listeners is measured through the hand of the writers [per manus scribentium vita mensuratur *auditorum*]" (II.2.7:173; translation modified). Such a strong version, in which cooperation is truly mutual, gives readers power over the text.

Although readers clearly do not write the biblical text, they can share in the authorship when they contribute to the unfolding and expansion of the text. I subscribe to Bori's assessment that the growth in question "is not only a spiritual progress measured according to Scripture. We also have here, at least according to Gregory, an objective growth and a forward movement of the sacred text that goes with the progress of the one who reads it: it is a '*virtus sacri eloquii*'" (1987, 59). Commenting on Ezekiel's vision, Gregory insists that the movement of the wheels does not obey the movement of the living creatures, but is in synchrony with them. The same spirit animates the living creatures and the wheels. Allegorically it means that the power of the spirit is both in the scriptures and the reader. This common presence is precisely what produces the act of reading. Within the text, there is thus an objective might or power dependent on the act of reading for increasing. The reader is moved by this power, recognizes the power of the text, and creatively contributes to this power.

One could say that the act of reading is the initial impetus for the wheels' movement, which leads the word to its proclamation through predication: the goal of reading is predication, but the movement has to be sustained. This sustained movement is only possible through a mutual contribution of both the text and the reader. Being addressed and moved by the text, the reader in turn carries the text further. Being read, the text grows or is increased: "When a reading of the holy scripture is sought, it is found at the measure of what becomes of the person by whom it is sought [*quaesita sacra lectio talis invenitur, qualis et fit ipse, a quo quaeritur*]" (Gregory 1971, I.7.16:332–33; translation modified). The reading links the text to what the reader becomes by virtue of reading it. The text causes the reader to change, and the changed attitude—the subjective growth—swings back to the text, which in turn becomes richer and is then read with more sophisticated questions and taken to hold deeper insights—objective growth. Still, since Gregory obviously does not want the Bible to be a product for personal and convenient consumption, what governs such cooperation between text and reader so that text and reader are mutually dependent on each other?

When readers ponder the biblical text, if their reading is nurtured by charity, they have the guarantee that continuity exists between the text to be interpreted and the reinscription of such a text in their living context. In other words, the principle of charity allows for a recontextualization of the scripture: a reading of the letter (*littera*) as a narrative (*narratio*) that tells us historical facts (*historia*), the meaning of which is to be configured in the light of the message of charity. For the letter refers not only to past words but also to future words, beyond the limits of the sacred history included in the biblical canon. Every biblical word also addresses the present of those who read it and who find there a prefiguration of their own existence. To that extent, the biblical context includes all the possible books, all the questions the reader asks the Bible. Charity as a hermeneutic principle amounts to recognizing a shared authorship of the biblical text in readers. Reading is now much more than an interpretation: the text of the Bible itself grows. Because it is the same spirit that informs text and reader, the different recontextualizations expand the text, in the sense that they make the text larger, broader, and richer: the divine words "literally" grow with the reader (*divina eloquia cum legente crescunt*; Gregory 1971, I.7.8:145; see also *quia igitur dicta sacri eloquii cum legentium spiritu excrescunt*; I.7.10:244–45). For the same reason, a recontextualization of the text does not amount to disfiguring it: the text has just grown larger.

A consequence of the cooperation between text and readers under the form of a shared authorship is that interpretation is a "machine of meaning," engineering and producing what the text says. Flowing naturally from the productivity of interpretation, Gregory seems to give his assent wholeheartedly to the possibility of a multiplicity or even infinity of valid interpretations. "In the interpretation of sacred scripture one need reject nothing that is not opposed to sound faith. For, as from one piece of gold, some fashion necklaces, others rings, and others bracelets, so from the one knowledge of sacred scripture various exegetes through innumerous interpretations compose various ornaments which all however contribute to the splendor of the heavenly spouse" (1982, III, 62:41–46).

Not only does Gregory accept a multiplicity of interpretations, he also accepts that a misunderstanding can be claimed to be right if it contributes to an increase of charity: "But if seeking the virtue in the divine words he has understood them differently from him by whom they were proffered, albeit he seeks the edification of charity beneath another's meaning, the words which he reports are the Lord's [*Domini sunt verba quae narrat*], because God speaks to us through the whole of scripture solely in order to attract us to the love of Him and our neighbor" (1971, I.10.14:216–21).

This echoes Augustine, for whom making a mistake that contributes to the edification of charity is like leaving the road by mistake during a trip and cutting across fields to reach the point where the road led (1962, 1:35–36, 39–41).

Because there is an intrinsic instability in the meaning of the text due to the interaction of the literal and the spiritual levels and because readers come to the text with their background, the background of Christians can take precedence over the meaning sought. Since the text follows the reader, as the image of the wheel following the living creatures indicates, what matters is what readers do with the text. We find such a view on the cooperation between text and reader expressed even more clearly in *In I Regum* in Gregory's adage on contemplation. His view suggests that the very materiality of the text, the fact that it has been written, is itself dependent on the background of those who read and that such a background is actually what made the text come into being. These ideas from *In I Regum* confirm the passage where Gregory positions the allegorical understanding as the solid foundation for the other senses. Although stronger and more explicit than what is found in the *Homilies on Ezekiel* or the *Morals on the Book of Job*, the passage from *In I Regum* remains in conformity with the latter.

Gregory not only explains his method of interpretation but also justifies it and makes a case for it both at the specific level of a Christian reading and at the general level of the necessity of a background. Regarding his specific way of interpreting the Bible from a Christian background under the auspices of charity, Gregory shows that such a reading has the advantage of accounting for the novelty of the New Testament. If the Bible is read only in following the old law, the New Testament is not fully integrated as a New Alliance. Reading the Bible while recognizing the novelty of the New Testament means acknowledging that the New Testament retrospectively leads us to see that what was before an integral whole (the Old Testament) was in fact a first stage—a literal meaning—that can now be read (and has to be) as the carrier of another meaning. Although such a view amounts to recognizing that the *littera* is a retrospective qualification (from the point of view of the New Testament), it is precisely what the New Testament— understood as a revelation of a New Alliance—demands. In other words, the hermeneutic decision to see the *littera* as in need of assistance derives from the very content of the New Testament. It is thus the New Testament that justifies putting the allegorical sense as a foundation, since allegorical understanding is not only one among different senses but also the very method to read the Bible in the right (Christian) way. Hence, the literal meaning is both a foundational sense at the beginning of the process of reading and a result, since the very process of reading is itself a hermeneutic stance.

The literal meaning is thus an overdetermination to the extent that readers come to the text with their whole history, their personalities, their needs, and consequently their beliefs and expectations. In the case of Christians, they implicitly make the hermeneutic decision to read the Bible in the light of the New Testament. It is not, however, a strict predetermination as if a set of religious assumptions could preempt the results of reading—as if readers, before reading, already assumed what the text says. Although the background will determine the direction the reading is going to take, Gregory seems to say, the text at one point becomes strong enough to find its way between overdetermination and predetermination. What prevents the background from becoming so intrusive as to erase the power of the text is the dynamic cooperation for which the text asks.

Since the cooperation between text and reader is under the auspices of charity, readers are accountable for their reading of the Bible. The literal meaning remains the level where interpreters have to justify their interpretation. Because it is too weak and unstable to serve as the motivation of an interpretation and needs a background to be meaningful as literal, the literal meaning cannot be first in the order of discovery. Nevertheless, the literal meaning remains first in the order of justification, since it anchors any claim made by interpreters that they interpret this text rather than that other text and why they interpret it the way they do. Any interpretation is ordered to charity and the well-being of the Christian community. As Markus notes, Gregory "was engaged in a truly communal exercise with his equals. Understanding the Bible was an enterprise carried out for the sake of the community, and within the community, drawing on its resources and its traditions of scriptural discourse" (1997, 42). The existence of a literal meaning makes it possible for interpreters to make claims regarding the validity of their interpretation—validity in the sense of being ordered to charity—and these claims in turn regulate the conversation that takes place in a community. In case of conflicts among Christian interpretations, the decision favors the one that contributes to the increase of charity and thus to the edification of the Christian community.

But Gregory does not simply confine the correct reading of the Bible to an actual Christian community. If we extrapolate, his framework also allows for a debate with non-Christians, and the literal meaning remains the space where the redeeming of claims can happen. When there is a conflict between two hermeneutic principles, for example, Christian and Jewish, the regulative role charity plays allows a decision to be made. The decision amounts, first, to recognizing that the Jewish reading belongs to another tradition, not the Christian tradition—an agreement to disagree of a sort, and second, as we can infer, a possible discussion about how the regulative idea of charity is manifested in the Bible and what God's will is. Gregory implicitly and retrospectively forces the Jewish reading of the Bible to recognize that such a Jewish reading is also a hermeneutic decision that is not self-evident and that it needs to make a case for ignoring the New Testament as a New Alliance: "The Gentiles bear in mind those precepts which the Jewish people could not keep so long as they hearkened only to the letter thereof" (1971, I.6.3:52–54).

The growth of the reader and the text, which is so troubling to many interpreters, can be seen as the growth of the community. Gregory does not say that individual readers have power over the text in isolation from their community. On the contrary, readers read with the standards of their community and from within their community. There is thus no radical arbitrariness in the sense that any reader can see anything in the text. As for the arbitrariness of a community—and Gregory acknowledges at least two communities of interpreters, Christian and Jewish—Gregory defends the Christian reading, which is guided by charity, since charity is precisely the message of the text of the Bible. It is thus almost by necessity that the text grows when the community of readers grows in its understanding of the text. They alone can make the text speak and respond to what they ask from it. It is thus not only unavoidable but also felicitous that the text falls in the hands of readers and risks being subjected to their whims. In the hands of readers, the text has a chance to make a difference. It needs to be struck to thrust its own fire upon those who read it. The text grows indeed, because it has been furthered, propagated, and even disseminated. But also, the fire of the text has spread, so that the reader's personal growth reverberates on the text: readers ask more sophisticated questions and are able to find more sophisticated answers. The fire coming from the text has kindled the spirit in the reader, which reciprocally makes the original fire of the text stronger and more powerful in its effect on other readers. In the end, the mutual growth of text and reader is a shared authorship by readers. The text is theirs because, transformed as they are by the text, they not only made it theirs, but, by fulfilling the very intention of the text, nurtured the spirit that is in the text.

The view that the interpretation of the holy scripture is infinite was accepted during the Middle Ages. However, this infinity has been redefined. There are many reasons for such a shift in hermeneutics that cannot be examined here. One of them is that the Bible becomes an object of academic interest in the different schools. Scholars look at the text, and more and more believe that, as Kenneth Hagen puts it, "what the Holy Spirit intended to say is there in Scripture, and all the levels of meaning are in the letter of the text, not in some other levels of meaning" (1985, 9). Such a change in the interest of scholars causes a change in the method of reading the Bible. There is a shift in theology from *sacra pagina* (the sacred page) to *sacra doctrina* (sacred doctrine). It is emphasized more and more that readers can only have a specific place within the circle of reading, in accordance with their capacity and their role. The Catholic Church, for example, has progressively seen itself as the only one able to cover the whole circle of interpretation because, more and more, the wheel has been seen as the church's reading. "Consequently, so that you can safely judge the letter, do not rely on your own intelligence," Hugh of Saint-Victor advises his readers. "This access [to the letter] should be asked from the doctors and the wise. Relying on the authority of the sacred Fathers and on the testimonies of the Scriptures, they can both provide you with such an access and open it to you as far as it is necessary" (1880, col. 804D–805A).

In a famous formula, Vincentius of Lerins writes, "that your treatment not your subject, your manner not your matter may be new [*cum dicas nove, non dicas nova*]" (1915, chap. 22, line 8:88). Some recent trends in theology, illustrated by Urs von Balthasar among others, have resisted these late moves and tried to reconnect with some of the insights of the early fathers of the church. Similarly, the revival of hermeneutics with Schleiermacher and then Gadamer has reopened the debate both about the status of the literal meaning and the contribution of readers to the text.

What is often missing in contemporary accounts of interpretation is the *discretio* Gregory values so much: the capacity to find a balance between what we take from the text and what we import into it. Gregory shows that readers read texts because somehow they are touched, affected, or concerned by what is said. Although as interpreters they are instances of discourse, functioning as a member in the equation for the meaning of the text to be carried further, readers are also involved in the act of reading as real persons with their own context, questions, and concerns. The background of readers is not just a set of beliefs, assumptions, or habits but also what makes them who they are, with the commitment they have toward fellow members of their community and toward their community. Despite those subjective elements in interpretation, Gregory also shows how a cooperation with the text or even a coauthorship on the side of readers does not necessarily amount to a devastation of the text and a radical relativity of interpretations. Literal meaning and background are interdependent, so that, first, literal does not amount to arbitrary—the background serves as a stabilizer of meaning for a given community—and, second, the existence of a background is an implicit acknowledgment of other possible backgrounds, so that the background itself is a possible object of discussion and has to be justified.

Because there is already an element of interpretation in what is literal, it makes little sense to speak of an unchanging literal meaning being applied differently, as Searle does. Gregory shows that any specification of a literal meaning is an application. There is, however, something that remains stable: the fact that there is always a correlation between what is literal and the background against which such a literal meaning is specified. What matters in interpretation is, thus, neither what the text says in itself, as many forms of monism claim, nor the background assumptions of readers, as pluralism contends, but the correlation between the two, so that a given interpretation can be situated: this is what this text means from this perspective with this methodology.

Is Gregory then a relationalist, in the sense defined by Gracia? Gracia writes, "I claim that theological interpretations are relational: A theological interpretation is not in fact, as many mistakenly hold, the understanding of what a divinity wishes believers to understand, but rather of what a theological tradition considers to be a divine message" (2001, xii). The divine text does not speak alone, but only when related to a tradition. "The interpretation of revelation depends on the theology that guides it, so that different theological assumptions necessarily result in different interpretations" (188). Gracia, however, is not ready to accept relativism. He considers two mechanisms at the disposal of theology to regulate interpretation: "The first consists of the beliefs and principles of the theology in question; the second consists of the general principles that govern all attempts to develop knowledge that goes beyond personal opinion" (188). Each theology has its own principles and conventions, which force any partner in the discussion to pattern any new interpretation in accordance with these regulations and conventions. The second mechanism belongs to the general rationality pertaining to any discussion.

If we were to reformulate Gregory's understanding of the cooperation between text and readers in Gracia's terms, we would lose two key elements of Gregory's hermeneutics. First, Gregory is not saying that each tradition—he only considers the Christian and the Jewish communities—of necessity will read the Bible differently, as Gracia claims. There is no necessity to read differently because of two different backgrounds. For Gregory one is clearly better and in fact the only one that is legitimate. That significantly limits the relationism of Gregory. Backgrounds can change, and a community can modify its background or adopt another one, which was for the preacher Gregory a constant hope, even of changing his own community. In sum, a background is not monolithic, but itself depends on the fire people can extract from the Bible. While Gracia sees biblical interpretation as an event determined by the background in which these events take place, Gregory is definitely on the side of reading the Bible as an act.

The second element of Gregory's hermeneutics that would not be captured by Gracia's views is the possibility of regulating the dialogue between communities. Gracia seems to believe that the rules of rationality are enough to prevent an encounter between different communities from turning into the cannibalization of one discourse by another. Although Gregory does not even mention rationality, what he suggests is that the only telos of any discussion, either intracommunitarian or extracommunitarian, is the good of the community. Given that the community in which he, Gregory, lives is based on the love of one's neighbor, the good of such a community can only be the extension of the community. And such an extension is not gained or made through arguments alone—although arguments are needed and Gregory himself was adept in preaching and convincing others—but through a sharing of a common good, which happens through a form of conversion.

Such is the *discretio* that makes an interpreter someone who emphasizes in the biblical text what contributes to the well-being of the community, while still allowing that well-being to be an object of discussion: are we really who we should be? The first aspect recognizes the import of the background in any act of interpretation, which is an event. The second aspect keeps the background itself in the discussion through the act the interpreter performs: am I myself contributing to the good of the community in the interpretation I provide?

5

The Representative Content of a Novel as a Set of Narratives

Grass as a Critic of Ricoeur

Besides the author's intention and the literal meaning, the third key concept in interpretation is the representative content of what is said: not only what was meant—the intention—nor what the words mean, but what is represented. Some kinds of texts aim at a perfect clarity of what they represent and strive toward avoiding any ambiguity and misunderstanding, such as journalism, history, law, and scientific papers (which does not mean that they always succeed in that endeavor). In most instances the means to assess the truth of an interpretation are readily available: a journalistic account has to be congruent with the facts otherwise available to other people; historical interpretation can be checked against available documents and sometimes witnesses; a legal interpretation by a judge can be appealed and scrutinized by other courts, with the Supreme Court functioning in the United States as the ultimate authority; and scientific papers will be dissected by colleagues who will verify the experiments and procedures. Some other texts, however, seem to encourage multiple understandings and rejoice in the ambiguities of what they represent or the consequent difficulties they cause to interpreters. Literary texts are of this sort. They are thus an ideal candidate for examining what the representative content of a text is and how it can be identified.

When we deal with literary texts, since most of their content is fictional, there is no real empirical data that can with some level of assurance assess the truth of what an interpreter says about a text, and there is no ultimate jurisdiction that is recognized as the ultimate arbiter for matters of interpretation. Authors do not have cognitive privilege regarding the meaning of their texts. In the case of literary texts, interpreters can stipulate their object of interpretation any way they please and choose their perspective and method. The task is thus rather daunting to defeat a given interpretation, especially of a novel.

The fact that literary texts do not claim to refer directly to the real world and thus cannot easily be transposed into a set of testable propositions led to the old belief that literature is not about truth or, in the more recent terminology of Jonathan Culler, "is something other than a statement about the world" (quoted in Juhl 1980, 154). I disagree. The representative content of a literary text can be, among other things, a set of narratives that readers extract from the text and apply to their situation, leading the text to configure their reality, or a set of intentional states that readers construe out of the text, colonizing the text for making sense of the world around them. My aim is to examine what interpretation does with literary texts, in particular, what kinds of decisions have to be made by interpreters when they explain what a novel means, a meaning that is not necessarily the author's intention and more than the meaning of the text. I examine the power of the text in terms of narratives, using Paul Ricoeur and Günter Grass.

Ricoeur's Theory of Narratives
Truth as Narrative Disclosure

If literature speaks to us, touches us, and moves us, it must relate to something beyond itself and known to us. Obviously, the way literature relates to us is not by providing us with information that we find vital about a certain Eugenie Grandet (Balzac 1976) or unveiling secrets about a certain Isabel Archer (James 1983). Whether literature makes sense politically at the heart of the Greek polis in the form of tragedies, in the former Soviet society through a virulent satire in Solzhenitsyn, or in the more confined circle of intellectuals in the case of Mallarmé's poetry in France, literature has always had the telos of saying something, of referring to something. Since Plato's presentation in *Ion*, poetry or literature is a message. Literary criticism has torn itself apart regarding the type of reference that literature provides: is it the social milieu, the author's experiences, universal archetypes, or the great library of the world, to use Jorge Luis Borges's famous expression? Does literature give us lessons or does it only provide manners of speaking? Does literature have a cognitive nature or merely an affective nature?

Philosophy and literature have had a long and rather strange history of interaction. Plato spoke of an ancient quarrel between them (*palaia diaphora*; Plato 1987, 607B; translation modified). He is suspicious about the social utility of poetry. Poets might be the interpreters of the gods and thus might practice a form of representation (mimesis), but, as argued in *Ion*, they do not know what they are doing. It is by virtue of a divine favor (*theia moira*; Plato 1925, 534C), a divine power (*theia dunamei*; 534C), or possession (*katokoche*; 536C) that poets are able to compose their works. In the *Republic*, Plato even decides to banish them from the ideal state. By representing things or events that are themselves copies of the truth, poetry is removed to the third degree from the truth and thus cannot know what it represents. Even worse, poetry imitates not only the highest virtues but also inferior passions such as anger, greed, and lust. Poetry "waters and fosters these feelings when what we ought to do is to dry them up, and it establishes them when they ought to be ruled" (Plato 1987, 606d).

In his *Poetics,* Aristotle (1927) nuances this harsh Platonic condemnation. Poetry is an affair of representation or imitation (mimesis) that, besides being a natural inclination of human beings, is also a way of learning. Aristotle shows how a form of poetry, tragedy, is superior to history, which is only concerned with particulars, to the extent that poetry reveals and makes intelligible the principles behind human action. Poetry is more philosophical than history. At the same time, poetry remains inferior to philosophy, which is only concerned with universals, to the extent that poetry shows the universal in particular instances of action, not conceptual and propositional modes. Poetry makes the principles followed by agents intelligible by providing a plot that links together in a coherent whole what was, before the imitation, a series of acts or episodes not explicitly concatenated. By being engulfed in the plot and sharing the fears and joys of the characters, listeners make the lesson manifested by the plot their own and are then part of a process of purification (catharsis). They have scenarios for making sense of their own experiences or of what can happen to them. The imitation performed by poetry is thus not a reproduction of what already exists, but rather the configuration of what happened or of what can happen. It is only after imitation has taken place that we see—we recognize—what was imitated. The original becomes meaningful once transposed at a distance in a representation.

On the basis of this view, an interaction between philosophy and literature is possible. It is remarkable that, in the history of such an interaction, the dialogue has usually been aborted. The recognition of the linguistic nature of both literature and philosophy at the end of the eighteenth century and at the beginning of the nineteenth (Foucault 1970, 299–300; Escarpit 1970, 1973; Ross 1992, 1996; Lacoue-Labarthe and Nancy 1978) seems to have prevented a fruitful dialogue. Literature became more interested in its own literary nature. And philosophy was divided into two trends after the linguistic turn initiated by Wittgenstein at the turn of the century, which was made possible by the scientific atmosphere of the nineteenth century. The new analytic trend focused on an analysis of language for solving philosophical problems, and the old continental trend continued its interest in metaphysical questions. Although this original chasm between analytic and continental philosophy is slowly narrowing, the damage done to approaching language and literature has been devastating. There was also a linguistic turn in continental philosophy, which took place quite early with J. G. Herder, who reacted against Immanuel Kant, followed by Wilhelm von Humboldt and culminating in Heidegger. Language went from being a "perspective on the world" (Humboldt's *Weltansicht*, 1963) to the language of being in Heidegger, that which speaks through what humans say.

Although the two traditions, analytic and continental, investigate the notions of meaning, intention, and interpretation, they do not use the same criteria of precision and do not agree on how to circumscribe the field of investigation. For the most part, analytic philosophy adopted the stance of methodological solipsism, which, broadly defined, consists in examining one's own mental states regardless of how others' mental states influence those mental states or how one came to have those states. The advantage of analytic philosophy is that it can provide detailed, sophisticated, and rigorous analysis of specific questions. In the study of language, such qualities have made analytic philosophy the only official philosophy of language. The problem such a philosophy has when approaching literature is that, since the analytic stance studies ordinary language, literature can only be investigated in terms of meaning, intention, or reference in the currency these notions have in ordinary language. The question then is about the cognitive power of literary fictions.

Frege nicely illustrates the issue of contention. First, he finds in literature, especially poetry, no interest in the sense of what is said, as in a normal meaningful use, but in "the shadings and colorings which poetry seeks to impart to the senses. These shadings and colorings are not objective" (2001, 201). Second, he reduces literature to aesthetic enjoyment, thereby excluding it from the search for the truth, given the concept of truth he proposes: "In listening to an epic, for example, we are fascinated by the euphony of the language and also by the sense of the sentences and by the images and emotions evoked. In turning to the question of truth we disregard the artistic appreciation and pursue scientific considerations" (203). Following the suspicion raised by Frege, Austin considers sentences uttered on stage or in a poem as nonserious and parasitic (1962). Searle also considers fiction to be a pretense to the truth.

While the analytic tradition offers narrow approaches to clearly delimited topics, continental philosophy has always been tempted to offer new systems or broad pictures of how problems develop and how they are motivated, whether it is a phenomenology of spirit (Hegel 1970), a genealogy of morals (Nietzsche 1984), a crisis of the European sciences (Husserl 1970), or a history of being (Heidegger 1989). In such a holistic approach to problems, continental philosophy has eagerly turned to literature as a manifestation of philosophical issues, as a specific perspective taken on the world, or as a resource for rejuvenating the usual ways of doing philosophy. Phenomenology itself found its first applications in literary studies, and existentialism was both a philosophical and literary movement.

This dialogue between continental philosophy and literature, unfortunately, suffered from an excruciatingly painful suspicion about conceptuality. It is indeed the creed of phenomenology that the conceptualization should come from what is observed and not be imposed on it. To surrender to the tyranny of the concept would amount to abandoning the phenomenological stance and engaging in rational reconstructions. The suspicion about conceptuality, however, also served as an excuse for some to indulge in conceptually nonrigorous writings under the plea that the margins of philosophy and literature had been blurred. The dialogue was promising and offered interesting and fruitful insights, but a conceptual articulation of the results of such a dialogue was late in coming. It is only with philosophers such as Ricoeur and Rorty, among many others, who manage to bridge the two traditions, that we benefit from a conceptually clear articulation of how literature and philosophy can interact with each other.

Among the different philosophical schools, phenomenology has been the one that has constantly and fruitfully engaged literature. One of the main contributions of phenomenology in the broad sense has been a reexamination of the traditional concept of truth and the correctives that have been suggested. In *Being and Time* (1962, 1984), Heidegger famously introduces a new notion of truth as unveiling or disclosure: the truth of assertions presupposes a prior opening made possible by human existence. Furthermore, the form such a disclosure takes is through what Heidegger calls a discursive articulation. This view has caused a radical change in continental philosophy, opening new areas of research.

In accordance with one of the basic tenets of Husserl's phenomenology, Heidegger in *Being and Time* (1984) considers that meaning (*Sinn*) is primordially the possibility for things to be articulated by humans or the susceptibility for things to matter to human beings and to make sense for them. Meaning is thus not strictly speaking what pertains to things independently of human involvement or what human beings project on an unformed world or an entity or a realm of entities floating between human beings and things. Meaning is an existential dimension: it is "that wherein the intelligibility [*Verständigkeit*] of something maintains itself" (193). The world itself is permeated by this dimension of intelligibility (*Bedeutsamkeit*). The capacity that human beings have to be sensitive to such intelligibility is a capacity to understand.

Meaning is thus the medium in which human beings encounter things around them and other people. This encounter does not take the form of a relationship between a subject and an object, as traditional metaphysics claims, but primarily of a receptivity: human beings find themselves (*sich befinden*) among things and people and are primarily affected by them. Understanding (*Verstehen*) and affectedness (*Befindlichkeit*) constitute two basic components of human existence. The existence of a dimension of meaning before anything can be the object of a theoretical gaze indicates that there is an opening allowing entities to become intelligible and, literally, to make sense. Human existence is such an opening. The mistake traditional metaphysics made was to forget this prior opening of meaning. Such an oblivion led metaphysics to consider presence at hand (*Vorhandenheit*) as the only basis on which objectivity and truth can be grounded, when an object is presented to the gaze of a subject who can then read off the properties of such an object.

Heidegger attempts to delineate the primordial opening made possible by human existence and thereby retrieve the possibility for a new ontology that would account for the primacy of meaning and the subsequent correlation between understanding and being affected by what already makes sense. Such an ontology is an ontology of readiness to hand (*Zuhanden-*

heit), where entities are primordially things of concern in the everyday world. Things reveal themselves primarily as objects of concern within a pragmatic network where they are things "for," ready to hand (*zuhanden*).

Because things are revealed through human concerns as something, such a revelation is a preunderstanding that provides a synthesis on the basis of which any theoretical act of judgment can be made. "Interpretation is carried out primordially not in a theoretical statement but in an action of circumspective concern—laying aside the unsuitable tool, or exchanging it, 'without wasting words'" (Heidegger 1962, 200). This hermeneutic synthesis—the "existential-hermeneutical 'as'" (201)—is different from, prior to, and at the basis of the propositional synthesis—"the apophantical 'as' of the assertion"—through which a thing is assigned properties in what becomes a propositional content (201). The propositional truth, thus, cannot be the primary locus of the truth, but is relative to the primordial opening of human existence.

Although human existence (*Dasein*) functions as the sense giver—Heidegger understands the word *bedeuten* in the strong sense of conferring (*be-*) an interpretation (*Deutung*; 1962, 120)—this capacity is not a privilege of the individual person but rather of human beings in general. It is a corporate capacity, so to speak. This capacity takes the form of what Heidegger calls discourse, which, along with understanding (*Verstehen*) and affectedness (*Befindlichkeit*), is an *existentiale* of *Dasein*'s openness to the world. These three components of human existence are said to be equiprimordial (*gleichursprunglich*; 203): none can claim to take precedence or to enjoy any priority over the others. Discourse belongs to the structure of human existence and even structures human existence, to the extent that it is a capacity or a competence: it is the active articulation of the significance of the world, which opens the framework in which the world can matter. Heidegger reformulates the formula *Zoon logon echon* as "man shows himself as the entity which talks [*Der Mensch zeigt sich als Seiendes, das redet*]" (208). The discourse that articulates things in their meaning already contains the voice of other people. The things that I encounter have already been encountered by others. It is only on the basis of such a shared world that I can find my way among things and people. Although the mediation exerted by meaning empowered human beings in their capacity to articulate the world, the preexistence of such an articulation prevents any radical semiotic revolution by an individual: on the side of things, they are "encountered from out of the world in which they are ready-to-hand for Others" (154), and on the side of other people, they "are not proximally present-at-hand as free-floating subjects along with other Things, but show themselves in the world in terms of what is ready-to-hand in that world" (160).

The fact that the significability (*Bedeutsamkeit*) of the world already resounds with the voices of people past or present indicates that the susceptibility of things to be meaningful is a possibility on the basis of what has already been laid out and articulated by other people. Discourse, besides being a competence, constitutes a background against which I, as a particular human being, have to find my identity and my place in the world. "The intelligibility of something has always been articulated, even before there is any appropriative interpretation of it" (Heidegger 1962, 203). The discursive articulation of the world is thus not merely a capacity but a historical and contingent fact for each and every *Dasein* out of which they will have to find their own voice. Heidegger calls such a historically sedimented discourse, holding together the background of any human endeavor, a public interpretation (*öffentliche Ausgelegtheit*). This public discourse, preexisting any individual action and even intention, "proximally controls every way in which the world and Dasein get interpreted" (165). From such a public discourse there is no escape: "This everyday way in which things have been interpreted is one into which Dasein has grown in the first instance, with never a possibility of extrication. In it, out of it, and against it, all genuine understanding, interpreting, and communicating, all rediscovering and appropriating anew, are performed" (213). Heidegger uses the term *das man* for naming the anonymity of the public interpretation: "one" or "they"; "The 'They' itself Articulates the referential context of significance" (167).

The drawback of being immersed in a dimension of meaning is now the looming specter of an anonymous machine of meaning against which individuals have to gain their own voice. "Proximally, it is not 'I,' in the sense of my own Self, that 'am,' but rather the others, whose way is that of the 'they.' In terms of the 'They,' and as the 'They,' I am 'given' proximally to 'myself' [*mir 'selbst'*]" (Heidegger 1962, 167). The "real dictatorship" (164) exercised by the "They" takes the form of a loose web of sedimented habits, customs, and ways of speaking, acting, and behaving, which "is expressed by being spoken out, and has always been so expressed; it is language" (211), a language in which "there lies an average intelligibility" (212).

I cannot pursue any further here Heidegger's detailed description of daily life, the way an individual can reach his authentic being, and the ultimate question Heidegger pursues in *Being and Time* concerning the meaning of the being that gives itself in this ontology of readiness to hand, a question that led Heidegger later to reject human existence as the primary openness of being and the primary locus of the truth (see Vandevelde 1994, 1999, 2003c). Heidegger's views underlie the notion of discursivity that became so prominent in postwar French philosophy, especially for philosophers such as Foucault, Derrida, Lyotard, and Ricoeur.

These philosophers essentially focus on the first part of *Being and Time*, which presents the dual aspect of the truth, as opening and as propositional, with an emphasis on truth as opening. To a large extent they strip Heidegger's views from the existential paraphernalia, putting aside the notion of anxiety, being toward death, and even temporality, thereby reformulating the ontological difference in strictly discursive terms: being is only a stratum of discursive practices that precedes whatever articulations individuals perform. Foucault, for example, has become famous for his reflection on discourse and discursive practices (1969, 1970); Derrida has made fashionable the notions of grammatology (1967a), *écriture* (1967b), and *différance* (1972); Lyotard and Ricoeur have developed a theory of narratives.

Lyotard (1979) argues that science itself is a narrative, contrary to the burning desire of scientific practices. Since Kant, the procedures that allow a science to delineate its object are supposed to be the application of universal concepts to a particular object. What Lyotard claims, however, is that the application of universal concepts to a particular object involves procedures that are selected, accepted, and valued. These procedures that allow a science to delineate its object are themselves linked into a legitimating discourse, a discourse that can justify the use of this procedure rather than another. As in any choice, values are involved. The discourse that legitimates scientific procedures can belong, for example, to a culture that values the comfort brought about by technological innovations or to a social or political group that sees progress as an augmentation of its power. In short, Lyotard calls into question the status of these universal concepts deemed sufficient to organize the particular, thereby putting scientific practices at the level of discursive practices.

The narrative, in Lyotard, is given back its fundamental role of being both *ratio* and *oratio*. A narrative not only tells stories but gives form and shape to what is said through it. Consequently, literature as a manufacturer of narratives eminently contributes to fiction, now understood in the sense of a process of invention—what the Latin word *fingere* means—which permits the articulation of reality. As German Romanticism proclaimed, language, reason, and literature are correlative. There is no reason outside a rational narrative; there is no narrative without words, figures of style, meanings—all are jewels that literature produces, refines, or modifies (Schlegel 1967, 1968, 1991; Lacoue-Labarthe and Nancy 1978).

The postmodern critique also results in the blurring of the opposition between the domain of the cognitive and the domain of the affective, where literature and art are generally classified as affective. As Stanley Rosen shows, Descartes represents the paradigm of the Enlightenment position in which the cognitive leads to the virtuous, and presupposes that the noncognitive is dangerous for the world order. This opposition can only hold true when there is a factual identity between theory and interpretation, when one trusts the self-evident truth of an interpretation. David Hume and Jean-Jacques Rousseau were the first to spread doubts and claim that theories are not only interpretations but also products of imagination (see Rosen 1987). Since imagination cannot strictly be called cognitive but is part of the process through which theories arise, the opposition between the cognitive and the noncognitive lost some of its redeemable value and became an irrelevant opposition. This disappearance of clear criteria and firm belief in what the cognitive order is also introduced a form of nihilism into the very heart of any intellectual process. As Rosen notices, the world has become an interpretation (220).

If the cognitive also belongs to the order of narratives, literature finds anew some privileges among the specialists of knowledge. As a correlate, fiction is no longer opposed to reality as a diabolic seducer menacing the omniscience of the learned person. Fiction is an inherent part of narrative and contributes to building knowledge. In this context, we remember that literature has the power to be a source of insight and illumination. There is also the ethical aspect: literature provides nonrationalized models that readers can use for representing themselves, understanding their needs, or evaluating their actions. The form of narrative as the organization of phrases can be a witness. Since its inception, literature has testified to the tensions and incompatibilities between different types of discourse, what is usually called conflict. Whether it is in tragedies, dramas, or novels, we can find many "differends" that have received total, partial, or no resolution at all. A differend, in Lyotard's terms, is "the unstable state and instant of language wherein something which must be able to be put into phrases cannot yet be" (1988, 13). In the differend, "Something 'asks' to be put into phrases, and suffers from the wrong of not being able to be put into phrases right away. This is when the human beings who thought they could use language as an instrument of communication learn through the feeling of pain which accompanies silence . . . that they are summoned by language, not to augment to their profit the quantity of information communicable through existing idioms, but to recognize that what remains to be phrased exceeds what they can presently phrase, and that they must be allowed to institute idioms which do not yet exist" (13).

Literature has the capacity to allow conflicts and incompatibilities to find their articulation, because it is a peculiar and exceptional mode of linking phrases. In this sense, literature is a resource. In a moment of instability in language, when a phrase tries to formulate itself and does not succeed in connecting with previous phrases because the connection is not apparent, literature has always been the laboratory where such new phrases are tried out and where themes are played out through characters made of paper. Through the treatment literature offers of such problems or situations, it can provide ways of linking or manufacturing new usages that do not fall under the control of one discourse. In other words, not only does literature "bear witness to the different conflicts between discourses, but it can also lend a voice. Literature allows us to escape established discourses through unheard of terms, through fantasies. In this sense, literature opens a new idiom" (Lyotard 1988, 13).

Narratives at the Heart of Reality

Pursuing his research apparently independently of Lyotard, Ricoeur has become one of the main theorists of narratives, providing us with the clearest and most detailed discussion of their power. He started out by applying narratives to the question of time (Ricoeur 1984), then extended his views to action (1986) and to self-identity (1990). The focus here is those aspects of Ricoeur's thought regarding narratives that are relevant to literature, especially their link with action.

Narrative belongs to a kind of a mediation. It is a string of sentences borrowing from different discourses that builds a recognizable plot where listeners can recognize who did what, when, how, with or against whom. Applying the notion of narrative to action, Ricoeur reformulates the notion of intention or intentional act. Intentional names the fact that any act of consciousness is directed toward an object. Narratives stop the directedness, so to speak; they slow down the movement of the mind toward the world. The challenge for Ricoeur is to deal with the pervasiveness of narratives: they invade everything. The object to be known is already caught in a web of narratives that have colored it, tainted it, provided it with its cultural attributes and social connotations. And worse: the subject attempting to know what is going on is also the result of a process of socializing, acculturation, finding his own voice in layers of sedimentation constituting a tradition. Ricoeur's challenge is to show that both object and subject arise out of narratives without any ontological loss: neither the object nor the subject loses its ontological status by being mediated through narratives.

Coming from what he himself calls the school of phenomenology, Ricoeur takes issue with a certain trend in Husserl that considers intentional acts to arise from a subject taken methodologically in isolation from other subjects. Ricoeur directly addresses the question of the genesis of such a subject by emphasizing the role narratives play both in action and in our understanding of ourselves. Any intentional act is interpretive in character. Against Husserl's view, when it happens that things are as I take them to be, for example in perception, the so-called fulfillment does not take place in my own mind, where there is an encounter between an empty intention and the givenness of something. To be fulfilled, Ricoeur suggests, an intention must have the potential to be articulated in signs and made understandable, and that means that the fulfillment of an intention is anticipated at the moment the intention is entertained: when entertaining an intention, I implicitly anticipate the concrete and relevant manners I can act upon such an intention. Intentional acts are thus no longer to be understood as purely mental acts but are already preformed by the way they can be fulfilled in a pragmatic framework. An intentional act includes an anticipation of its pragmatic fulfillment. Similarly, to act means to act upon intentions, so that action is the embodiment of intentional acts. In such an interplay between intention and action, a narrative has pervaded and articulated action. Action has become a quasi text, just as a text—as a conglomerate of intentional acts—is already pervaded by the potential for action.

The mediating role of narratives represents a response to the two alternatives that Gadamer proposes in *Truth and Method* (1998): a methodic analysis that leads to objectivity by putting the object at a distance, as natural sciences do, and an interpretation that acknowledges the involvement of the subject in the object of investigation, as human sciences do. Method is characterized as an alienating distanciation and interpretation as belonging, which leads to truth. Ricoeur has argued at length in his long debate with Gadamer against such an alternative. "My own method," Ricoeur writes, "comes from a refusal of these two alternatives and from an attempt to overcome them" (1986, 101). The problem of the text offers Ricoeur the possibility of escaping from these two alternatives or of even reconciling them. It offers an encompassing view that does justice to the ontological concreteness of our belonging to a life world and to the objective method of a science. Despite the distanciation it requires through signs, a text permits one to think of human experience as a communication between humans, i.e., as a historical belonging through and within this distanciation.

Language is an anonymous system of combinations of signs. Only in a discourse, when signs are brought together in a sentence uttered by someone, can something happen. Language, then, becomes discourse. As such, this linguistic event takes place in time and discourse becomes a work under someone's responsibility. The work might well be a projection by a cogito. However, unlike Athena, it does not arise fully shaped from the head of the utterer. It is only through discursive work that a cogito can come back to itself, in what Ricoeur calls a narrative identity. For narrative identity to take place, speech needs to be sedimented into writing. The cogito loses itself in the production and deciphering of signs. It loses itself and dies—disseminated in the world—in order to construe itself and understand itself in terms of a journey of a life of reading, writing, and interpreting. "There is no self-understanding which is not *mediated* through signs, symbols, and texts" (Ricoeur 1986, 29). Only through this semiotic mediation can the cogito, construing itself, come back to itself and rediscover itself such as it was "always already." Ricoeur writes, "The question of self-understanding which, in romantic hermeneutics, occupied the fore-stage, is now postponed until the end, as final factor, and not as introductory factor, and even less as center of gravity" (103).

The cogito belongs to the same category as the author of a work: as a craftsman—the *auctor*—it is responsible for the work. The author, however, is a category originating from the interpretation of the work. The author is what the interpretation discovers as its source. Only from the interpretation of the work can meaning arise; and only in interpretation can this meaning be referred to and attributed to its author. There is thus correlation and precedence between author and work or between cogito and thought: like the author, and as an author, the cogito is "a human being individualized by producing individual works" (Ricoeur 1986, 110). There is thus no mutual exclusion between truth and method, as Gadamer claims. Distanciation, which is on the side of the method, is, Ricoeur claims, the detour that alone permits one's coming back to oneself and understanding of oneself. Works allow authors to understand themselves because, before the arising of works, there was no author.

If authors have to construe their own self-understanding through and in their works, and only there, then the notion of the author's intention becomes ambiguous. If what is meant by intention is an articulation that preceded the work, such an understanding only focuses on the genesis of a work, reduces the work to the processes of its production, and overlooks the proper self-understanding of the author that articulated itself in the work. Once they have been written, works have freed themselves from the constraints of a living dialogue and their authors can thus survive or escape their own present. Authors' authority then does not pertain to their intentions but is itself contextual. Against romantic hermeneutics, and against Dilthey, Ricoeur firmly states that distanciation "is not only what understanding can overcome, but also what conditions understanding" (1986, 112). As a result, a work can only become what it is in contextualizing itself—in being written in a network of texts constituting a culture—and the work, conversely, can be decontextualized as well as recontextualized. Gregory the Great, for instance, anticipated some aspects of such a view.

A narrative has thus a function that exceeds the traditional *oratio*, which is just supposed to convey a preexisting *ratio*. Narratives give shape and form to that which would be unformed, handicapped, and impoverished without them. "What would we know of love and hatred, of ethical feelings and, in general, of all that we call the Self, if all this had not been brought to language and articulated by literature?" (Ricoeur 1986, 116). Narratives configure and mediate in a threefold schema that Ricoeur calls mimesis.

Borrowing the general qualification of poetry as mimesis from Aristotle, which means representation as imitation, Ricoeur builds a three-stage model leading from action to text and back to action. The first level of this schema, called mimesis 1, is the level of a prefiguration. There is a narrative quality of the world, which makes it susceptible to be told within its own articulation. "Life is more than experience. There is something in experience that demands the assistance of narrative and expresses the need for it" (Ricoeur 1991, 28). There is a nascent narrative in life. At this first level, Ricoeur mentions three points at which narrative is anchored in life.

1. The first point of anchor is manifested by the very structure of action itself. Human action is indeed structured around projects, plans, goals, means, and circumstances that we implicitly understand and that constitute a conceptual network with which we are natively familiar. Experience

is already structured semiotically, so that the framework of action is already predelineated within experience. To this extent, there is a semiotic dimension that pervades practical life. It is what Ricoeur calls a semiotic of action.

2. Human action itself, inscribed in a structured experience, in turn finds its articulation in signs, rules, and norms that determine or qualify capacities, modes, and means for action. This symbolic mediation "makes action a quasi-text for which symbols provide the rules of signification in terms of which a given conduct can be interpreted" (Ricoeur 1991, 29).

3. The third point of anchor of narrative in life is called "the pre-narrative quality of human experience" (Ricoeur 1991, 29). Action takes place in an experience that is already structured and involves plans and goals that can be achieved (first point of anchorage); action itself has to follow some patterns, obey some rules, and submit to some norms, so that performing an action is analogous to writing a text (second point of anchorage). As a chain of actions, life is a story in its nascent state, an activity and a passion in search of a narrative. One can see how the level of mimesis 1 as a pre-semiotic moment is a reformulation of Heidegger's view of the world as a significability articulated by discourse or speech.

The second level, mimesis 2, is the properly narrative level of a configuration where the symbolic mediation of language and discourse permits a story to be told. Borrowing the notion of *muthos* from Aristotle, Ricoeur calls emplotment the act of linking together in a story the different components and the sequence of what took place. The plot provides an explicit structure to what was already prestructured. Since the story highlights symbolic structures already embodied in the practical life of action, the story does not merely render action or life as an imitation through a mirroring effect. The explicitly semiotic aspect of the story shows in a particular fashion the implicit semiotic potential of action and of the life world. The narrative is thus not imposed on a set of actions as their possible explanation but is claimed to match the very structure of actions.

Stories thus make us aware of the narrative articulation of our world and represent a reserve of narratives that can be applied to the life world and can be used to configure new types of actions. According to Ricoeur, the possibility of an iconic increase of the world, the possibility for the world to be enriched by some new alternatives, is opened by narratives. This is the level of mimesis 3: a refiguration, or the way narratives reshape practical life. The reader can be affected by narratives and act accordingly. As a symbolic discursive mediation, a text opens to action and configures action, so that we have a cycle between mimesis 1, 2, and 3. The means through which we think and live, by being brought explicitly in front of us through stories, lead us to reexamine our life, gain awareness, and modify our ways of being. Literature not only configures (mimesis 2), but can also refigure (mimesis 3).

This is the aspect I want to investigate: How can fictional narratives, such as literature, lock onto our way of life? By what mechanisms can a story that is not true have a direct effect on how I behave or act or see myself? As a first element of response, Ricoeur argues that what allows the passage from mimesis 2 to mimesis 3, in the case of fiction, is "a second degree reference" (1991, 85; Ricoeur also uses the expression second-order denotation, 1975, 279). In oral discourse, the reference is guaranteed by the ostensive function. Ultimately, a discourse can be made understandable by going back to a reality, a thing, or a state of affairs that is common to the speakers and thus can be shown. When it cannot be shown, it can at least be situated within a network of relationships understandable to the interlocutors through what they can remember, what they can check in official documents, and so forth. Ultimately, the parameters of reference of all discourses are the here and now of the speakers.

By contrast, in the case of fiction, the possibility of returning to a here and now that could be used for situating the object of reference is, by definition, foreclosed. It is a fiction, a poem, a play, or a novel. In fiction, Ricoeur claims that what is abolished is the first-degree reference. This abolition opens a new reference, at a second degree. If we read and enjoy fictions, we must be able to relate what is invented to what we live. Fictional narratives, such as literature, offer a rearticulation of the world, "the projection of a possible inhabitable world" (Ricoeur 1975, 119). "For what must be interpreted in a text is a *proposed world* that I could inhabit and wherein I could project one of my ownmost possibilities. That is what I call the world of the text, the world proper to *this* unique text" (1991, 86). Literature does not impinge on the world at the level of manipulable objects alone, but at a level that Husserl designated as *Lebenswelt* and Heidegger as being in the world (see Ricoeur 1986, 114).

The second element of response Ricoeur offers regarding the link between fictional narratives and life is the use we make of narratives when living our own life. The three levels of mimesis in their interrelationships show that "fiction is only completed in life and that life can be understood only through the stories that we tell about it," so that "an *examined* life, in the sense of the word as we have borrowed it from Socrates, is a life *recounted*" (Ricoeur 1991, 30–31). This last comment opens a new ethical dimension: a narrative "turns out to be the first laboratory of moral judgment" (1990, 167). Literature just increases the number of narratives available among which we can choose those that fit the situation to be understood. "Our life . . . appears to us as a field of constructive activity, borrowed from narrative understanding, by which we attempt to discover, and not simply to impose from outside, the narrative identity which constitutes us" (1991, 32). Mario Valdés has applied and reformulated Ricoeur's views in what he calls the "literary truth-claim" (1992).

Ricoeur contends that narratives are not just stories told after the fact. Our life has a prenarrative quality, whether it is in our actions and behaviors or in our self-identity. Without that presemiotic character, it would indeed be difficult to understand how stories can speak to us, affect us, or cause us to change. However, the flip side of the presemiotic character of life is the danger of derealizing reality by overemphasizing the discursive or narrative articulation at the heart of the raw reality. Can Ricoeur prevent the presemiotic character of life from leading to a textual idealism, so that everything becomes a text, even if it is only a virtual text? Ricoeur believes that the circulation between the three levels of mimesis is the answer to the objection. The circulation has a direction; it is a spiral ascension, so that the real is enriched by narratives and the semiosis permits the attainment of a higher altitude. Gregory presents a similar figure of interpretation as a wheel moving forward and upward. Gregory speaks of texts, however, not of the real.

This question of a semiotic derealization of reality is actually an ontological question, which has two components: (1) Do we have any guarantee that the circulation of the levels of mimesis will gain a higher altitude, so that life in its raw reality cannot become worse after the semiotic operation? This question bears on what I call Ricoeur's narrative optimism. (2) Is there any mechanism that would allow an evaluation of narratives, so that a distinction could be made between those narratives that are honest in the ascending spiral and those that are strategic, trying to orient a course of action toward a predetermined goal? I turn to Günter Grass's novel *Dog Years* in order to answer these questions.

A Novel of Disfiguration

Günter Grass's *Dog Years* (1965, originally published in 1963) is the last volume of the *Danzig Trilogy* and was preceded by *The Tin Drum* (1962, originally published in 1959) and *Cat and Mouse* (1963, originally published in 1961). In *Dog Years* Grass expends gigantic efforts to describe, through the life of people of the working and middle classes, the rise and establishment of Nazism in Germany, its fall, and the reconstruction. Often in a cruel light, he indirectly lets us see how normal and average people allowed and contributed to the rise of Nazism. He also ironically and sarcastically depicts old Nazi sympathizers after the war as they borrow democratic clothes, purchase the outlook of decent citizens, rebuild Germany, and eagerly embrace a capitalism of consumption. Grass was awarded the Nobel Prize for literature in 1999.

The novel *Dog Years* nicely illustrates the power narratives have to configure a certain part of reality and to create an iconic augmentation, in the sense of revealing the complexity of the interactions between the Nazi regime and the life of average citizens. The novel offers an iconic increase in at least two ways: (1) It offers a particular view, and thus a configuration of that dark and painful part of German history, the Nazi era. (2) The fiction puts on trial, through fictitious characters, a real person: Martin Heidegger, who appears as a character in the novel.

These are also two manifestations of the irruption of reality into fiction. Grass's fiction has thus a particular status as configuration: it is a political critique of Germany, of its people and its intellectuals, especially Heidegger. The iconic increase Ricoeur speaks of takes a particular form, to the extent that it brings back the past in its unbearable atrocity, it makes the configuration a disfiguration, and the iconic augmentation takes the form of a virulent critique.

A Configuration of the Past as a Disfiguration

The writing style of the novel is at times tortuous, exaggerated, or even parodic. The narrative structure is highly complex and difficult to analyze. Grass holds this novel to be the best of the *Danzig Trilogy*. "I consider *Dog Years* to be more complex and also more daring with regard to the narrative process" (Grass 1991, 27). The novel presents itself as a narration through proxy. It is an order placed by a certain Brauxel, who owns a mine, so that writing is mining. Thirty-three shifts work under his command and produce this novel, going down every morning into the mine. This is the first part of the novel, "Morning Shifts." Brauxel assigns the narration of the second part, "Love Letters," to a certain Harry Liebenau, who, after an exam, is hired to write to his cousin, Tulla. The third and last part, "Materniads," is written by Walter Matern. These three sections of narration correspond to three distinct temporal slices, respectively: the rise of Nazism, the establishment of the Nazi regime and its fall, and the reconstruction. As always in Grass's novels, the tone is lighthearted or cruel but not reflective. Through the daily and banal facts and acts of the characters, the three temporal slices unveil themselves, often unbearably.

The novel describes a real descent into hell in a caricatural parody of Dante's *Inferno*, to which there are several explicit references. Three themes articulate this hell: the mine, the dog, and the scarecrow. The mine first represents writing itself. It is where the shifts of narrators, hired by Brauxel, go down to produce the narrative. The mine also represents the hell into which Germany descends, a hell from which, after Nazism, people emerge having to face their past and confronting those who contributed to the making of such a hell. "What is extracted from mines: coal, iron, potash, scarecrows, the past" (Grass 1965, 81). To extract the past means to try relentlessly to unmask what happened, to tell what happened, and to find words so that it becomes speakable. It means to accept facing hellish forces: "This is hell, indeed!" (543) Matern says down in the mine at the end of the novel. The hell that the mine was has been converted, in the reconstruction after the war, into the production of articulated scarecrows that have been made in the image of people living on the surface, such as Heidegger. When Matern sees what scarecrows represent, such as a board of directors meeting on the stock market floor, he says: "This is hell. Hell Limited Inc." (555; translation modified). The goal of writing is to mine the past and to make that past intelligible for what it was, to force readers to acknowledge, as Matern, the former SA (*Sturmabteilung*, storm trooper) member does, that it was indeed hell.

Just as in Dante's *Divine Comedy*, the number three is central: the novel includes three parts and three narrators. The first part is drafted by thirty-three morning shifts, which provide structure to this part. Since three works as a symbol, one cannot help but hear a historical fate in the Third Reich and the year 1933, which saw Hitler reach power. The symbol reflects the circumstances that provided the novel with its material. Nineteen thirty-three was also the year Heidegger gave his rectorate's speech, symbolizing the alliance of most intellectuals with the Nazi machine: "They get out in Freiburg in Breisgau and drop in at the university. The environment is still ringing with the turgid speech he delivered in '33—'Our own selves: that is our goal!'" (Grass 1965, 392). In his address, Heidegger explicitly asks students to support Hitler and help Germany assert itself.

Hell—the mine where the narrative of hell is threaded, the place in the fiction where scarecrows are built—finds a continuation in the importance of the dogs in the novel. "Every dog comes from below and has to be lowered again in the end" (Grass 1965, 537). Many of the episodes of the novel are narrated according to a genealogy of dogs. "In the obscure beginnings there is said to have been, there was, in Lithuania a she-wolf, whose grandson, the black dog Perkun, sired the bitch Senta; and Pluto covered Senta; and Senta whelped six puppies, among them the male Harras; and Harras sired Prinz; and Prinz will make history . . . " (57). Prinz will be offered to Hitler, and in the novel his escape will be the impetus for the last action of the Third Reich, which seeks to find him in Operation Führer's Dog. It is the same Prinz who, after his escape, will accompany Matern when Matern engages in a quest for revenge against those who led him to become what he was during Nazism. Heidegger counts among those who contributed to Matern's Nazism, and Heidegger must pay. At that moment, Prinz becomes Pluto. Pluto was actually one of Prinz's ancestors, the one who sired Senta, but now Prinz becomes the Pluto of infernal origin, like Cerberus of Hades. "And Harras hearkened to the name of Pluto as if he had always been a hound of hell" (162). The link between the dog and the powers of the underworld becomes clearer: "Never has a dog, unwilling to leave his self-chosen master, had an opportunity to learn so much about the dog's function in mythology: is there any underworld he doesn't have to guard; any river of the dead whose waters some dog doesn't lap up? Lethe, Lethe, how do we get rid of memories? No hell but has its hellhound!" (362).

The lineage of the dogs emphasizes the infernal structure of the events and represents a monstrous theogony: "In the beginning there was a Lithuanian she-wolf. She was crossed with a male shepherd. The outcome of this unnatural act was a male whose name does not figure in any pedigree" (Grass 1965, 502). This mythical act, where the pure German blood—of a German shepherd—is mixed with the savagery of the wolf, without any record of it, gives rise to a "cynogony," where dogs represent the irruption of the world from below into the world of the surface. As a parody of the racial pedigree so dear to the defenders of a pure race, this cynogony encompasses the history of Germany. The dog is very much in the blood of Germans. When Prinz is given to Hitler as a gift, it is the continuation of a long tradition, and Hitler will bequeath the dog to the German people. This cynogony gives legitimacy to the cynicism of the novel in depicting those "dog years" of the German people, which are in line with history.

When writing endeavors to render hell as a mine and a dog as the link between the underground and the surface, a straight story becomes impossible to tell. Only a caricature can express what the narrators endure: descending into the mine, facing hell, and threading it into a plot. It should be no surprise if some characters take the form of stuffed people used as scarecrows, because the story is as much an articulation of what happened as it is a disarticulation of an entire world.

The scarecrow, we are told, was created in the image of humans. "Of course," Brauxel-Eddi Amsel explains later to Matern, "you may say that every man is a potential scarecrow; for after all, and this should never be forgotten, the scarecrow was created in man's image" (Grass 1965, 533–34). To configure, which is a function of narrative, also means to disfigure. And Grass opts for literality when Germany finds itself put to the question: "All nations are arsenals of scarecrows. But among them all it is the Germans, first and foremost, even more so than the Jews, who have it in them to give the world the archetypal scarecrow someday" (534).

Even as a child Amsel, who is half Jewish, had a knack for building efficient scarecrows: "His creatures, though built for no purpose and with no enemy in view, had the power to instill panic in birds" (Grass 1965, 30). Of his scarecrows, it is said, "They seemed to be alive, and if you look at them long enough, even in process of construction or when they were being torn down and nothing remained but the torso, they were alive in every way" (31). Amsel's goal was merely the pleasure of building: "Nevertheless Eddi Amsel built no scarecrows to ward off the sparrows and magpies with which he was familiar; he built with no adversary in mind, on formal grounds. At the most he wished to convince a dangerously productive environment of his own productivity" (182).

Because he needs uniforms for his creations, Amsel, who cannot belong to any organization since he is half Jewish, asks his old friend Matern to become a member of the SA. Amsel will then have a way, through his friend, to get his hands on SA uniforms. The tactic works, and Amsel has almost finished his work: a group of mechanically articulated SA soldiers with the uniforms Matern provided. And with, in place of their faces, pig bladders. These mechanically articulated soldiers can walk and salute. Amsel is rehearsing a mechanical SA march when a group of real SA confronts him and beats him up, breaking all his teeth. As he hears one of his attackers grind his teeth, which is Matern's habit, Amsel, his old friend, asks him: "'Is it you? Si ti uoy?' But the grinding fist doesn't speak, it only punches" (Grass 1965, 213). Amsel, like his friend Jenny, the little girl who is of gypsy origin, becomes a snowman and waits there for a thaw, like so many people who are not rounded up. When the thaw takes place—when the war is over—Amsel is searching in the snow: "What was he doing when he stopped poking and bent straight-kneed from the hips? Was the young man with his very long fingers looking for something in the snow? Beech-nuts? A key? A five-gulden piece? Was he looking for goods of another, intangible kind? The past in the snow? Happiness in the snow? Was he looking in the snow for the meaning of existence, hell's victory, death's sting? Was he looking for God in Eddi Amsel's thawing garden?" (218).

All these questions are questions that real people asked after the horror was over. Searching their past, wondering "how could that happen?" And in the past, or in Grass's formulation, in the snow, the object of the question is the meaning of existence (how can human beings do that?), hell's victory (is there not anything intrinsically good in human beings?), and death's sting (these millions of exterminated human lives). These questions indirectly point to an all-good and powerful creator: where was God and what was he doing? ("Was he looking for God in Eddi Amsel's thawing garden?")

Although it is Amsel who encourages Matern to enter the SA movement, he means it as a joke: he just wants to have SA uniforms. The SA takes over his old friend and turns him into an anti-Semitic fanatic who does not hesitate to beat his childhood friend, his blood brother. One episode of their childhood foretells what could happen to their friendship. Amsel offers a pocketknife to Matern and they use it for becoming blood brothers. One day Amsel watches his friend looking for a stone to throw in the Vistula, which is one of his habits, but Matern does not find any. The urge to throw something becomes irrepressible, and Matern, feeling the knife in his pocket, throws it in the Vistula, throwing away a gift, the instrument of their blood brotherhood, as he will later throw away his friendship with a half Jew. At the end of the novel, Amsel, who has become Brauxel and owns a mine, offers Matern another pocketknife, which is actually the same one that he offered Matern when they were children. He explains to Matern that he drained that part of the Vistula to recover the knife. Matern listens to his former friend, who, in passing remarks, puts him on trial for his own, German, past. "No, my dear Walter, you may still feel bitterness toward your great fatherland—but I love the Germans. Ah, how mysterious they are, how full of the forgetfulness which is pleasing to God!" (Grass 1965, 533).

This qualification of forgetfulness also applies to Matern, who deals with his past by accusing others, Heidegger among them. And he accuses Heidegger for speaking of forgetfulness of being at a time when real human beings were murdered. When Amsel-Brauxel goes on to say that the Germans have the potential to give the world the archetypal scarecrow some day, Matern starts to grind his teeth, a sign of irritation. His odd habit of throwing stones when he was a child reappears, and "Matern throws—well, what do you think?—the newly recovered pocketknife far away" (Grass 1965, 534). Immediately, Amsel-Brauxel ironically consoles him: "Don't worry, my dear Walter. For me it's a mere trifle. That section of the canal will be drained. There isn't much current at this point. You'll have your good old pocketknife back in two weeks at the most.—It made us into blood brothers, you know" (534). Matern, who has seemed reluctant to recognize that Brauxel is his old friend Amsel, the same Amsel he beat up when he was a member of the SA, is now confronted by his old demons. "O impotence brooding eggs from which rage will hatch: naked and without fuzz. Matern releases a word. O human rage, always looking for words and finding one in the end. Matern flings a single word, which aims and strikes home. . . . Several times in succession the word . . . Leitmotive slips into murder motive. Matern takes aim and says: 'SHEENY!'" (534).

Eventually, Matern acknowledges his old friend and, worse, his own deeds by focusing on his resentment toward Jews. Sheeny is the translation of *itzig*, a slang name for Jew.

Next, Amsel-Brauxel forces Matern to visit the mine that he, Brauxel, owns, where scarecrows are produced on an industrial scale in the image of real people living on the surface. This episode takes place during the reconstruction of Germany after the war. Brauxel reproduces the past, so to speak, in the sense that he wants to preserve the former selves of these new capitalist Germans who have reinvented themselves. The copies he produces of the new people are scarecrows, and among them we find Heidegger.

Heidegger as a Character

From the book's vast fresco, which covers several painful decades of German history, only the references to Heidegger are analyzed here, references that may appear minor in the novel taken as a whole. Such use of a historical person in a novel turns the traditional perspective upside down. Fiction is usually understood as imitating historical data in order to produce a plausible story. Sometimes it even exploits the historicity of a person so as to increase its plausibility through the credence of real persons. In this novel, however, Heidegger is not an object of reference whose historicity would provide some credibility to the story that is told. It is rather the contrary: a story told that indirectly offers a devastating attack on Heidegger the person. What the story suggests, through the actions of its characters, is that Heidegger, by his example, through the kind of ideas he proposed and by the kind of jargon he crafted, has been a key factor in the unfolding of the Nazi history. In the story told, Heidegger is plunged into the plot through the use other characters make of his name, his thought, or his philosophical language. The novel undermines the credibility of the person Heidegger through a rather implausible plot.

This standpoint taken by the narrative of not using the real attributes of a real person for narrative purposes but of caricaturing this real person in what presents itself as a fiction, illustrates best the subversion of which the second-degree reference is capable. The novel *Dog Years* appears then as a configuration, at the level of Ricoeur's mimesis 2, of the impact an intellectual such as Heidegger can have, even if that person is not directly aware of how he can be understood. The sarcastic tone of the novel, the outrageous accusations made by Matern against Heidegger, and the use of Heidegger's vocabulary for speaking of concentration camps also show the ambition of the novel to be a refiguration, at the level of mimesis 3, of what political life should be. Ricoeur's theory offers us a means to articulate the extent to which a novel can provide narratives that catch the reality of a person in their web so as to cause that reality to unravel in the plot provided.

To hold Heidegger captive to a fiction requires the novel to accept an ironic challenge and to engage in a parody. It is ironic to retrace the thread of the life of someone such as Heidegger, who has always presented himself as a professional thinker, entirely devoted to the task of thinking being. Regarding the problem of being, "one should not tell stories about it," Heidegger reminds us at the opening of *Being and Time*, quoting the Foreigner in Plato's *Sophist* (Heidegger 1984, 6). Similarly, Heidegger constantly maintains that the life of a philosopher is irrelevant. It is precisely, Heidegger says in "The Origin of the Work of Art," when nothing is known of its author that a work speaks best (1950, 53). As a professional thinker, Heidegger, it seems, is no material for a novel, neither for what he thought nor who he is. And yet!

Mercilessly, the narrative recalls the scheme with which this professional thinker associated himself, a professional thinker who, in his own words, only concerned himself with the question of being. Heidegger's concern for being developed and was elaborated in the twenties, leading to the publication of *Being and Time* in 1927. In 1933, Heidegger accepted the rectorship of the University of Freiburg-in-Breisgau—and became a member of the Nazi party—a tenure that lasted ten months until he resigned from this position. As rector he made his famous rectorate's speech, in which, among other things, he encouraged students to follow the führer. Even if he dissociates himself progressively from the Nazi leaders, he still speaks in 1935, in his *Introduction to Metaphysics* (1959b), of the "greatness of the movement."

One can say that Grass's novel puts Heidegger on trial and, by virtue of a fiction, demonstrates Heidegger's responsibility at three levels. First, Heidegger is guilty of associating his name with Nazism, with what Nazism did, and with its leaders. Second, Heidegger is guilty of crafting a philosophical discourse or a philosophical logic that became blind to what was really taking place or that legitimated, in the name of history or of the unfolding of being, what Nazism was doing. Third, Heidegger is guilty as a person and has to account for what he did toward others, without the luxury of seeking refuge behind the mask of the thinker.

The references and allusions to Heidegger are established according to three mechanisms that happen to correspond to the three counts of accusation in the book. These mechanisms can be formulated as association, discourse, and character. In each of these, which follow from one another, there are duality and progression. In association, the name of Heidegger is inserted into the plot as a marker or impression of reality, before becoming a target: the name Heidegger is associated with Hitler and the Holocaust. In discourse some characters borrow the Heideggerean jargon. Sometimes this jargon is used when speaking of trivia, but it also serves some characters for thinking, or rationalizing or trivializing horror. Lastly, Heidegger is the object of a search by Matern, a former Heideggerean disciple blinded by ontological language who wants to take his revenge against Heidegger. At the end, Heidegger becomes a scarecrow of which Brauxel has manufactured one hundred copies. These different mechanisms of the narrative, in their progression, catch Heidegger in the plot, and the plot, increasingly darker, becomes the trial of the philosopher in absentia. The second-degree reference—Heidegger inside the novel—comes to haunt the first-degree reference—the real philosopher.

Association

Matern is a fervent disciple of Heidegger. His half-Jewish friend Amsel offers him a copy of the first edition of *Being and Time* "dedicated to little Husserl" (Grass 1965, 392). Amsel offers him the book, but without taking it seriously. "Eddi passed him on to me as a joke. Words that read like soft butter. He was good for headache and warded off thought when Eddi ratiocinated about sparrows. . . . I read him aloud to Langfuhr SA Sturm 84. They were doubled up at the bar, I had them whinnying out of *Being and Time*" (392). But just as Matern took his SA mission, to which Amsel introduces him, seriously, he takes Amsel's gift seriously. "I took him [Heidegger] with me in my musette bag from Warsaw to Dunkirk, from Salonika to Odessa, from the Mius front to Kaiserhafen battery, from police headquarters to Kurland, and from there—those are long distances—to the Ardennes; with him I deserted all the way to southern England, I dragged him to camp Munster, Eddi bought him secondhand in Tagnetergasse: a copy of the first edition, published in 1927, dedicated to little Husserl" (392).

Matern will cling to this book, even after being expelled from the SA (Grass 1965, 361). He has become a master in Heideggerese and can explain to Liebenau, the narrator of the second part, "Heidegger's calendar mottoes" (469).

Heidegger is also used as a temporal marker for situating some events. For example, Tulla, the character who serves as a transition between the first and the second part, was born in 1927: "When Tulla was born, the book *Being and Time* had not yet appeared, but had been written and announced" (Grass 1965, 113). The association of the name Heidegger with events of the novel loses its triviality and innocence and becomes overdetermined by the other associations present in the novel: Tulla's birth also corresponds to the call to workers for unification by the National Socialist Party. Tulla—whose story is the material of the second part, as told by her cousin Liebenau—is also intimately linked to the genealogy of the dogs, which also serve as markers for the whole story and the events narrated. "When Tulla was born, Harras, her uncle's watchdog, was one year and two months old" (113). Tulla will have privileged relationships with this dog, Harras, who will father Prinz, the dog offered to the führer and the very same dog who will later hunt down Heidegger with his new master, Matern.

After the war, Matern, as a former SA member, wants to take his revenge against those people he holds responsible for what happened to him. Before every punitive expedition he finds the name of his former accomplices and torturers in the urinals of the Cologne train station, near the cathedral. Of this cathedral and train station we read, "They go together like Scylla and Charybdis, throne and altar, Being and Time, master and dog" (Grass 1965, 369). The sequence of conjunctions suggests a connivance, even a complicity, between these symbolic entities. The railroad system served to deport Jews to concentration camps, and the proximity of the cathedral to the train station suggests that the church was an accomplice in the mass killing done in concentration camps. Not only can we understand a passive complicity of the church in that the church did not oppose Nazism, did not speak out against it, but sometimes encouraged people to rally behind it. Grass even suggests a murderous complicity: "Ultimate Führerintimations, recorded by General Burgdorf and in Führertestament: 'Dog Prinz will try to reach Vatican City. If Pacelli raises claims, protest immediately and invoke codicil to will'" (349). The führer indeed makes a will in the novel, according to which "Führer's favorite dog Prinz, black, short-haired shepherd, is Führer's gift to the German people" (349).

The dog represents the power of evil, the irruption of hell into the world. The genealogy of dogs, where a German shepherd interbred with a she-wolf, indicates that it has always been part of the German heritage to have dealings with hell. Hitler is the one who opened the gates of hell, establishing a realm of dogs. And, as he himself says, "Never will the dog be negated" (Grass 1965, 348). This is his gift to the German people. The acidic irony in the mention of Pacelli, who was Pope Pius XII and who has been accused of not doing enough against Nazism, is that Hitler sees his dog trying to reach the Vatican and suspects the pope of having some views on the realm of the dogs, on hell itself. Since Hitler believes that this is his achievement and what he wants to bequeath to the Germans, he wants to protect his own achievements from being taken over by the pope. Hitler sees Pius XII as a competitor for hell.

Regarding the role of the church, there is also mention of twelve headless knights and twelve headless nuns who drink and fornicate. The headless knights evoke the Teutonic Knights, a military and religious order serving the expansion of Christendom in the fourteenth century. Hitler revived the cult of the Teutonic Knights and saw those knights as the forerunners of the Nazis attempting to expand Germany. The fornication with nuns suggests a satanic rite, even a pact through which both the military and the religious leaders lose their heads, accept blood as a necessary price, and confuse hell with the future of Germany.

Such a murderous complicity between throne and altar is reinforced by the mention of Charybdis and Scylla, two monsters in Greek mythology guarding the strait of Messina, the former causing whirlpools that sink ships and the latter, a six-headed monster, devouring the men. As the saying goes, avoiding one of them might lead you to even worse. Avoiding Nazism or escaping Nazism, in other words, might lead you to fall into even more treacherous hands. The train station, the engine of the Nazi killing machine, goes with the cathedral, the complicity of the church, like two monsters. *Being and Time*, the title of Heidegger's main work, goes with them, in the same enterprise of silent passivity and active acquiescence. The last pair, dog and master, recall the story of the dog Prinz, which was offered to the führer. The proximity of this association with *Being and Time* also suggests the submission of Heidegger to the führer, like a dog following his master's voice: as Matern puts it plainly, "Get this straight, dog: he was born in Messkirch. . . . He and the Other had their umbilical cords cut in the same stockingcap year. He and the Other Guy invented each other. One day He and the Other will stand on the same pedestal" (Grass 1965, 392). Heidegger was born in Messkirch in 1889, the same year Hitler was born. "He and the other Guy invented each other" indicates that just as Hitler needed the support of intellectuals to reach power and fulfill his task, intellectuals such as Heidegger saw in Hitler the agent of a cultural and political renewal of which they would become the spiritual guides.

After the association of his name with the events told, the vocabulary of being is the second mechanism used by the narration to catch Heidegger in the net of the narrative.

The Discourse of Being

When Liebenau, the second narrator, becomes warrant officer of the Luftwaffe in an antiaircraft defense battery, the tech sergeant of the battery gnashes his teeth like Matern used to and thus appears as Matern's double. The tech sergeant is a disciple of Heidegger who "uttered quotations . . . from one and the same philosopher," Heidegger (Grass 1965, 297). His auxiliary, called Stortebeker, "repeated his quotations and created a philosophical schoolboy language that was soon prattled by many, with varying success" (297). For example,

- The auxiliary begins his sentences with "I, as a pre-Socratic" (297): a reminder of Heidegger's interest in the pre-Socratics.
- "But if Harry said: 'Being,' Stortebeker corrected him impatiently: 'There you go again. What you really mean is beings'" (297; translation modified): Heidegger asks the question of being anew and makes a distinction between anything that is, a being, and what makes it what it is, being. This is what Heidegger calls the ontological difference.
- "After all, the essence of being-there is its existence" (319): this is a fundamental view of *Being and Time*, which considers existence (*Dasein*) not only as an opening but also as what matters most to *Dasein*.

Heideggerean vocabulary is applied to the operation of capturing all the rats that have invaded the battery where Liebenau and his auxiliary work. During this operation, which is called deratification, the auxiliary speaks to himself "in his own tongue, which however had been infected with obscurity by the tech sergeant's language, rat propositions and onto-logical rat truths" (Grass 1965, 303). The auxiliary, for example, states, "The rat can endure without the ratty, but never can there be rattiness without the rat" (304). Retranslated in Heidegger's language, such a statement makes a parody of the ontological difference between being and beings: "Clearly being unfolds without beings, but never can beings be without being." Even more sarcastically, "The rat withdraws itself by unconcealing itself into the ratty. So the rat errates the ratty, illuminating it with errancy ... the rat errs and so fosters error. That is the essential area of all history" (303). All the terms used in the quote have Heideggerean undertones. Sub-stituting rat for being, Grass is indirectly suggesting that being, which was Heidegger's own concern and led him to try to overcome metaphysics, can be the realm of rats, an infestation of what is most abhorrent. Correlative-ly, beings, those that are made possible by being and among which we have to count human beings, can be ratty, manifestations of rats.

Heidegger made what exists (beings) subservient to a prior openness of being and thereby both derealized what exists (it only matters because of this first opening of being) and relativized what exists to its condition of possibility. Of such a view, Grass sarcastically asks, what if being is a rat, if it is hell? Is it still an opening? Can Hitler contribute to the unfolding of being? And in this hypothetical state (and for Grass all-too-real possibil-ity), Heidegger can only talk nonsensically at best and outrageously at worse: The "rat errates the ratty," which means that it is being that causes human beings to err. Human beings are not responsible and error is "the essential area of all history" (303).

It is also about rats that we read on the next page, "When they grew wise, as long as poems . . . When they announced the beginning of the world and made leaks in hell" (Grass 1965, 301). The mention of poetry is another allusion to Heidegger's growing interest, after *Being and Time*, in a poetical mode of speaking. The association of poem, wisdom, and rats sug-gests that the thinker, by abandoning his task of thinking to the poet, gave up any rational scrutiny of what happens, and allowed the world to be invaded by rats and to fall into hell. The fall into hell would only be anoth-er manifestation of the opening of being.

Besides replacing being with rat in some formulations that are almost perfectly Heideggerean, Grass sometimes replaces being (*Sein*) with dog in the term *Dasein*. *Dasein* means existence, but Heidegger uses the term to name the fact that human existence is the place where being manifests itself. *Dasein* is the being there (*Da-sein*) in the sense of the there of being. Grass speaks of *das Hunde-da*, the dog there: "Dog-being—the very fact of it—implies that an essent dog is thrown into his there. His being-in-the-world is the dog-there" (Grass 1965, 312). Being, or the vocabulary of being, which Heidegger questions as a professional thinker, is now presented as what gave its status to the dog: to pass through human undertakings and focus on what permeates them, such as being, or to make the real life of people a place for the manifestation of something else, such as being, can also be a way of opening the gates of hell. Being can take the form of a dog, and dogs, the realm from underneath, can take over human beings, the world of the surface. In Heidegger's framework, there is no evaluator of being as opening, by definition, and the question Grass suggests is a what if: what if the opening of being invites hell to take hold? "The question of the dog is a metaphysical question. . . . And never will the dog be negated" (348). As Hitler himself says, "The dog itself—as such— was-there, is-there, and will remain-there" (349).

The accusation leveled against Heideggerean discourse becomes unbearable when the auxiliary adopts such a discourse for making sense of a mound near their antiaircraft battery that emits a foul odor. In her blunt speech, with an animal sense for things, Tulla expresses what everybody thinks: "Bet you it's bones. And what's more, human bones. Everybody knows that" (Grass 1965, 306). Stortebeker, the auxiliary, "evades the proffered bet with a grandiose gesture of blessing that takes in the battery and the mound of bones: 'There lies the essence-ground of all history'" (307). But the tech sergeant, Matern, eventually accepts the bet: "I bet they're not" (307). When Tulla comes back with a skull, and says, "See? Do I win or not?" (308), the tech sergeant becomes irritated and slaps her on the face: "The tech sergeant stood rigid and rectangular with dangling carbine, self-conscious as on the stage. Behind him held geometrically still: placedness, instandingness, nihilation, the essence-ground of history, the difference between Being and beings—the ontological difference" (309; translation modified). The last six expressions are Heideggerean expressions, with which the tech sergeant is left for making sense of what he has to see now as an extermination camp close to his battery.

There is one last mention of Heideggerean discourse. When Prinz escapes, and Hitler, to recapture him, launches the last big operation of the Third Reich, the code used by the headquarters of the army is of Heideggerean tone: "Not until April 25 did General Wenck, Twelfth Army, reply from the Nauen-Ketzin sector: 'Nothing being after-accomplished on double and substantivized. The Nothing attuned to distantiality discloses dread in every sector of the front. Dread is there. We are speechless with dread. Out'" (Grass 1965, 346). Dread (*Angst*) is a key concept of *Being and Time*, and "we are speechless with dread" is an accurate quotation of Heidegger (*Die Ansgst verschlägt uns das Wort*; Heidegger, 1976, 112).

Being, the dog, and the führer: this summarizes the association of Heidegger with this descent into the hell of Germany, into these dog years where the dogs, literally and cynically, make history. The association is founded in the Heideggerean discourse borrowed by the Nazi soldiers and their leaders. As a result, Heidegger has become an accomplice at a third level: he is liable as a character within the novel.

The Character Heidegger

In the last part, "Materniads," former SA Matern intends to take his revenge against those who led him to become a part of the dog years. Heidegger is one of his targets. Since Matern seeks him, Heidegger can only fall into the plot. In the urinals of the Cologne train station, where Matern finds the instructions for his vengeful saga, he reads that "the Alemanic Stockingcap is capping between Todtnau and Freiburg" (Grass 1965, 392). The Alemanic stocking cap is a direct reference to Heidegger, who was very proud of his roots in southwestern, Swabian Germany, occasionally wearing the traditional outfit with the particular cap, which Matern calls the stocking cap. The text continues in German: *Das Seyn wird fortan mit 'y' geschrieben.* (Grass 1974, 486): "The word for *Seyn* (Being) will henceforth be written with a 'y.'" This sentence, which has been left out in the English translation (and which is also absent from the French translation), alludes to Heidegger's use of an old spelling for "being": *Sein* as *Seyn*, to show that the question Heidegger asks about being is older, or more primordial, than the level at which we can think or speak of beings.

Matern, the same tech sergeant, will be tried and court-martialed by the Nazis because, while drunk, he insulted the führer "in sentences marked by such locutions as: forgetful of being, mound of bones, structure of care, Stutthof, Todtnau, and concentration camp" (Grass 1965, 325). With these expressions Matern directly associates Heidegger with the concentration camps. Forgetful of being is what Heidegger considers to be our present situation, where we are caught in a metaphysics of presence and have forgotten that what exists has been made possible by an openness that preceded anything that is. *Being and Time* is the work that claims to ask anew the question of being. Part of the book was written in Heidegger's retreat at Todtnauberg. Structure of care serves to describe human existence: we are concerned with things around us and are living with other human beings with whom we share a world where we work. Matern now groups each Heideggerean formula with concentration camps: forgetful of being and mound of bones; structure of care and Stutthof, which is a concentration camp close to Matern's air force battery; Todtnau and concentration camp. This association suggests that an interest in being had caused in Heidegger and others a blindness or a distraction such that the current political and social situation was not seen for what it was. The retreat to Todtnauberg to write about being was a retreat from the public sphere and indirectly allowed the rise of concentration camps, in the sense that the intellectuals who should have been vigilant and courageous in speaking up abdicated their responsibility.

Matern also uses forgetful of being as a direct accusation against Heidegger of having been complicitous in the final solution: "In what cap have you hidden the lime-sprinkled forgetful of Being?" Matern asks in front of Heidegger's house in Freiburg (Grass 1965, 394). The lime-sprinkled are the people exterminated in concentration camps and buried in mass graves. Forgetful of being names our situation, in which we have forgotten the openness at the origin of the world as we know it. There is, Heidegger says, an oblivion of being for which we are responsible because being itself, somehow, has withdrawn and thus fallen into oblivion. Heidegger attempts to articulate this interaction between a being that we help manifest through reflection and action and a being that opens a framework within which we can be who we are. The rage of Matern, who was a believer in Heidegger, explodes when this metaphysical framework of thinking is confronted with the real atrocities of bodies destroyed on an industrial scale and buried in mass graves. Did these people die because we forgot being or is it being that forgot them? The question appears out of place at best and insulting at worst. By searching for Heidegger, the person, Matern wants to remind him of his responsibility, because Heidegger, under the guise of an oblivion that would permeate us, forgot even the most basic decency that a human being owes to other human beings.

Convincing Heidegger of his responsibility, however, is no easy task. Not only can Heidegger not be found, but what kind of argument would he accept? "How many of my teeth do I have to pull to turn throwness into a Being that is, stockingcapped?" (Grass 1965, 394; translation modified). We are, Heidegger says, thrown into the world and have to reconquer our own self. What is the price for being recognized as existing, as a manifestation of being, Matern asks. The question of how many teeth again evokes the concentration camps, where gold teeth were pulled from the victims. When is it, Matern asks, that a human being is a human that exists, in Heidegger's framework?

Heidegger did not play his role and worse, provided a vocabulary for speaking of the unspeakable. "You ontic dog! Alemannic dog! You dog with stocking cap and buckled shoes! What did you do to little Husserl? What did you do to tubby Amsel? You pre-Socratic Nazi dog!" (Grass 1965, 325). In Heidegger's framework, ontic is related to what really exists, whereas ontological characterizes the conditions of possibility for what exists. Heidegger was interested in ontological questions, not ontic questions. It is thus all the more sarcastic when Heidegger is qualified as an ontic dog, as a really existing cause of evil. Alemannic refers to the culture and dialect of southwest Germany, where Heidegger was born and lived. The reference to Husserl is also particularly hard on Heidegger. In 1933 Husserl, who had retired some years earlier, lost his pension and was forbidden access to the university library because he was Jewish—the very same university at which Heidegger accepted the rectorship (although Heidegger was not the one who made the decision to forbid Husserl access to the library). When *Being and Time* was reprinted, Heidegger deleted the dedication to Husserl. The expression "What did you do to little Husserl?" can be found several times in the novel. Grass accuses Heidegger of having strangled Husserl. Matern says, "How long was the stockingcap you strangled little Husserl with?" (394). By cultivating his regional roots, Heidegger, Grass suggests, invited an ideology of fanaticism for land or blood, which meant an exclusion of those, like Husserl, who do not belong because of their difference.

Matern is on a vengeful mission and shows up at Heidegger's home: "Matern is here, manifesting himself as the call of care. Open up!" (Grass 1965, 393). Matern's irony is to ask Heidegger to open the door to a person who, though motivated by the desire for an authentic existence, is before all else a person who wants to understand what happened to him. The irony or parody continues when it turns out that Heidegger cannot be found: "If he isn't erring below, he's enacting his Being up above; if he isn't coming-to-be up top, he's grounding on a slip of paper beside the iron gate: 'Down below Stockingcap manifests Nothing'" (394). Faced with this character, who refuses the rules of the game and remains invisible and thus unseizable, Matern can only assuage his anger by smashing the door of Heidegger's garden and doing what dogs do: he urinates in the mailbox, marking a dog's territory.

Heidegger is rebellious to fiction: he is a character who cannot be found, who is present only by his multiple absences, who shies away from any interaction with other characters. He does not lend himself to being a reference of second degree through the mediation of his character. Although he does not allow that a simile of himself offers, in a fictitious narrative, possibilities for a new configuration, he lends himself to caricature. The story of the novel recovers Heidegger as a scarecrow. Brauxel, the owner of the mine, reconverts his plant into manufacturing scarecrows, among which one can find one hundred replicas of Heidegger as an articulated scarecrow. "He, the pre-Socratic, he multiplied a hundredfold. He capped with a hundred caustic-degraded, once Alemannic stockingcaps, He in buckled shoes, in a linen smock: a hundred times He, coming and going. And thinks. And speaks. Has a thousand words for being, for time, for essence, for world and ground, for the with and the now, for the Nothing, and for the scarecrow as existential frame. . . . A hundred matching philosophers come and go on the salt floor, greeting each other essentially: 'the scarecrow exists self-grounded'" (Grass 1965, 551).

Heidegger finds himself stuffed by a fiction while his language becomes disarticulated. At that moment, he can appear in the terror he could cause. Brauxel concludes at the end, "Of course you may say that every man is a potential scarecrow; for after all, all this should never be forgotten, the scarecrow was created in man's image" (Grass 1965, 533–34).

The Blindness of Narratives

The power of a plot in which Heidegger is put on trial is, in Ricoeur's terms, to tell in the thread of a story what has been kept silent, what Heidegger himself refused to discuss. The narrative of this novel offers a configuration, at the level Ricoeur calls mimesis 2: the narrative provides an articulation of what was potentially told and articulated. In our case, the configuration is a disfiguration. It is a disfiguration because the narrative forces Heidegger and his work to face what was prenarrative in all the events referred to—in the rise of Nazism and the language of being that unfolded at the time hell took hold. The effect on the reader, at the level of mimesis 3, is a shock caused either by the new light shed on the life world of the thinker of being, or by the ferocity and unfairness of Grass' caricature.

Ricoeur's theory of narrative is thus helpful for showing how Grass's novel grafts onto a real political situation (the rise of Nazism and the tacit complicity of many Germans), how it configures such a situation by making some of its elements unbearably visible. In this sense the novel refigures the political situation by reminding people that the past has to be confronted. However, Grass underscores some elements that can be seen as a critique of Ricoeur. He criticizes two aspects of Heidegger's way of doing philosophy: (1) the production of a certain vocabulary that, according to Grass, blinded, deceived, or distracted people regarding the political situation and (2) the view that a paradigm or an epoch always precedes whatever articulation human beings are capable of, so that any articulation remains relative to the paradigm and the paradigm as an opening escapes discussion and cannot be questioned. These two elements also elude the scope of Ricoeur's theory of narratives. Narratives too can tend toward propaganda, and they too can serve the interest of a given worldview. Indirectly, Grass raises the question of the power narratives can have or the limitations to which they are submitted. This critique is thus, ironically, Heideggerean in nature.

The first Heideggerean question concerns language. For Ricoeur, language is simply a combination of signs, and to this extent it is anonymous. A narrative, in contrast, which is a discourse put in a text, belongs to the ontological order, to the extent that it articulates or configures what takes place. However, Heidegger has shown that language itself, before being embodied in narratives, already provides possibilities for articulation. The play of deconstruction and reconstruction that language allows has the advantage, prior to the establishment of a narrative, of offering a proposal about what can be put into phrases. Grass, in his use of language, sides with Heidegger on this issue. The virulent attacks of Grass against Heidegger essentially bear upon the Heideggerean vocabulary, as if Heidegger was guilty first of using a vocabulary that blinded people regarding what was really taking place and second of allowing them to somehow legitimate what was going on in the name of a hidden destiny.

The play that language allows does not, of course, play itself. Partners who have identified themselves through narratives are needed—Ricoeur is right on this point. A sociolinguistic environment is needed as well, where some stakes have been identified and recognized—Ricoeur again is correct.

However, the fact that the play is played does not seem to pertain to the narrative itself but rather to the possibilities of language. Because it is still free of any articulation, language offers the possibility of a subversion of the paradigm, a subversion that, for Heidegger, is the meaning of thinking. Narratives and language do not exert their effect at the same level. Narratives offer an articulation at a conscious level and are thus open to discussion. Once we question, as Heidegger as well as Grass does, the level of words and their political or cultural connotations, we question a level that is beyond narratives and not treatable or discussable directly at that narrative level. In the wake of Heidegger's deconstruction of metaphysics, deconstructionism, for example, has initiated a trend in reading, making readers aware of the cultural and rhetorical baggage involved in discourses (de Man 1983, for example, 102–41; Derrida 1967a, for example, 203–26).

In one of its forms feminism has attempted to highlight male prejudices inscribed in the way writers describe their female characters and urged a "reading as a woman," which is a revision of the canon and a resistance to dominant values: "There has been a strong emphasis in feminist literary criticism on the need to become resisting readers, to learn to read against the grain of emotive language and imagery and to construct oppositional narrative positions within the text from which to challenge its dominant values and gender assumptions" (Morris 1993, 29).

These efforts focus on a level where meaning is produced that is not narrative in nature and is not a direct object of discussion. This indicates that narratives configure not only by articulating (what Ricoeur calls emplotment) but also by imposing values, rhetorical effects, and connotations, and these values, rhetorical effects, and connotations do not obey the rules of narratives. They belong to a prediscursive level. Heidegger considers that this prediscursive level cannot be completely brought to a discursive and predicate level. Derrida famously speaks of differences in the system of signs that allow conceptual differences and even self-identity, so that concepts and self-identity are rather relative to a system of semiological differences: "The subject (identity with oneself or possibly consciousness of identity with oneself, self-consciousness) is inscribed in language, is 'a function' of language, only becomes speaking subject in conforming one's speech . . . to the system of prescriptions of language as a system of differences" (1972, 16). Pam Morris sees what she calls "the patriarchal logic at the centre of the meaning system" in this prediscursive level (1993, 159).

Grass indirectly identifies a second blind spot in Ricoeur's theory of narratives. Ricoeur sees the narrative as the space of human freedom in a horizontal dimension—narratives are the laboratories of history. In contrast, Heidegger thinks that any human work, narratives included, takes its relevance from within a paradigm, in a vertical dimension. It is what he calls the openness of being or the unconcealment of being, where human freedom has already received an orientation, where it is already contaminated, if not determined. Even if he completely changed his perspective about the status of language, Heidegger always confined the linguistic articulation within its revealing function over and against a givenness that is not a matter of articulation. He calls this givenness "being." In all his works he clings to the view that a principle or event opens whatever articulation becomes prevalent. As a consequence, such an articulation (a narrative, for example) is prevented from alone accounting for the being of what is threaded in the plot. A preposition in all its ambiguity always comes between articulation and being: the discourse of being or the language of being. This is a direct consequence of the ontological difference, that what is has conditions of possibility that cannot be brought back to the level of what is.

Although I do not accept Heidegger's "new ontology," I follow him in thinking that narratives carry with them values and interests that are not visible at the level of the narrative itself but are ordered to nonnarrative aims and goals. Thus, I am not ready to surrender to Ricoeur's narrative optimism. Ricoeur seems to suggest that the iconic increase provided by narratives is not relative to the narratives that provided it, so that a faith in narratives seems to ensue. The three levels of mimesis are caught in an ascending spiral, crossing each other but at an higher altitude, Ricoeur tells us. Grass accuses Heidegger of providing a type of philosophical narrative that yielded not iconic increase but a veil of symbols that prevented people from realizing what was going on in Nazism and legitimated what the Nazi were doing. Similarly, Grass wonders, asking a nice, if somewhat cruel, Heideggerean question, what if being, which is a narrative of a sort, is a rat or a dog? What kind of iconic increase, in Ricoeur's terms, would that be?

There are less dramatic examples available. The advertisement discourse, which has invaded even the sphere of academia in the realms of productivity and marketing, seems to obey goals and interests that do not belong to the order of narratives, as if an economic and technological paradigm selects those narratives that are acceptable and efficient. Even if the paradigm can become an object of reflection, as in a narrative, ultimately what will allow this narrative to become public and accessible is the set of criteria established by the paradigm. With Heidegger it is thus not narratives alone that configure, and it is not narratives themselves that offer an iconic increase. Against Heidegger, however, and siding with Grass on this point, I am wary of the mystical talk of a being that unfolds, toward which anything real is relative, or of an epoch that opens up and allows a world to set in. I do not believe, in other words, that what precedes narratives is already articulated, as if a hidden narrative had infiltrated the current narratives. Even if Heidegger adamantly maintains that being is not something, his talk of event, of unfolding of being or history of being, of being having abandoned us, clearly indicates that events occur where a new world opens, an event that is not the making of human beings.

If I refuse the talk of paradigms or paradigm shifts that occur independently of human beings, what sense does it make to claim, as I do, that something precedes narratives, that they do not have in themselves their own light? I minimally claim that narratives in themselves are blind. They configure, but such a configuration only has as norm what is conventionally accepted, so that any talk of iconic increase, iconic decrease, or iconic abolition is relative to whatever framework is in place. The question always remains: iconic increase for whom and from what perspective? Because narratives are blind, they are in need of evaluation. What allows an evaluation to take place is the claim to rightness that binds people to the good of the community. The iconic increase itself has to be qualified according to the good that is pursued.

Grass was clearly animated by a desire to encourage or even force his contemporaries to reflect on what Apel has called the German national catastrophe (1988, 370). Grass was one of the first writers to broach the topic of the role of the German people in Nazism. "Literature is in itself engaged; even when literature tends toward *l'art pour l'art*, it also tends against something and is in this sense also political" (1991, 19). From his novels it is obvious that he is animated by a claim to write what is right for the present political situation. It is an attempt to stimulate the German conscience, to prevent people from forgetting, to force them to face what they willingly or unwillingly let happen. And what Grass accuses Heidegger of breaking is precisely, even if implicitly, his responsibility: Heidegger broke the implicit contract that people have with their community, failing as a person. The motivation for the character Matern to hound Heidegger and ask him to account for what he did comes from the conviction of Matern that what Heidegger did "was not right." Heidegger forgot his commitment to his community and ignored his commitment to the well-being of his people. He may have been blinded by the events of the time, since not many intellectuals could see clearly what was happening. But he owed an explanation or an apology, which he always refused to offer. In the novel Matern never succeeds in having a face-to-face discussion with Heidegger about what happened. As a character and a person Heidegger is elusive, and this unwillingness to be part of the discussion is what seems to enrage Matern most. By not offering a word in response, Heidegger opts out of the discussion and refuses to redeem his claim to rightness.

Narratives can kill. The configuration of narratives and by narratives is blind and needs some other mechanism for guaranteeing that readers "read right." Ricoeur suggests that the circulation between the three levels of mimesis (a world presemiotically articulated in the potential of narratives; the configuration provided by explicit narratives, such as literature; and the actions of readers enriched by their readings) is enough to guarantee a safe navigation of narratives and the attainment of a higher and richer config-uration of life. By contrast, *Dog Years* is an illustration of how a narrative— for example, Heidegger's discourse of being—can lead to a disfiguration and sclerosis of, for example, political life. Of course, I gain this view from reading Grass's novel as a narrative. I certainly followed Ricoeur's cycle of the threefold mimesis. What is refigured by this novel, however, is the fragility of narratives. Either they can fall in the wrong hands—a Nazi such as Matern using *Being and Time* to justify concentration camps—or they are composed by blinded people and help configure worlds we should not inhabit.

If we apply these views on the limits of narratives to the question of what interpretation is and how it works, what clearly appears is that inter-pretation cannot content itself in construing what is represented by the text, at the expense of losing any possibility of assessing its validity. If Ricoeur claimed that interpreting a text is nothing more than construing narratives out of it—which he does not—*Dog Years* would have an easy objection: readers can construe whatever they want out of any text. But what *Dog Years* also shows is that writers bear responsibility for how their texts can be construed. Heidegger is responsible, in Grass's novel, not only for his own involvement with Nazism but also for how his type of philoso-phy, the discourse of being, could be understood. The narratives generated by a novel are thus an undeniable component of what a novel means—and our reading of Grass's novel clearly construes narratives out of it. Howev-er, because these narratives are blind, can be construed arbitrarily, or can be devastating, the writer remains a parameter of interpretation. Those narratives can be construed out of a novel that the writer allowed. The author's intention, as the first level of meaning, limits the construction of what the text represents. What mediates the narratives readers of necessity construe from a text and the author's intention is the second level of meaning: what the text says. Interpretation, if it claims validity, uses these three parameters of author's intention, text's meaning, and representative content.

The text of *Dog Years* is not always clear, allusions are sometimes obscure, the narration is not linear. I construe several narratives out of what the text says in order to figure out what the novel means in terms of what it represents: a critique of Germans and their intellectuals before, during, and after the war. I follow what Ricoeur says happens in the reading of novels. Of course, there are other possibilities. Since these possibilities originate from readers, it would make little sense to imagine all the possible readings of a novel. The construction of narratives out of a novel is arbitrary, if it is left to itself. What limits the arbitrarines of my construction of the narratives I present here is the justification I provide by using Grass's text (quotes, passages, or words); for example, the sentence that is missing in the French and English translations and that is a direct and unmistakable reference to Heidegger's use of the old written form *Seyn* for naming being (*Sein*). This meaning of the text only finds its stability if it is anchored in what the author, Grass, could have meant. If *Sein* were the name of a new treatment for breast cancer, we could imagine a directive of the German company saying, *Das Sein wird fortan mit "y" geschrieben* ("Sein" will henceforth be written with a "y") to avoid embarrassment in France, where *sein* means breast (to avoid the ridicule the Totes company suffered when it launched its German advertising campaign with the slogan *Totes Deutschland*, which means in German "Dead Germany"). What links this sentence to Heidegger in *Dog Years* is the fact that Grass is German, writes about contemporary Germany, mentions the name "Heidegger," quotes Heidegger, and knows Heidegger's philosophy. We thus need the three levels of meaning together in some form of interaction to have an interpretation that can claim validity.

6

The Representative Content
of a Novel as a Set of Intentional States
Sabato as a Critic of Searle

Readers construe the representative content of a novel by extracting narratives and applying them to their own situation. Readers also colonize the text with their own intentional states, continuing the text in a way that speaks to them. The literary text appears then as an invitation for readers to graft onto the text and make the text their own. This is a second way a literary text has a reference, besides the second-degree reference obtained through narratives. Narratives manifest a conception of truth as disclosure: narratives unveil some aspects of reality and provide meaningfulness to other aspects. Another truth involved in the act of writing exists when a writer invites readers to colonize her text with their intentional states. The Argentinian writer Ernesto Sabato explicitly states that the duty of a writer of fiction is to tell the truth (1991, 241). Obviously, Sabato does not mean that literature has to be a faithful reflection of the world. Rather, he suggests that in the act of writing fiction a specific claim is made by writers that they are faithful to their task. I understand Sabato's claim pragmatically: the claim to truth lies not in what is said—it is fictitious—but in the performance of writing. When writers write, they perform an act that consists in making statements, which themselves relate, in the story told, assertions, promises, questions, and so on. Readers relay the fictitious assertions, promises, and questions they find in the text and construe the representative content of the text. The truth of which Sabato speaks thus concerns the responsibility of the writer, who made such a colonization possible at the moment he wrote his fictional text, that is, in the act of writing.

To identify the performative nature of the act of writing, two questions have to be answered. Since literature is essentially made of fiction, and fiction means what is not real, literature defines itself in relation to what is accepted as real and as the norm. The question is thus whether there is something like a normal use of language or a normal situation of discourse that can be identified and to which literature relates or onto which it grafts. Once that question has been answered, the next question concerns the order of priority that exists between the two: is fiction derived from and thus a mere modification of the normal situation of discourse, or can fiction influence or even change the normal situation of discourse? The first question, I submit, is to be answered positively: there is a normal situation of discourse that can be identified fairly clearly. We immediately know that there is a difference between what is real and what is fictional, even if at times the distinction is not clear (in the case of some journalistic accounts reinterpreting facts, some biographies speculating on some aspects of someone's life, or some fictions referring to real people and events). The second question has a mixed answer. Fiction is not just a derivation and modification of the normal situation of discourse. If that were the case, fictions would always be subservient to what is normal and would never have the capacity, as they sometimes do, to question this normality, to change it, or to undermine it.

The task I have to perform in this chapter is thus a twofold demonstration. The first part of the demonstration consists in defining the rules of the normal situation of discourse and showing that these rules are in part interpretive and thus susceptible to change. There is thus a normal situation of discourse, which provides the means to refer, but this normal situation is itself dependent on conventions. The second part of the demonstration consists in showing that fiction, which does not have a referent in the terms of the normal situation of discourse, can have an effect on the conventions determining the normal situation of discourse, so that fiction has some sort of referential potential.

The Normal Situation of Discourse according to John Searle

John Searle has been, with Austin, the champion of the thesis that speaking is a form of action, so that when I say something I perform an act that involves me as a person in the world. In his book *Expression and Meaning* (1979) Searle provides a detailed analysis of the different classes of what he calls illocutionary acts, acts through which something is done. The first class comprises what he calls assertives, which assert something about the world, such as "It is raining." When saying "It is raining," a speaker not only conveys the propositional content that a rainy state of affairs exists near the speaker but also performs an act of asserting. The second class includes the commissives, which commit the speaker to a certain course of action, such as a promise. The directives belong to the third class and name acts that attempt to have the hearer do something, such as an order. The fourth class includes the expressives, which express the psychological state of the speaker named in the propositional content, such as thanking or congratulating. Finally, Searle analyzes the declarations, the fifth class, which bring about the correspondence between the propositional content and reality, for example, to baptize or to declare a war. For each of these classes Searle specifies the different rules for the realization of the illocutionary act. I focus here only on one of these classes, the assertives.

According to Searle, there are four rules at the core of an act of assertion. When I assert something,

1. I commit myself to the truth of what I say. This is the essential condition, and failing to satisfy it amounts to telling something false.

2. I claim to be in a position to provide evidence or reasons for the truth of what I say. Not being in such a position amounts to making unsubstantiated claims.

3. I claim to have a point that is not obviously true to the person I talk to. Failing to fulfill this claim means to make a pointless statement.

4. I commit myself to believing that what I say is true and thus to being truthful. This is the sincerity condition, and failing to fulfill this condition amounts to lying.

Regarding the status of these rules, Searle makes two points. The first consists in presenting these rules, which are semantic and pragmatic, as embedded in the spoken language. A speaker makes those commitments by virtue of the rules of the illocutionary acts. If he does not want to make those commitments, either he has recourse to a form of strategy or he does not know what it means to speak English; if he does not know what it means to speak English, he cannot really speak English.

The clear advantage of such a view is twofold. First, the rules of language catch any real person in their web and make it the case that the speaker, as an instance of discourse, for example, in the guise of a personal pronoun such as I, is the real, flesh-and-blood person who uttered the words. Second, these rules, which involve a real person as speaker, connect words and the world so that a reference has been made. Thus, my saying "It is raining" first involves me as a person in what I said. Then, my words, through the rules of assertion, lock onto the world and make it the case that a reference has been made: there is a rainy state of affairs in the real world nearby the speaker.

The second point Searle makes regarding these rules of illocutionary acts, in our case an assertion, is to present fiction as the performance of a nonserious and parasitic illocutionary act. Fiction is a pseudoperformance in which the author pretends to make illocutionary acts of, for example, assertion. Traditionally, if a statement does not have a reference, it is beyond the realm of what can be true or false. Any assessment of a statement has to presuppose the possibility of a correspondence between what is said and what is the case. The question of reference is crucial for the question of what a text means and what the intention behind the text is. If there is no reference in fiction, it is difficult to assign it a meaning and as difficult to find out the intention inhabiting such a fiction.

By seeing fiction as pretense, Searle follows a long philosophical tradition of suspicion about what literature can achieve. Searle embraces the position and even the vocabulary of his mentor, Austin, the father of speech-act theory, who believes that in sentences uttered on stage or in a poem, "language is not used seriously . . . that we have a parasitic use of language compared to the normal use" (1962, 55).

We expect, Searle says, a journalist to follow the rules of the normal situation of discourse. If a journalist cannot substantiate assertions in an article or if he takes assertions made by others as his own, it is a sufficient reason for the newspaper—for example, the *Boston Globe* or the *New York Times*—to fire such a journalist. An assertion binds the person to make the four claims Searle mentions. In contrast, making up things, inventing stories that are not true, is perfectly acceptable for writers of fiction; we even admire them for doing so. The reason for such a distinction between journalists and writers, Searle says, is that in fiction there is a contract between the author and the reader that suspends or brackets the normal situation of discourse. In the form of horizontal rules, the contract loosens the grip that words normally have on the world by virtue of the vertical rules of assertion and other speech acts. These vertical rules are linguistic and belong to

English or French as it is spoken; the horizontal rules are not linguistic and are not in the text.

The net result for fiction is that it presupposes the normal situation of discourse on which it feeds—as a parasite—and derives from this to the extent that it is by virtue of extralinguistic conventions between writers and readers that the rules of the act of assertion, which are linguistic, do not connect the words to the real world. In fiction there is, because of the contract and out of convention, a set of nonserious assertions or other speech acts, so that no reference is possible and, as a matter of necessity, no truth, in the sense of propositions verified by their states of affairs.

Searle acknowledges that, although fiction is nonserious, the writing of fiction can be serious. But he confesses that "there is as yet no general theory of the mechanisms by which such serious illocutionary intentions [when writing fiction] are conveyed by pretended illocutions" (1979, 75). In other words, there is no theory, Searle argues, that explains how pretended assertions, pretended questions, and so forth, which we find in novels, can serve as the means for conveying an aesthetic, social, or political message.

Although I agree with Searle's analysis that, when saying "It is raining," claims are made—for example, to tell the truth and to be truthful—I do not agree that such a rule of assertion de facto makes the speaker directly committed to the truth of what is said or to being truthful. I question whether the rules of speech acts, which indeed involve claims to tell the truth and so on, guarantee a commitment of the real person. Searle believes that by being spoken by a particular person language automatically commits that particular person to the claims that are embedded in the use of that language, whether that particular person knows it or not.

"Agrammaticality" traditionally undermines the meaningfulness of a sentence and thereby prevents it from being an instance of assertion. "The girl is cone the ice cream shopping buying the man" is an agrammatical sentence. If uttered, it would not satisfy a possible claim to intelligibility and would not qualify as an assertion. We do not see what could be meant, and the rules cannot thus connect the words with the world. This sentence, however, was uttered by a real woman, Chelsea, who is deaf but who was misdiagnosed as retarded when she was a child and who began to learn a first language at the age of 31, when fitted with hearing aids (Pinker 1994, 293). For her co-workers, who are familiar with her speech, there is no doubt that she means something, and she most likely means, "The man buys the girl a cone of ice cream while shopping." The claim to truth or even intelligibility, though, does not immediately follow from the utterance of the sentence, by the magic of English syntax. The claim, rather, is based on the fact that speakers and their audience share a common background. The claim to tell the truth or to be truthful then depends, for being intelligible, on the community in which the speaker lives as an agent. Therefore, it is in part interpretive. Claims at the level of discourse stabilize the situation of discourse and allow for meaningful assertion or promise—Searle is correct—but such a function is subservient to those claims being recognized within a given community.

The same criticism holds for the claim to tell the truth in general, even when intelligibility is not a factor. Such a claim depends on the criteria and standard of what is meant or understood as an account. A natural event or a disease can be accounted for by appealing to hidden forces in the universe, the will of God, or scientifically established natural laws. Even in one community these criteria can somehow coexist. For example, some people, by distinguishing different domains of their life ruled by different principles, can be "enlightened" and still believe in one almighty God. These two sets can even intermingle: some product warranties in the United States do not cover damage due to acts of God. Or the two sets of criteria can conflate, as in the debate between evolution and creationism, where the proponents adhere to two different frames of reference for accepting facts and evidence: scientifically established facts and the scriptures.

Let it be clear that we speak of claims to the truth and not of truth itself. Claiming, as I do, that there are several interpretive frameworks for making claims to the truth does not commit me to a stance on the question of whether truth is relative to different frames of reference. My contention is much more limited, in that I only contend that the claim to the truth is to be recognized as a valid claim within a frame of reference where such a claim is admissible. This is, for example, how someone in the early seventeenth century refuted Galileo's discovery of the moons of Jupiter: "There are seven windows given to animals in the domicile of the head, through which the air is admitted to the tabernacle of the body, to enlighten, to warm and to nourish it. What are these parts of the microcosmos: Two nostrils, two eyes, two ears and a mouth. So in the heavens, as in a macrocosmos, there are two favourable stars, two unpropitious, two luminaries, and Mercury undecided and indifferent. From this and from many other similarities in nature, such as the seven metals, etc., which it were too tedious to enumerate, we gather that the number of planets is necessarily seven" (quoted in Taylor 1985, 141).

Galileo is supposed to be refuted. Both Galileo and this particular opponent claimed to be intelligible and to tell the truth, but their claim was not enough to make them committed to reaching a consensus on what was said. They disagreed on what intelligibility meant and what the truth can be. In other words, it is not clear that they would recognize what the opponent says as a meaningful assertion.

Searle's mistake is to believe that the commitment derives from the utterance of the assertion, because he sees in an assertion a fusion between the psychological moment—when I intend to convey something, for example, that it is raining—and the conventional moment—namely, what the English sentence "It is raining" is taken to convey. When I speak, I take responsibility for the words as I use them as expressing what listeners will take them to express. At that moment, I implicitly acknowledge that there is no discrepancy between what the sentence I use means, which is publicly available and conventional, and my intention, which gives it life at the moment I borrow that particular sentence for expressing what I mean. The sentence meaning matches the speaker's meaning. Searle says that linguistic conventions, in their literal sense, express conventional intentional states, so that they represent one moment in the execution of a speech act. There are conventional mental states. In intention there is thus for Searle no difference between a psychological moment of, for example, intending to place myself under an obligation by making a promise, and a conventional mental moment when I borrow the conventional linguistic expression "I promise" as the expression of the conventional intentional state of placing myself under an obligation.

Against such a view, I contend that there is a difference between, for example, the linguistic expression "I promise" and the conventional intentional state, just as there can be a discrepancy between the psychological moment of intending and the conventional moment of what people take me to intend. The fusion that indeed exists most of the time is not due to language as spoken but to a commitment by a real person. The person chooses an available expression as the expression of a conventional mental state current in his community because he implicitly recognizes such a conventional use of the expression "I promise" and accepts the conventional intentional state expressed by such an expression. For people speaking the same language and having been socialized in the same linguistic community, there is indeed an implicit matching of my psychological state when using the words "I promise" and the conventional mental state expressed by such words. When asked why I am committed by uttering these words, I can say meaningfully that I speak English. The fact remains, though, that such a conflation between psychological state and conventional mental state has a genesis. The conflation has been made possible by a socialization process through which real speaking persons have implicitly pledged allegiance to the conventional intentional states current in their community.

In a given community—in synchrony—there is a guarantee that speakers most of the time (and implicitly) recognize the same claims. This guarantee, however, does not originate solely from the pragmatic use of language but also from a shared background. Borrowing these claims when speaking makes the speaker a partner in the dialogue that takes place in a community by imposing rules for asserting, giving orders, making promises, and so on. The commitment of speakers, however, does not derive from those accepted usages, from the mere fact that they speak, as Searle believes. Rather, the commitment derives from the assent a speaker gives to the intentional states expressible, and this assent itself originates from the conviction that those intentional states serve the good of the community. I am not even suggesting that it is the rules of the speech act that serve the good of the community or that we can somehow change the rules of making assertions or promises. I only contend that the rules of assertion, for example, are not enough to commit a person to the truth. Another act takes place, what I call giving one's assent to—for example, placing oneself under an obligation.

Put in another way, the rules of assertion connecting words with the world and engaging the speaker as an agent in the world only work on the basis of a contract somewhat analogous to the contract between writer and reader. Whereas the latter contract takes place on the basis of a normal situation of discourse and suspends the rules of assertion, the former contract is the moment when speakers most of the time implicitly give their assent to conventional mental states current in their community and to the expressions of such conventional mental states. Just as the horizontal rules, which dissolve the rules of speech acts according to Searle and thus give rise to fiction, are not linguistic rules and are not in the text, the contract between speakers and their community is not linguistic either and is not submitted to the rules of language or the rules of discourse. The initial contract, however, is made visible by rules. These are the rules that govern the approval or disapproval of what is said and thereby involve speakers in their responsibility toward the community regarding what they say. These rules of assent determine, apart from the issues of truth and truthfulness, whether an assertion is right.

A way to express this notion of assent given to a norm would be to distinguish between the claims involved in the speech acts and the claim to rightness when these speech acts are performed. Apel and Habermas bring together elements of Searle's theory of speech act and Bühler's philosophy of language and reformulate the components of a speech act in terms of claims, one of them being the claim to rightness. When I speak, I implicitly claim that what I say is appropriate given the circumstances at hand.

Although I share Apel's and Habermas's views, I contend that such a claim to rightness does not derive from a speech act alone but from the commitment of the person who speaks. The particular status that I see for the claim to rightness is that it represents, at the level of the speech act, a nodal point where there is a fusion between the speaker as an instance of discourse in the speech act and the real person who performs such an act. As a nodal point, the claim to rightness at the level of the speech act is also what makes the normal situation of discourse vulnerable and susceptible to change, for example, when a discrepancy can be felt or a critique drives a wedge between what is said, with its implicit claims to truth and truthfulness, and whether it is right. In movies from the 1930s or 1940s, we see evidence of stereotypes and patronizing attitudes manifested by the characters toward women or some ethnic groups. Although such attitudes were deemed acceptable at the time and might not have been seen as discriminatory, even by those who were victims of them, we now feel that they are not right: we would not give our assent to those conventional intentional states by borrowing their linguistic expressions. It is because such attitudes implicitly were claimed to be right then that we can criticize them now: it was wrong even at the time to assent to those intentional states. The basis for criticizing an earlier use of language is not the speech acts themselves but rather our conviction that it was wrong to borrow such intentional states. And it was wrong in the sense that, as we see it, such attitudes did not contribute to the common good and did not make the community a better and stronger community.

The claim to rightness, which is a pragmatic claim, is embedded in a specific community where there is a commonly accepted understanding, most of the time implicit, of what is and is not good for the community. The claim to rightness is the point where there is an exchange between the claims regulating speech acts and the convictions of the real persons. It is because there is a feeling that it is right that claims to truth are accepted and current. It is because people believe implicitly that these claims bind people so that they can be trusted that a conversation takes place and can go on.

A normal situation of discourse can be identified and is governed by rules, essentially claims. Such a normal situation of discourse does not have the status of an a priori but relies on a form of implicit contract to the extent that it depends on the assent members of a community implicitly give to such a norm. A claim to rightness is embedded in any speech act through which the speaker, as an instance of discourse, is connected to the real person living in a community of fellow citizens. Such a claim to rightness allows for an exchange and mutual influence between the rules of the normal situation of discourse and the convictions people have regarding what is good for their community.

Ricoeur makes a case for the idea that fiction configures the realm of action and self-understanding, so that there is a mutual exchange between fictions, which offer scenarios and a laboratory for possibilities of life to be tested, on the one hand, and the world to be rearticulated by fictions when readers act upon what they read, on the other. In this sense, literature is clearly connected with the real world. Ricoeur speaks of a second-degree reference.

My thesis is stronger than Ricoeur's in that I claim that fiction has referential potential not only as a configuration but also as a performance. As a performance the writing of fiction involves speech acts, which make it the case that a writer makes claims. Among the different claims writers make when writing fiction, there is a claim to rightness: writers claim that their works fit the situation at hand and the empirical circumstances. Through such a claim that their work is right, they implicitly claim that their fiction has something to say regarding the world as it goes. Whether meant for entertaining, exploiting the situation at hand, or criticizing it, fictions present themselves as connected with reality, not at the level of a claim to truth or truthfulness in the sense of fitting existing empirical conditions, but at the level of a claim to rightness. Through their claim to rightness writers refer to the conditions of the normal situation of discourse.

Contrary to Searle's view, fiction is more than the result of a contract between writer and readers: fiction can influence the initial implicit contract through which speakers give their assent to the conventional mental states that are current in their community. Fiction might be defined by contradistinction to what is the case, but it is not just a derivation from the normal situation of discourse, as Searle believes. There is a mutual interaction between fiction and the normal situation of discourse, so that fiction can have an influence on what people perceive as appropriate or inappropriate mental states and therefore on what can be expressed. Described in traditional terms, literary fictions shape the conscience of a nation. It is through a claim to rightness that fiction, which does not correspond to real states of affairs, refers to what matters to the real speaking persons, because what matters for real speaking persons is precisely what will determine the verdict on the claims they make in the normal situation of discourse.

A negative manifestation of that implicit claim to rightness operates when a work of art creates a controversy: it is found to be at odds with what some members of the community consider the good of the community, whether it is about pornography or about religious beliefs. Similarly, the reason artists have always appeared suspicious to dictatorial regimes lies not just in the content of their work but in the fact that they dare represent what they represent. They break, so the dictators think, the implicit contract that members have with their community by not contributing to the stability or the betterment of the community. They allegedly undermine the fabric of society.

Through their claim to rightness, writers engage their responsibility. It is for assuming his responsibilities that Sabato is hailed as a hero in Argentina for his daring fictions and essays written in a time of authoritarian regimes. It is also on the basis of a claim to rightness that Grass relentlessly and painstakingly depicts the everyday life of German people during and after the Nazi era. Similarly, the responsibility of philosophers or literary critics suddenly becomes an issue when a controversy arises. One of the major philosophers of the twentieth century, initiator of a specific brand of phenomenology and existentialism, Heidegger was also the rector of the University of Freiburg for ten months in 1933, during the Nazi regime, and remained a party member until 1945. De Man, the famous Yale scholar, father of deconstruction in literary criticism, was also a young journalist writing racist and anti-Semitic comments in his regular literary column for the Belgian newspaper *Le Soir* when Belgium, his native country, was occupied by the Nazis during World War II. These two authors are professional thinkers, in philosophy and literary criticism, respectively. Heidegger has always claimed that philosophy is its own ground and that the philosopher's biography or the history of the time is irrelevant to philosophical thinking.

Analogously, de Man is at the origin of a movement of literary criticism that has spread from Yale to cultural studies and philosophy as deconstruction or deconstructionism. In its basic form it is the thesis that the language we use for speaking about the world provides the grid through which we can see the world, so that we basically see what we can articulate in words. Derrida, a close friend of de Man, has formulated such a view by saying that the subject is a function of language. The subject, which is traditionally seen as the source of meaning and the possibility for taking responsibility, is thus a mere construct that only has a linguistic existence through the signs such an entity uses. The task of criticism is therefore to undo the web of words used in a text and reveal a hidden system of oppositions, of values, of the mechanisms involved when sense is generated by words, and so forth. What is remarkable in the case of Heidegger and de Man is that life caught up with them, so to speak, where they did not expect it. Nazism with its oppression, the sterilization of the public sphere, the illusion it brought of a new beginning, the cowardice it generated among those who just wanted to get by, and the opportunity it provided for the ambitious posed a retrospective and cruel challenge to Heidegger and de Man. Clearly, they did not pass the test as persons. They lacked courage at best or became opportunistic at worst, all through their work.

Although Heidegger's and de Man's involvement as persons is not an argument against their theories, it is legitimate to ask whether there is a deficit in their theories. The deficit might be precisely the fact that they did not recognize the claim to rightness involved in any theory. They recognized neither their responsibility as persons living in a given situation nor the impact their theories might have on real people. In the case of Heidegger, his philosophical views might have encouraged the political situation by providing a narrative for embracing, without scrutiny and in the name of a historical opportunity, the aberrations of the Nazis. By willingly associating his name with the Nazis he unwittingly gave credence to what the Nazis did. This is one of the charges Grass levels against him. In the case of de Man, who was still a student when he wrote his infamous columns, the theory he provided came after the aberration he committed, as what can be seen as a retrospective justification. He, who never mentioned the infamous writings of his youth, let alone apologized for them, could argue, quoting his friend Derrida, that the subject is a function of language, thereby exculpating the real person who is merely the host of those thoughts.

As part of the performative nature of literature, a claim to rightness is made, which engages the responsibility of the writer and causes the work to connect to the normal situation of discourse. Sabato, who has always been involved in politics in his native Argentina, is most famous for his works of fiction. One of his claims is that the duty of a writer of fiction is to tell the truth. I understand this truth telling in the case of writers of fiction as a claim to rightness.

Politics and Responsibility in the Writing of Fiction

Sabato's second novel was *On Heroes and Tombs* (1981, first published 1961, reprinted in Sabato 1997b). The third part of the novel, "The Report on the Blind," tells the strange story of a secret sect. Although commentators such as Ángela Dellepiane (1973), Marcelo Coddou (1973), and Carlos Catania (1973) do not even mention the political connotations of the work, I find them quite striking. As the first evidence that this fiction is a parody of a dictatorship, the novel can be linked to Sabato's environment. Sabato has always been linked to the politics of his country, whether inside the government or outside. In his youth, he was involved in anarchist and communist student groups and became the secretary of the Communist youth of La Plata. When a military coup took place, he was forced into hiding. "In 1930 the first military coup took place [in Argentina], terrible and bloody. It was the consequence of the danger that social movements represented for the military and the capitalists. . . . That first coup was decisive in my life since I had to enter into clandestinity: first, because of my status as a militant—I have always despised the salon revolutionaries—and second, because I became the Secretary of the Communist youth and was thus very much wanted by the repression" (Sabato 1999, 54).

He fled to Brussels, left the Communist Party in part because of the revelation of Stalin's purges, and lived for a while in Paris. He came back to Paris later with a scholarship to work in the Curie laboratory. While in Paris, wondering whether to pursue a career in physics or to turn to literature, he met French surrealists. In 1940 he accepted a professorship of theoretical physics at the University of La Plata in Argentina. After some years of teaching and doing research in physics, he decided to dedicate himself to literature. Juan Perón hastened the decision by forcing him to resign from his professorship in 1945. Perón was offended that Sabato had publicly criticized the violent repression of students' demonstrations. In 1955 Sabato was forced to resign from his position as editor of *Mundo Argentino* because his support of free speech and freedom of the press brought him into conflict with the military government of Pedro Aramburu. The situation repeated itself in 1959, for a different reason, when Sabato grew dissatisfied with the policies of the government of Arturo Frondizi and resigned as director of cultural relations (Constenla 1997).

On Heroes and Tombs caused Sabato some problems when it appeared: "I believe I once mentioned to you that the publication of *On Heroes and Tombs* openly unleashed the powers" (Sabato 1991, 253). Throughout his career Sabato wrote opinion pieces in newspapers. Through his opposition to undemocratic regimes and his courage in speaking up, Sabato became a kind of conscience for his country. After the brutal reign of a military junta that caused the death of an estimated thirty thousand people, Sabato was appointed by the new president, Raul Alfonsin, in 1984 as head of the National Commission for the Disappearance of Persons (*La Comisión Nacional sobre la Desaparición de Personas*). The report he wrote has come to be known as the Sabato report.

But what does it mean for a novel to be political? There are at least four ways a work of literature can be linked to politics. At a minimum and trivial level, since the author is the efficient cause of the work, the work is political in the sense that the author participates in the public sphere of her time and contributes to the public sphere by producing a work. If that were the entire political effect of writing, strolling in the street would also be political and politics would lose much of its meaning. In a second sense a work can be political through the impact it has among readers who interpret it politically, regardless of whether the work was so intended. Daniel Auber's opera *La muette de Portici*, exalting the patriotism of Neapolitans against their Spanish oppressors, caused riots in the streets of Brussels in 1830 that led to the revolution against Belgium's Dutch occupiers. This is clearly a political impact of a fictional work. But Auber, a French composer, probably did not intend his opera, written in 1828, to have such a political appeal and cannot be accountable for or credited with the Belgian revolution.

A third manner in which a work is political is through the intention of the writer. Some elements in works by Aimé Césaire, Grass, and Solzhenitsyn make an unmistakable reference to political events and present critical perspectives that are also unmistakably political. In this sense only works with direct references to political situations would qualify as political.

A fourth manner in which a work is political—in a general, but not trivial, sense—is as a performance by a person (the author) who designs through her work possible intentional states that become available to readers. Such a political sense is not trivial as with the first sense, in which any production is de facto political; it belongs to the work and not to its effect, as in the second sense; and it applies to all works, and not only to some particular works making explicit references to political events. If the political character of writing fiction consists in the performance of the act of writing, we have to further examine what is involved in such an act, especially the status of what is represented by the text.

In a conversation, when we do not understand a sentence uttered by someone, we feel a certain amount of frustration and try again, by asking the speaker to reformulate the sentence. We need to know what someone meant in order to find out what the sentence he uttered means. If someone tells us, "The building is running away," we understand the sentence in terms of its components: the act of running is predicated of the building. What we do not understand is the intentional state of the person who would utter such a sentence. "What on earth do you mean?" Quite remarkably, the same does not hold true for works of art. We can understand works of art while ignoring what the author meant or even who the author is. We do not need an exact interpretation for enjoying the works, and we can even find pleasure in them while not being able to express what we understand. However vaguely, they speak to us. But what is that "word" coming from the work, apparently coming in addition to the work?

There are at least three differences between an interpretive situation dealing with a conversation and a novel. First, the author of a novel is most of the time not available to tell us what she meant by writing down those sequences of words; second, even if she were available, most of us would not grant her the privilege to determine what her novel means. We are thus left with two levels of meaning: the word and sentence meanings and what is conveyed. Since we cannot or do not want to appeal to the author as the one who conveys a message by the word and sentence meanings, we have to come up ourselves with that which is conveyed.

But there is a third difference between a conversation and a novel. In a conversation we understand someone and trace back the word and sentence meanings to the intentional state our partner must have. In the back-and-forth of the sentence exchange, we and our partner can at any time correct the understanding of our words and sentences: "I take it back," or "Why do you say that?" The starting point and the end point of a conversation is what the speaker means in terms of what he wants to say. Of course we can also analyze the style, implications, and unconscious motivations of our discussion partner. Since in a novel the author is for most of us not granted a privileged position of authority, we can only start, not with what the author wants to say, but with what is said. Starting with words and sentences, we have to construe possible intentional states that make the word and sentence meanings coherent and plausible. When we read a novel or part of a novel, we understand the words and the sentences and most of the time can summarize the story told, but sometimes we wonder, "What does it all mean?" This question bears on what is represented. Once we have a satisfactory answer to that question, what have we done? We have translated what we read in terms of intentional states.

I call intentional state that which is conveyed by word and sentence meanings. When reading, we thus construe the intentional states that allow us to make sense of the word and sentence meanings. "It is raining" conveys the intentional state of believing that it is raining and being willing to assert it. When reading a novel, we understand the words and the sentences. Since we know neither what the author meant otherwise than through the sentences we read nor what specific characters in the novel mean because they only exist at the surface of the text, we have to construe the intentional states bringing to life the sentences we read. For example, we understand the words of Isabel Archer in *The Portrait of a Lady*, "I shall not have success if [the English people are] too stupidly conventional. I'm not in the least stupidly conventional. I'm just the contrary. That's what they don't like" (James 1983, 52). But we need to find out what is represented. We colonize those statements and imagine what she means, leading us to figure out who she is. And at the end of the novel, we have to connect that assertion of nonconventionality with her resolution to go back to Rome, where her husband, whom she just left, lives. After turning down the proposal of Caspar Goodwood: "In an extraordinary short time—for the distance was considerable—she had moved through the darkness (for she saw nothing) and reached the door. Here only she paused. She looked all about her; she listened a little; then she put her hand on the latch. She had not known where to turn; but she knew now. There was a very straight path" (559).

The sentences we read in the novel are invitations for us, readers, to imagine what she thinks, believes, hopes, or fears. In a way, what we do is analogous to finding a background for the literal meaning of those sentences. In this case, however, because these characters and events are fictitious, the application to a background is our responsibility. Only by construing the intentional states animating the sentences we read can we understand what the novel means, in the sense of what it represents.

Interpreting a novel is thus a colonization of its meanings by intentional states originating from readers, and a novel appears as an invitation for readers to construe the intentional states that bring the meanings to life.

Some readers are quite good at this, continuing the story after the end of the novel: "Do you think they will see each other again?" It does not matter to these people that the text has ended, that the characters of the novel as creatures made of paper are exhausted and have been retired.

Because readers invest in the literary text some of their beliefs, hopes, and desires, literature is not confined to a description or an illustration of already existing intentional states. Literature can also create something new, offer indirectly, through what readers do with the text, a new way of looking at a situation or of behaving. The many novels describing love relationships in their passion, jealousy, treachery, tragedy, or redemption can serve as warning or enticement: "This can happen to you too, beware or enjoy!" But how can an intentional state be something new? How can a new intentional state become part of the current pool? The answer is not easy to formulate for the simple reason that literature usually does not explain what it does, but rather represents, so that readers have to take responsibility for what it is that they understand.

But clearly the words written on the page have been put in a certain order so as to signify something. Whatever the imagination of readers configures in terms of a significant story, what nurtures the frantic imagination of readers is the words written on the page. Readers do not rearrange the sequences of letters in words nor the sequence of words in a sentence, even though their reading might leap from one part of the novel to the end and back. The author's intention remains crucial as the hand or the efficient cause in choosing specific words and sentences and putting them in specific sequences. Denying this level of meaning would amount to denying the fact that the novel has been written by someone.

Thus, the fact that sentences once severed from their original background gain a life of their own and become the mercenaries of any background that will receive them is only half the story. These sentences have been meant as bearing that possibility of being mercenary. If such a large array of possible intentional states can be generated by a work, what kind of intention is involved in the making of the work? If the work is a set of possible intentional states, what is the responsibility involved in the design of those intentional states? Can writers of fiction be held responsible for whatever a reader will construe out of their productions and, if yes, to what extent?

The fact that the story is designed as a set of intentional states made available to an audience constitutes one political dimension of literature that is, in my view, the most fundamental and to which the other aspects are related. What is political is precisely the design, the act of putting together words and sentences that invite readers to colonize them. This political aspect engages the responsibility of the author, a responsibility that is limited by the existence of a mediation (the story as a set of intentional states) between what the author means and what readers interpret. Although responsible for the availability of intentional states, the author cannot be fully responsible for how these intentional states will be borrowed, acted upon, or interpreted.

It is thus a matter of necessity that a novel yields many possible different understandings. What we read is the sentences on the basis of the meaning of their components, and those cannot determine a clear univocal understanding without some form of background, as Gregory the Great and Searle convincingly show. Readers have the choice of reinhabiting the author's background or of dispensing with it.

What troubles many critics and philosophers is the fear that, if we recognize the relevance the act of writing has for the meaning of the text, the meaning potential of the work will be tamed. This was the motivation at the heart of Barthes's essay "The Death of the Author" (2002) and Foucault's text "What Is an Author?" (2002). Worse! The responsibility of writers will be engaged, free speech is threatened, and the spectrum of censorship looms on the horizon. These are indeed dangers, but responsibility also presupposes authorship. If we deny responsibility, we deny authorship. Authors do not have much to gain in such a bargain.

To avoid misunderstandings, a distinction must be made between the act of writing, which is a political act and which then engages the responsibility of writers, and whatever readers construe out of the work, which is the readers' responsibility. The author's responsibility is limited. It does not originate so much from the content of the work (which is susceptible to multiple interpretations) as from the bringing into existence of the work. It was not so much the fictions of Gustave Flaubert's *Madame Bovary* (1971) or Thomas Mann's *Buddenbrooks* (1981) that alarmed the good citizenry and the authorities and challenged the social order, but what readers could construe out of their fictions in terms of intentional states—retrieving repressed intentional states or construing new ones. As for the specific question of when a writer is liable for what readers interpret, this is a legal question that can receive different answers depending on the norms in particular countries. My concern is not with a specification of the criteria for assessing the responsibility of writers, but only with the general view that their responsibility is engaged through their act of writing.

An example of such political writing, *On Heroes and Tombs* probably constitutes Sabato's most comprehensive and powerful novel. Dellepiane calls this a total novel, in the sense that Sabato expresses in it all of his preoccupations, observations, and knowledge, his cosmovision (1973). The third part of the novel, "The Report on the Blind," describes the investigation Fernando Vidal Olmos pursues of the blind people of Buenos Aires, whom he suspects of being part of a sect running an underground network and governing what takes place at the surface. Obsessed with blind people, Vidal decides to infiltrate the sect. He befriends a man who has just lost his sight in an accident and waits to see how this newly blinded man will be approached by the Sect of the Blind. Vidal describes in detail his plans, his long wait, his trailing of blind people or people associated with them, his descent into the Buenos Aires sewers, his discoveries of strange and horrible events. Meticulously he writes a report of his findings.

At first glance, this part of the novel seems separated from the other three sections, which relate the interactions of three characters: Alejandra, Martin, and Bruno, none of whom appear in the third part, narrated by Vidal. Similarly, Vidal does not play a substantial role in the other parts. It even takes the reader some time to realize that the narrator, Vidal, is the same Vidal as the evanescent character mentioned in the other parts, who is Alejandra's father. Sabato addresses this structural rupture of the novel in a short essay, "A propósito del *Informe sobre ciegos*" ("On 'The Report on the Blind'"). In the essay Sabato acknowledges that this third part is "one of my pieces of fiction that produced for me the most headaches and misunderstandings" (1997a, 947; my translation). One of those misunderstandings is precisely the feeling that this third part is a separate and independent part of the novel. Sabato responds, "I had the intention of making a novel in which the central character, as the saying goes, 'would shine by his absence.' This character is Fernando Vidal, because everything turns around and about him. . . . After writing the fiction in such a manner, I thought that in this way only the 'diurnal' side of this character would remain, whereas the other part, the more enigmatic, would remain absent: the part about his profundities, his deliriums, and dreams. I then decided to narrate his great nightmare, as a horrible, infamous, and cathartic vomit: the 'Report on the Blind' (947; my translation).

Vidal, the narrator of "The Report on the Blind," is by all accounts, his own included, an obsessed, even paranoid man. There is no clear indication in the report of what that story stands for. The narrator only speaks of blind people, underground tunnels, clandestine rooms, psychological phobias, perverse sexual acts. It looks like a parable or an allegory. There is not even a clear sense that the narrator really believes in what he writes. Vidal speaks of his hallucinations, of his nightmares, and even of his split personality. And at the end of the report, the narrator finds himself in the same room where he started the investigation. Even in the context of fiction, it is not clear that there is an attempt to make us believe in the story.

This is confirmed by the author's note at the beginning of the novel: "There exists a certain type of fictional narrative whereby the author endeavors to free himself of an obsession that is not clear even to himself. For good or ill, this is the only sort of fiction I am able to write" (Sabato 1981). Sabato formulates the problem of this type of fiction in *The Angel of Darkness* (1991, originally published in 1974), in which his persona Sabato appears as a character in the novel:

> What was he trying to say with his fiction? Almost ten years after publishing *On Heroes and Tombs* students, intensely curious ladies, clerks in government offices, kids doing their dissertations at Michigan or in Florence, typists would ask him that. And navy officers going into the Officers Club now looked with intrigued suspicion at that old Blind Man dressed like an English gentleman. . . . Yes, those sailors too wanted to know what that famous "Report on the Blind" meant. And when he told them that he could add nothing more to what he had already written there, they would grow insistent. . . . Because how could the author himself not know things? It was futile to try to explain to these people that some facts, some realities, some *things* can only be explained with mute and inexplicable symbols, just as the man dreaming does not always understand what his nightmares mean. (1991, 26–27)

If the story does not even try to make us believe in the reference of what is narrated, what other kind of reference can this fiction have? Since literary fictions have a reference through the claim to rightness their author makes, what is the claim to rightness present in this fiction? In *Angel of Darkness*, Sabato, as a character, meets a young friend who is fond of literature. "'What is the writer's first duty?' S. asked him suddenly. . . . I'm talking about a writer of fiction. His duty is no more and no less than telling the truth" (1991, 241). I understand Sabato as saying that telling the truth for a writer of fiction is fulfilling his duty as a writer and, in my terms, redeeming his claim to rightness. In an earlier essay, "Sartre contra Sartre. La misión trascendente de la novela" (Sartre against Sartre. The transcendental mission of the novel, 1968), Sabato vehemently reacts against Sartre's avowal that a novel such as *Nausea* does not have much sense when a child dies from hunger. Sabato argues that "art has other possibilities and other missions" (64) than being of direct utility to people. Writers of fiction can offer people a "catharsis" because they are "those beings condemned to dream for the whole community" (85). In a modern world they offer alternatives to what a particular economic and political system makes available. In response to Sartre's pessimistic views on the power of literature, Sabato writes, "Human beings write fictions because they are incarnate, because they are imperfect. A God, Sartre, does not write novels" (93).

To describe what Sabato calls the truth of the act of writing, we need to describe the content of the act, namely, the story told or what is said. The story told in "The Report on the Blind" can be understood as a parody of a dictatorship, a religious parable, a psychological exploration, and a narrative of the writing of a novel. These four levels represent the different forms the claim to truth can take on the side of the writer, which in my view is a claim to rightness and which causes the act of writing to latch onto the normative realm of readers, thereby turning the act of writing into a political act.

The tunnels, hidden rooms, entries, and exits that Vidal describes and tries to follow can be seen as an image of the hidden ways a dictatorial regime exercises power, through infiltration and spying. The descent into the sewers, into filth and suffering, the fear of the narrator of having his eyes plucked out, and the description of what that would be like, all this, in unbearable detail, makes us think of the methods of torture that are all too common in dictatorial regimes. At one point Vidal, the narrator, flees to Paris to escape the power of the blind (Sabato 1981, 337), just as Sabato fled to Paris in the 1930s after a military coup. The blind would then stand for the obscure power that can dictate to people what to do and think, make them lose any clear vision, and maintain itself through fear, suspicion, and self-censorship. The paranoia of the narrator would then be the effect of the terror exerted by a dictatorship, leading people to fear any unusual movement or person and thereby losing the sense of what is real and what is not.

At the same time, Vidal, the investigator, can be seen as part of the dictatorship. Vidal is the one who investigates and decides who is suspicious. The obsession of the narrator that a conspiracy is taking place can be seen as an attempt to legitimate the investigation, rather than as a motivation for the investigation. Blindness as the criterion for being investigated seems as arbitrary as being a Jew for the Nazis or being an intellectual in Mao's China during the Cultural Revolution.

The report Vidal is writing also reminds us of the files that dictatorial regimes usually keep on some of their citizens as leverage. Self-censorship is the most efficient guarantee of the status quo. The paranoid character of Vidal parallels the paranoia of a dictatorship through the self-fulfilling aspect of the investigation. For Vidal, it is enough that people are suspect for them to be worthy of suspicion. Since it is the investigator who decides who is suspicious, there is no possibility for the investigator to be proven wrong. In any given fact Vidal sees a motivation to investigate further: if the fact fits his expectations he praises his cleverness for having seen through the plan of the blind, and if the fact does not fit the plan he had envisaged, this is sufficient evidence that his own plan has been seen through and that the blind are trying to throw him off into a dead end. Vidal is on a mission where everything feeds the hypothesis he has and nothing can ever falsify it. Once started, the mission can only move forward.

"The Report on the Blind" is replete with religious references as well as a religious vocabulary, so that it can also be read at a religious level, as an allegory. Vidal, for example, can be seen as an inquisitor: "I am an investigator of Evil" (Sabato 1981, 282). The object of suspicion is called a secret sect, the secret sect of the blind, which is sometimes called the forbidden realm (338). "If, as they say, God rules heaven, the Sect has dominion over the earth and the flesh. It is evident that the universe is in its absolute power, that of life and death, which it exercises through pestilence or revolution, sickness or torture, deceit or false compassion, mystification or anonymity. . . . I do not know if, in the final reckoning, this organization must one day account for its actions to what might be called the Luminous Authority. . . . I am not a theologian and am not qualified to state whether these infernal powers can be explained by way of some sort of contorted Theodicy" (245).

This sect is an instrument of the prince of darkness: "In my view the conclusion is obvious: the prince of Darkness continues to rule with an iron hand. And the instrument of this rule is the sacred Sect of the Blind" (Sabato 1981, 247). Sometimes, the blind are associated with hell: "the labyrinths of Hell, or rather, the universe of the Blind" (279). Vidal compares himself to Tiresias, someone who has a power of clear sightedness. He presides over a holy war, and his role is to denounce the prince of darkness by writing a report.

Besides reading the novel as a parody of a dictatorship or as a religious allegory, we can read it at a psychological level. Vidal is a narrator who brings to the fore our worst fears and obsessions: claustrophobia evoked by the different episodes he narrates of being locked in a small dark room with little air, of a couple locked in an elevator for a whole winter and dying, of being lost in a labyrinth, of hearing somebody tell us something vital, a matter of life and death, and not being able to understand. He also describes in detail how his eyes are plucked out by a bird (Sabato 1981, 318–20). With great relish he details his uneasiness with serpents, snakes, and other reptiles. A woman, a blind person, or someone who is different irritates him or makes him suspicious. And he likes to justify his own short-comings—he is, he says, a bastard—by appealing to a greater cause and a greater good: "I am an investigator of Evil, and how can Evil be investigated without plunging into filth up to one's neck?" (282).

The novel makes it quite clear that Vidal is himself a psychologically troubled man. He is subject to recurrent nightmares or hallucinations, from which he emerges "struggling like a person who is drowning, someone who fears that he will again be swept up by the dark and tumultuous river from which he has just begun to emerge, after painful effort, by clinging to the edges of reality" (Sabato 1981, 358). A character, Bruno, who knew Vidal closely when they were kids and later on when they were anarchists, calls Vidal "an alienated man" (387), whose mind "was totally absorbed by his mad obsessions with the blind" (410). Vidal himself acknowledges that in his youth he was involved with a "band of gangsters and armed holdup men" (246), that he was even the leader of such a gang (251). This is confirmed by another character, Vidal's cousin and wife, Georgina, who says that around 1930 Vidal organized a "gang of thugs and armed bandits" (410). Even worse, although the information is scattered all through the novel, Vidal turns out to be the father of Alejandra, the main character of the first part of the novel, and had an incestuous relationship with her.

This information retrospectively makes intelligible the foreword of the novel, which is a police report saying that Alejandra killed her father, locked herself in the house, and set it on fire. We know from Vidal himself in his report that he expects to be killed, but he suspects the blind. The police report also mentions the fact that a report on the blind, drafted by Vidal, was found that "lends itself to certain interpretations that throw light on the crime and make the hypothesis of an act of madness less plausible than another more sinister, more obscure explanation" (Sabato 1981, 3). The report suggests that such a line of reasoning could explain why Alejandra did not use the two bullets left in the pistol to kill herself and chose instead to burn herself alive (3). The irony of this report by the police is that it adds credibility to Vidal's report of a conspiracy, whereas Vidal himself undermines the plausibility of his own story. Or that the police are ready to believe the writings of a paranoid man.

The most important of these obsessions, which the novel highlights and which could justify a psychological reading, is obviously blindness. There is, first, Vidal's projection that blind people are the instruments of the prince of darkness. There is also Vidal's hallucination that he himself loses his sight. He describes himself walking and crawling in the sewage of Buenos Aires. At one point he falls:

> I struggled to keep my head out of the mire, raising my forehead in the direction of the cavern, as the rest of my body began sinking into those nauseating waters.
> "I have to be able to breathe," I thought.
> But I also thought: "By keeping my head up I am enabling them [the birds circling around] to get at my eyes."
> The thought came to me that it was as though there were a curse upon me and I was condemned to this horrible operation, and yet at the same time I was freely consenting to this hideous and apparently inescapable rite. (Sabato 1981, 319)

One of the birds pierces his eyes. This loss of sight, to which he himself somehow consents; his designation of this as a rite; the feelings he has of having arrived at the truth (Sabato 1981, 319); the "curious repugnance that I now felt toward myself" (320)—all that, allied with allusions to the prophet Tiresias and to Oedipus (360–61), who also decided to lose his sight because of his incestuous relationship with his mother, makes Vidal another Oedipus, who has to be mutilated for a sexual transgression: the incestuous relationship with his daughter.

This reading of "The Report on the Blind" illuminates Sabato's statement that the duty of a writer is to tell the truth: this duty can consist of unmasking the mechanisms of a dictatorship, warning against any form of inquisition or witch hunt, and exposing deeply hidden obsessions and fears that seem common to human beings. I do not suggest that this represents a message, only that the writer writes what he sees. There is a fourth level at which "The Report on the Blind" can be read: as a description of the very process of writing.

A first indication that Sabato refers to the act of writing is offered by several self-references in the novel, most of them ironic. Vidal, the investigator, was born in 1911, like the real Sabato. Vidal is afraid of losing his eyesight and eventually loses it, like Sabato, who has become almost blind. It is said in the novel that "Vidal Olmos" is an assumed name, which, in light of the references to Sabato and the similarities between Vidal and Sabato, is quite true. The report Vidal writes in the novel is motivated by another report written by an insane murderous painter, Castel, who confesses that he has always been obsessed with blind people. The title of Castel's report is "The Tunnel," which is the title of Sabato's first novel (1997c, translated into English as *The Outsider*; Sabato 1950, 331). As a writer, Sabato creates a fiction of a paranoid character writing a report and being influenced by a mad murderer who, in the fiction, writes what Sabato in reality wrote. Reference is also made to Madame Curie, in whose laboratory Sabato worked in Paris when he was a physicist. At the time, the laboratory was directed by Marie Curie's daughter, Irène Jolliot-Curie. In the novel, and possibly related to Vidal's stay in Paris, a lady talking with Vidal speaks of the genius of Curie. Reporting the conversation with that lady, Vidal notes, "It was inevitable that Madame Curie's name should come up" (Sabato 1981, 272). Given the self-references that Sabato puts in Vidal's story, we understand the irony: since Sabato worked in Curie's laboratory, people around him cannot help but bringing up the name "Curie." And what Vidal says is also ironic, if not sarcastic. Vidal argues that the term "genius" does not apply to Curie: "Madame Curie, Señorita, did not discover the law of the evolution of species. She went out with a rifle to hunt tigers, and happened to meet up with a dinosaur. If we were to use this as a criterion, the first sailor who spied Cape Horn would also be a genius" (273).

Sabato's self-deprecatory remarks under the borrowed name of "Vidal" weaken Searle's position, since for Searle an author who says "I" is an author pretending to be someone else. Sabato abundantly plays with that pretense, casting doubt on the truth of what Vidal narrates and taking in part the role of a murderer (Castel, who writes *The Tunnel*) and an obsessed man, even a sexual offender (Vidal, who is the same age as Sabato, flies to Paris like Sabato, and fears the loss of and actually loses his eyesight, like Sabato).

A second indication of a reference to writing comes from the manner in which Vidal understands his task as a writer. He presents himself as entrusted with a mission of revelation. There are two worlds, he believes—a view Sabato often expresses—the world of light and the world of darkness. Science is interested in the world of light and tries to explain it.

Literature, in contrast, explores the realm of darkness. The descent into Buenos Aires sewers can thus be seen as a metaphor for what writers do. They explore what sustains the world of light, which is like the sewers carrying away the wastes of the world above:

> Here below, in obscene and pestilential tumult, there rushed along, mingled in a single stream, the menstrual blood of those romantic, beloved women, the excrement of those ethereal young girls dressed in tulle and chiffon, the condoms used by dignified bankers, aborted fetuses by the thousands, the remains of meals of millions of homes and restaurants, the immense, the immeasurable Refuse of Buenos Aires.
>
> And everything [in Buenos Aires' sewer] was heading toward Nothingness of the ocean by way of secret subterranean conduits, as though Those Up Above wanted to forget, to refuse to recognize the existence of this side of their reality. As though heroes in reverse, such as myself, were condemned by fate to the infernal and accursed labor of bringing this reality to light.
>
> Explorers of Filth, witnesses to Refuse and Bad Thoughts.
>
> Yes, I suddenly felt myself to be a sort of hero, a hero in reverse, a black and repugnant hero, but a hero nonetheless. (Sabato 1981, 354–55)

In his search for the blind, he compares what he experiences to heroes in combat: "I abandoned myself to the heady, mad pleasure of vertigo, that sensual pleasure that heroes in combat experience at the most dangerous moments" (Sabato 1981, 279). He places himself among doomed poets: "those few who may have succeeded in entering the forbidden world, writers who also ended their lives as madmen and suicides (Artaud, Lautréamont, Rimbaud, to name three)" (361).

Such a view of the writer, as someone who dares plunge into darkness, is a deep conviction of Sabato's. This in fact was the reason he decided to dedicate himself to literature, abandoning a promising career as a physicist who had worked in the Curie laboratory and taught theoretical physics at the university. To reach this underworld, which is the source of appearances, a new sight has to be gained, and this new sight occurs by sacrificing the normal sight. "Wasn't Homer himself blind?" (Sabato 1981, 360). Tiresias too became blind and received the gift of foresight. Vidal presents himself as such an explorer of darkness, who has to dive into darkness in order to understand it and report on it: "The blind rule the world, by way of nightmares and fits of delirium, hallucinations, plagues and witches, sooth-sayers and birds, serpents, and in general, all the monsters of darkness and caverns. It was thus that I was little by little able to make out the abom-inable world that lay behind appearances. And it was thus that I began to train my senses, exacerbating them through passion and anxiety, hope and fear, so as to be able in the end to see the great forces of darkness as the mystics are able to see the god of light and goodness. And I, a mystic of Refuse and Hell, can and must say: 'BELIEVE ME!'" (361).

Losing sight is a punishment for a sexual transgression, as in the case of Oedipus. The transgression can also consist in facing the powers of dark-ness, the punishment for such a transgression being the loss of sight. With the punishment, however, comes a gift, like that of Tiresias: the power to see what caused the transgression.

Not only does the narrator present himself as a writer, but he also explains the status of the story we read. This is the third indication that this story offers a direct reference to writing. The story, Vidal tells us, originates from a split of personality: "The thought sometimes occurs to me that per-haps reincarnation is a fact and that in the most hidden depths of our self memories of these beings that preceded us lie sleeping, just as our bodies preserve traces of fish and reptiles; dominated by the new self and the new body, yet ever ready to awaken and emerge the moment that the forces, the tensions, the screws and bits of wire that hold the present self togeth-er work loose and give way, for some reason unknown to us, and the wild beasts and prehistoric animals that inhabit us are unleashed" (Sabato 1981, 253).

The narrator experiences this when his self explodes and the world of an older brain irrupts into the world of the social self. Literature does not aim at describing what appears, but rather the magma of forces that sus-tains and keeps together what appears. Writers have to take the risk of making that trip underneath, below the surface of the social self, and con-fronting the fissure between the present social self and "the screws and bits of wire" that hold it together. The narrator goes on to say,

> This has happened to me very often, as though I were a region
> devastated by an earthquake, with great yawning fissures opening
> up and the telephone wires down. And in such instances, anything

may happen: there is no police force, no army. Any and every sort of calamity may occur, any and every sort of pillage and plundering, any and every sort of depredation. As though my body belonged to another, and I, mute and powerless, were observing the birth of suspect movements, of tremors presaging a new convulsion in this alien territory, until little by little catastrophe takes possession of my body and, finally, of my mind.

I set all this down so that my readers may understand me.

And also because many of the episodes that I shall recount would otherwise be incomprehensible and unbelievable. But it so happens that for the most part it was because of this catastrophic slip in my personality that they came about; not despite it, but because of it. (Sabato 1981, 253–54)

The story originates from a split in the personality of the narrator. He tells the story after a catastrophic split in his personality takes possession of his mind. The episodes he narrates came about, he tells us, not despite the split in personality but because of it. It is the splitting of personality, normally a mental disease, that causes the narration of the story. At the same time that the narrator gives up his role of narrator by telling us that it is all untrue; at the very moment the character Vidal gives up being a narrator, because he himself doubts the truth of what he said, the narrator becomes a writer.

From that moment on I am unable to distinguish between what actually happened to me and what I dreamed or what they [the blind] made me dream, to the point that I am no longer certain of anything, not even of what I think happened in the years and even the days immediately preceding this, so that today I would even doubt that the entire Iglesias episode ever took place, except that I know for certain that he lost his eyesight in an accident that I myself witnessed. But everything else that happened after this accident I remember with that feverish clarity and intensity that events have in a long and horrendous nightmare; the pension on the Calle Paso, Señora Etchepareborda, the man from the electric company, the emissary who looked like Pierre Fresnay, entering the apartment in Belgrano, the Blind Woman, being trapped in that room waiting for the verdict. (Sabato 1981, 357–58)

The episodes mentioned are the key events of the story. The "entire Iglesias episode" is the starting point of Vidal's investigation: Vidal befriends him in order to watch how Iglesias will be approached by the blind and become a member of the sect. Now unable to distinguish what happened from what was dreamed, Vidal is only certain that Iglesias lost his eyesight in an accident and remembers the episode that followed like fragments of a nightmare. If, however, the entire Iglesias episode did not happen in the story just told, nothing happened, since the episode following the accident was the starting point. But, again, at the moment the narrator as a character is telling us that his true story does not correspond to events that took place, the narrator as a writer describes how he creates, and he creates out of what does not exist as such in the real world. At the end of the story, when the story cancels its own existence as a story, because the narrator doubts everything narrated, the narrator in so doing describes the very act of writing.

On the last page of the report, Vidal wakes up in his room, the same room in which he was at the beginning of the story. He is, he says, "as blind and deaf as a man rising from the depths of the sea" and he "emerged into everyday reality once again," speaking of a "frenetic magic spell":

> The nightmare of the apartment in Belgrano has ended. I do not know how it is that I am free, here in my own room; no one (it would seem) is keeping watch on me. The Sect must be immeasurably far away.
>
> How did I arrive back home again? How did the blind let me out of that room in the center of a labyrinth? I do not know. But I do know that all of that happened, exactly as I have recounted it. Including—most importantly—that last dark day. (Sabato 1981, 374)

The narrator ends the report by saying,

> I therefore end my Report here, and shall hide it in a place where the Sect cannot find it.
>
> It is midnight. I am going there now.
>
> I know that it will be waiting for me. (Sabato 1981, 375)

Although the narration, when nearing its end, erases its own material and lets the fiction unravel, canceling its own fictitious reference, the narrator still makes a claim to truth: "I do know that all of that happened." He has just told us that all that was the fruit of his split in personality, that he is not sure whether it was real. The split in personality is that split when a real person as a writer takes part in a representation and becomes a narrator who is a character of the novel. The narrator as a character can only make pretended claims to truth, so that the story is coherent and interesting. Our character Vidal does not even bother to do that. He himself doubts that all that really happened. But the writer, a hero in reverse, Sabato tells us, a writer who has to tell the truth and who speaks through the narrator, can make such a claim: "I do know that all of that happened." "All of that" did not happen in the narrative but is the product of the claim to rightness made by the writer: to tell a story that fits the pragmatic situation, a story that is appropriate, a story that speaks to people. And people can connect to that claim, because they themselves make such claims when they speak in the normal situation of discourse

When we read, we cannot just read the words. We make out sentences, and we understand those sentences as expressions of intentional states. Sabato's novel presents us with a series of sentences that call for being understood as an allegory: the blind and their behaviors as a political power, as a religious empire, as a psychological theater, or as the drama of writing. We read the sentences and construe intentional states that make the set of sentences coherent. We thus let a world take shape, generated by those intentional states: we see what is happening in the tunnels, we are frightened when Vidal is locked in the room with the blind woman. Once we are in this world and see how it works, we can make connections with our world and see in our world what we did not see before, or we may wish that some aspects of our life were different. Sabato, however, tells us that it is our responsibility to see whatever we want in the novel. He writes the sentences, and we construe the intentional states with the world connected to them. He is not telling the truth about the world we construe, since it is a construct. He intends those sentences, though, with their possibilities for being construed as we do.

Since the novel does not claim to refer to anything real, does not even try to make us believe in a reality of the narrative, it would seem that there would be no cause for a dictatorial regime to be alarmed if this novel is published and disseminated. What could be and what was the cause of alarm is that someone wrote it with the possibility of being interpreted as presented here and that someone will read it with the intention of finding out what is meant, thereby construing intentional states and a world connected to them. The publication of the novel stirred some emotions, Sabato said. He claims that he does not know what the parable of the blind stands for, but it was quite easy for readers at the time to see how Sabato referred indirectly to the undemocratic situation in Argentina. From the point of view of such regimes, it is not right to write such stories, because the story by Sabato unmasks the mechanisms used by dictatorial regimes to modify, sterilize, or even suspend the rules of the normal situation of discourse.

Not only can fiction make visible the mechanisms for thwarting and impeding the normal situation of discourse, it can also thereby reawaken a political consciousness among readers who can say, reading the novel, "It is so true." When readers say that, they do not mean that they have recognized what the fiction refers to—the story here is not even clear to Sabato himself. What readers mean by saying that it is true is that the novel is right, that it touches on something in their world. This fiction by Sabato might then remind readers that they give their assent (and can then withdraw it) to publicly available intentional states, for example, those that are permissible in a dictatorship. This might impel readers to assent to other intentional states, those that are not permissible, in order to question how and at what human cost power is exercised. Readers could then try to lay claim to the situation of discourse, attempting, as Sabato did in some of his nonfiction writings, to defend freedom of speech, basic human rights, or economic justice. The truth that writers ought to tell consists in giving readers those resources that will help them configure a world they deem hospitable. What Sabato calls a claim to truth is what I call a claim to rightness: agreeing to link one's own act, in this case writing fiction, to the normative realm of human interactions and fulfilling one's commitment.

What Sabato has shown, albeit indirectly, is that the normal situation of discourse is itself submitted to conventions, what Searle denies. The claims made in any speech act are submitted to the assent speakers give to these values of truth, truthfulness, and so forth. It is because speakers find what is said right that the normal situation of discourse is normal. The claim to rightness, however, points to nonlinguistic conventions at the core of the implicit or explicit beliefs that speakers have regarding their community, its well-being, and its future. While fiction is indeed not real in relation to the normal situation of discourse as accepted and is a set of "as if" speech acts, fiction is also part of the discourses available in the community and can offer threats or resources to the conventions that lead to the acceptance of any normality. As a performance—an act of writing and publishing—

fiction also makes a claim to rightness and, as an act, locks onto the conversation that takes place in the community and is part of the normal situation of discourse. In a moment of instability in language—for example, under a dictatorship or in times of cultural crisis—phrases are tentatively and inchoately tried and do not succeed in connecting with the established situation of discourse. In these moments of instability, literary fictions can be the laboratory where phrases are tried out and where themes are played out through characters made of paper. Through the treatment literary fiction offers of problems or situations, it can provide scenarios for making sense of what is going on or it can manufacture new uses of language that do not fall under the control of one established discourse. The act of writing is political as a commitment a person makes to serve the truth, thereby becoming part of the conscience of a nation.

If we claim validity for our interpretation of this novel, we have to support any colonization by elements of the novel's text, and we can only correlate a passage of the text with a particular interpretation by providing evidence that Sabato as author could have meant that. My interpretation negotiates a agreement between the first level of meaning—Sabato's intention—the second level of meaning—what the text says—and the third level of meaning—what we take the story to tell us. Sabato himself in a way has theorized for us this necessary negotiation. As a writer he does not want to claim any privilege regarding the third level—what the novel is about—but he claims responsibility for the text as written with its potential to be understood in different ways. This is his claim to truth in writing fictions. I call it a claim to rightness. And the same claim to rightness falls upon interpreters. The negotiation we perform of the text and its levels of meaning is regulated not by accuracy or meaningfulness alone but also by rightness. And this claim, like the claim to truth for writers, allows for a discussion of the validity of what is presented in the public sphere: in what sense does this text or this interpretation serve the common good?

7

Navigation and Negotiation

ᔥ

Interpreting a text is not so much a straightforward process of construing or retrieving the meaning of a text as it is a negotiation interpreters lead with a text that offers several ways to be approached as well as to resist. The different examples of practices examined here indicate that a text does not directly present itself as a set of clearly identifiable units of meaning that are waiting to be interpreted. There is thus no direct correspondence between components of the text and interpretive constructions. Interpretation itself can decide what to take as its object. Instead of being neatly framed by a hospitable text, interpretation has to invade the text and map it by attaching to it at the edges, usually its beginning and end. The rest is a process of navigation where nearly everything has to be negotiated. The process, however, is not blind and random. There are tools of navigation and clear objects of negotiation. The tools are the claims made by interpreters at the moment they state their interpretation and are necessary if they desire public recognition for their interpretation. If interpreters want more than just to enjoy a text or muse about it, they are bound to justify the different decisions they make when interpreting.

There are three main areas of negotiation where decisions have to be made, what I call three levels of meaning: (1) the author's intention—what someone meant by writing the text to be interpreted, (2) the literal meaning—what the text says given the individual meanings of words and the composed meaning of sentences, and (3) the representative content—what the text as a whole means, in the sense of what it represents. Interpreters can choose to focus on one of these levels of meaning and downplay or even ignore the others, or they can attempt to do justice to them all. The wide range of what interpreters can do with a text is only limited by the claims they implicitly make to be intelligible, to tell the truth, to be truthful, and to be right.

Because the content of claims can change, they do not offer a definitive way to assess the validity of what a particular interpreter says about a particular feature of a text. What they guarantee is that the interpretation remains bound to the text, mapping it, instead of roaming aimlessly between the margins. The metaphor of navigation aptly helps us visualize what interpretation can and cannot be: it cannot be a univocal and exhaustive rendering of the components of a text, as if there were only one way to reach a destination, but it can achieve a negotiation of selected aspects of a text as it chooses one of many routes and maneuvers around the obstacles along the way.

Because any object of interpretation can be stipulated according to the interest or qualification of the interpreter, the idea of a univocal and all-encompassing interpretation of a text is a theoretical fabrication. The existence of three main levels of meaning renders irrelevant an expression such as "the meaning of this text is this and that." Such an expression presents itself as a definite description, as if it were true that there is an entity that can be the meaning of a text; in reality it can be the meaning intended by the author, the meaning of what the words and sentences say, or the meaning of what the text represents, with all the possible candidates for each of these levels. It is thus not of decisive value to differentiate elaborative interpretations from elucidative interpretations, as Novitz does (2002), or meaning interpretation from relational interpretations, as Gracia suggests (2000). While the general distinction is quite pertinent and has been around for a long time—Schleiermacher (1977) is a thoughtful and reputable predecessor—the difficulty begins when we try to identify them: how can we isolate an elucidation of a passage from what we see in this passage once we elaborate it, as Novitz believes we can? Or how can we identify an interpretation that bears on the meaning of the text without that meaning being in some way related to a framework, as Gracia claims is possible? Gregory the Great shows that the cooperation between text and reader renders those distinctions relative. What is literal must be preunderstood as bearing that capacity for being literal. We need to know what can be done with it (what we can elaborate or to what we can relate it) to see it as literal. As to the question of the difference between elucidative-meaning interpretation and elaborative-relational interpretation, the unfortunate answer is, "It depends."

But it depends on something. The metaphors of navigation and negotiation indicate that there is always a goal in sight and rules to abide by, so that the give and take of a negotiation does not yield arbitrariness. Although the decisions made at each level of meaning (author's intention, literal meaning, representative content) disseminate the process of interpretation, the claims made by interpreters unify the process of interpretation. The dissemination only affects the content of the interpretation, not the process of justification. Interpreters have to be ready to redeem the claims they implicitly make when focusing on this aspect of the text rather than that other aspect, or this method to the exclusion of others. The effect of the claim to rightness is that ultimately interpreters are committed to the good of the community. This commitment ensures that the line of defense against arbitrariness is fairly strong and forces interpreters to justify the hermeneutic decisions they make if they claim validity for their interpretation. These claims must be made in different discourses, not just academic or artistic. Interpreters act as virtual citizens of an unlimited community.

While the existence of three levels of meaning where hermeneutic decisions can be made and the liberty of interpreters to stipulate the object of their interpretation as they see fit lend support to critical pluralism, the claims interpreters have to redeem, if prompted, bring the pendulum back toward a form of monism. However, what matters is not choosing between pluralism and monism. What matters is recognizing their purview. Interpretation is both an act and an event, but not from the same perspective. To the event belongs the wide range of possible hermeneutic decisions, and to the act belongs the firm requirement to redeem the claims made. There is a clear partition between the first-person perspective—that of an interpreter facing the puzzles offered by a text—and the third-person perspective—that of theoreticians of interpretation reflecting on what happens when interpretations are made. Pluralists focus mostly on the latter and tend to identify this third-person perspective with what interpretation in fact is. By doing so, they commit the future-perfect fallacy. They qualify the interpretation taking place from a future perspective the interpreter cannot have, when it will have been shown that the interpreter, at the time of interpretation, was influenced by values, habits, and interests specific to his community of interpreters—and which do not pertain to the text. Monists, on the other hand, tend to focus on the first-person perspective without considering the range of hermeneutic decisions that have to be made and thus believe that one level of meaning is sufficient for ascertaining what a text means.

Besides the advantage of not having to choose between the two faulty positions of monism and pluralism, a view of interpretation as negotiation offers an explanation for the problems at the three levels of meaning in a text. Regarding the first level—what is meant—we can understand how, for example, translators negotiate a text in order to remain truthful to two masters, the original voice of the author and the ear of the audience. Translators start with what the text means to them—given their ear—but claim to render the first voice, so that their own voice presents itself as a place holder for the author's voice. This dual voice creates the harmony of the translation, as it maps the text, covering it at the edges, while at the same time negotiating individual problems of meaning.

Regarding the second level—what the text says at its minimal level— interpreters identify such a meaning by applying it against a background. What prevents the meaning from changing in its different applications—a point Gadamer overlooks—is its constant link to a background, so that the meaning found is always a meaning that has to be justified. Interpreters again negotiate a literal meaning against a particular background they happen to have or they adopt, but the negotiation is precisely the process that allows others to see how the literal meaning is relative to the background chosen. This enables others to enter the discussion, to object or to offer alternatives. Negotiation, as in the case of Gregory the Great, indicates that literal meaning and background cannot be identified in their self-identity and related to each other. We start from within—we navigate—so that literal meaning and background are themselves the result of an interpretive process. What matters is to make clear the rules followed in the negotiation and the goal the interpretation attempts to achieve.

Finally, regarding the third level of meaning—the representative content—interpretation as negotiation allows us to recognize the power writers have, especially writers of fiction, to contribute to the shaping of the public sphere. This effect of literature in general could also be recognized by monism and pluralism. In the case of monism, we would have to state that the writer intended to use her fiction, which already means something, with a particular end in mind. And in the case of pluralism, whatever the writer intended would become irrelevant: the text itself, sustained by readers, would be granted this power. But we are able to ascribe to writers of fiction both the power to shape or reshape the public sphere and the right to claim that it is their fictions that perform this. As in the work of Grass and Sabato, fiction accomplishes this task as a set of narratives readers apply under their responsibility or a set of intentional states readers construe in colonizing the text.

To understand interpretation as a negotiation allows an interpreter to remain lucid about other possible manners of identifying the levels of meaning and adjudicating their importance. After all, interpretation is an event taking place in the partly uncharted territory where we have to start. Negotiation also means that interpretation is an act, making interpreters committed to be good-faith partners in the discussion. Given their decisions about the different levels of meaning and the goal they pursue, their interpretation is the best they can think of, and they are ready to justify it in an ongoing conversation. While the goal of the discussion will not be to arrive at a factual final agreement—everything can be renegotiated—the effect is a strengthening of the community. A community becomes stronger not only and not essentially in the enrichment provided by new interpretations—for interpretations can be disastrous for a community too, as Grass reminds us—but in the community's capacity to scrutinize new interpretations. The community becomes a stronger critical community. If, as Sabato claims, the duty of a writer is to tell the truth, the duty of an interpreter is to negotiate in good faith the interests of his threefold allegiance: the demands of an original intent in the text, the constraints of the literal meaning of the text, and the indeterminacy, sometimes invited by the text, of the representative content.

Works Cited

Apel, Karl-Otto. 1976. "Sprechakttheorie und transzendentale Sprachpragmatik zur Frage ethischer Normen." In *Sprachpragmatik und Philosophie*, ed. Karl-Otto Apel, 10–173. Frankfurt: Suhrkamp.

———. 1980. "Zwei paradigmatischen Antworten auf die Frage nach der Logos-Auszeichnung der menschlichen Sprache." In *Kulturwissenschaften. Festgabe für Wilhelm Perpeet zum 65. Geburtstag*, ed. H. Luetzeler, G. Pfafferott, and E. Strohmaier, 13–68. Bonn: Bouvier.

———. 1988. *Diskurs und Verantwortung. Das Problem des Übergangs zur postkonventionellen Moral*. Frankfurt: Suhrkamp.

———. 1994. *Selected Essays*. Vol. 1, *Towards a Transcendental Semiotics*. Ed. E. Mendieta. Atlantic Highlands, NJ: Humanities Press.

———. 1996. *Selected Essays*. Vol. 2, *Ethics and Theory of Rationality*. Ed. E. Mendieta. Atlantic Highlands, NJ: Humanities Press.

———. 1998. "Regulative Ideas or Truth Happening? An Attempt to Answer the Question of the Conditions of the Possibility of Valid Understanding." In *From a Transcendental Semiotic Point of View*, ed. M. Papastephanou, trans. R. Sommermeier, 183–215. Manchester, UK: Manchester University Press.

Aristotle. 1927. *Poetics*. Trans. W. Fyfe. New York: G. P. Putnam's Sons.

Augustine. 1894. *De Genesi ad litteram libri duodecim*. Corpus Christianorum Series Latina 28.1. Vienna: Tempsky.

———. 1962. *De Doctrina Christiana*. Corpus Christianorum Series Latina 32. Turnhout, Belgium: Brepols.

Austin, J. L. 1962. *How to Do Things with Words*. Cambridge, MA: Harvard University Press.

Les auteurs grecs expliqués d'après une méthode nouvelle par deux traductions françaises. 1855. Paris: Hachette.

Balzac, Honoré de. 1970. *Sarrasine*. In Barthes 1970, 227–58.

———. *Eugénie Grandet*. 1976. In *La comédie humaine*. Bibliothèque de la Pléiade. Paris: Gallimard.

Banniard, Michel. 1986. "Luxta uniuscuiusque qualitatem. L'écriture médiatrice chez Grégoire le Grand." In *Grégoire le Grand. Colloques Internationaux du CNRS*. Paris: CNRS.

Barbin, Claude, trans. 1682. *L'Odyssée d'Homère. Nouvelle traduction*. Paris: Claude Barbin.

Bareste, Eugène, trans. 1842. *L'Odyssée*. Paris: Lavigne.

Barnes, Annette. 1988. *On Interpretation: A Critical Analysis*. Oxford: Blackwell.

Barthes, Roland. 1970. *S/Z*. Paris: Éditions du Seuil.

———. 2002. "The Death of the Author." In Irwin 2002, 3–7.

Bassnett, Susan. 1991. *Translation Studies*. London: Routledge.

———. 1993. *Comparative Literature: A Critical Introduction*. Cambridge: Blackwell.

Beardsley, Monroe. 1992. "The Authority of the Text." In Iseminger 1992, 24–40.

Benjamin, Walter. 1968. "The Task of the Translator." In *Illuminations*, trans. R. Zohn, 69–82. New York: Harcourt, Brace, and World.

Bérard, Victor, trans. 1972. *L'Odyssée*. Paris: Armand Colin.

Bitaubé, Paul-Jérémie, trans. 1883. *L'Odyssée*. Paris: Librairie de la Bibliothèque Nationale.

Booth, Wayne. 1961. *Rhetoric of Fiction*. Chicago: University of Chicago Press.

Bori, Pier Cesare. 1987. *L'interpretazione infinita. L'ermeneutica cristiana antica e le sue trasformazioni*. Bologna: Il Mulino.

Bourdieu, Pierre. 1977. *Outline of a Theory of Practice*, trans. R. Nice. Cambridge: Cambridge University Press.

Bryant, William Cullen. 1871. *Odyssey of Homer. Translated into English Blank Verse*. New York: Houghton Mifflin.

Buckley, Theodore Alois. 1851. *Odyssey of Homer Literally Translated*. London: Henry Bohn.

Bühler, Karl. 1965 (originally published 1934). *Sprachtheorie. Die Darstellungsfunktion der Sprache*. Stuttgart: Gustav Fischer.

Burkhardt, Armin. 1990. "Speech Act Theory—The Decline of a Paradigm." In *Speech Acts, Meaning and Intentions. Critical Approaches to the Philosophy of John Searle*, ed. Armin Burkhardt, 91–128. Berlin: Walter de Gruyter.

Butcher, S. H., and L. A. Lang. 1937. *The Odyssey of Homer*. New York: Collier.

Butler, Samuel. 1900. *The Odyssey, Rendered into English for the Use of Those Who Cannot Read the Original*. London: Longmans, Green.

Cabassut, André. 1960. "Discrétion." In *Dictionnaire de spiritualité. Ascétique et mystique. Doctrine et histoire*, 3:1311–30. Paris: Beauchesne.

Carroll, Noël. 1992. "Art, Intention, and Conversation." In Iseminger 1992, 97–131.

———. 2000. "Interpretation and Intention: The Debate between Hypothetical and Actual Intentionalism." *Metaphilosophy* 31:75–95.

———. 2002. "Andy Kaufman and the Philosophy of Interpretation." In Krausz 2002a, 319–44.

Carruthers, Peter. 1996. *Language, Thought and Consciousness. An Essay in Philosophical Psychology*. Cambridge: Cambridge University Press.

Catania, Carlos. 1973. "Sabato informa sobre ciegos." In *Homenaje a Ernesto Sabato*, ed. H. Giacoman, 231–57. New York: L.A. Publishing.

Chapman, George. 1956. *Chapman's Homer, the "Iliad," the "Odyssey" and the "Lesser Homerica."* Ed. A. Nicoll. Vol. 2. New York: Bollingen Foundation.

Chomsky, Noam. 1975. *The Logical Structure of Linguistic Theory.* New York: Plenum.

———. 2001. "Language and Problems of Knowledge." In *The Philosophy of Language,* ed. A. Martinich, 581–99. New York: Oxford University Press.

Clark, Francis. 1998. "Authorship of the Commentary *In I Regum*: Implications of A. de Vogüé's Discovery." *Revue Bénédictine* 108:66.

Coddou, Marcelo. 1973. "La teoría del ser nacional argentino en *Sobre héroes y tumbas.*" In *Homenaje a Ernesto Sabato,* ed. H. Giacoman, 105–26. New York: L.A. Publishing.

Constenla, Julia. 1997. *Sabato, el hombre. Una biografía.* Buenos Aires: Seix Barral.

Cotterill, H. B. 1911. *Homer's Odyssey: A Line-for-Line Translation in the Metre of the Original.* London: George Harrap.

Cowper, William, trans. 1910. *The Odyssey of Homer.* London: Dent and Sons; New York: E. P. Dutton.

Cummings, E. E. 1994. *Selected Poems.* New York: Liveright.

Dacier, Madame. 1815. *L'Odissée d'Homère. Nouvelle édition.* Paris: Delaunay.

Dagens, Claude. 1977. *Saint Grégoire. Culture et expérience chrétiennes.* Paris: Études Augustiniennes.

Dahan, Gilbert. 1999. *L'exégèse chrétienne de la Bible en Occident médiéval.* Paris: Éditions du Cerf.

Davidson, Donald. 1980. "The Material Mind." In *Essays on Action and Events,* 245–60. Oxford: Clarendon.

———. 1984. *Inquiries into Truth and Interpretation.* Oxford: Clarendon.

———. 2001. "Truth and Meaning." In A. P. Martinich, *The Philosophy of Language,* 98–109. New York: Oxford University Press.

Dawe, R. D. 1993. *The Odyssey: Translation and Analysis.* Sussex: Book Guild.

Dekkers, Eloi. 1984. "*Discretio* chez Saint Benoît et Saint Grégoire." *Collectanea Cisterciensia* 46:79–88.

Delègue, Yves. 1987. *Les machines du sens. Fragments d'une sémiologie médiévale.* Paris: Éditions des Cendres.

Dellepiane, Ángela. 1973. "'Sobre héroes y tumbas': Interpretación literaria y análisis." In *Homenaje a Ernesto Sabato,* ed. H. Giacoman, 29–104. New York: L.A. Publishing.

de Lubac, Henri. 1959. *Exégèse médiévale.* Vol. 1–2. Paris: Aubier.

———. 1993. "Typologie et 'allégorisme.'" In *Studies in Early Christianity,* ed. E. Ferguson, 224–70. New York: Garland.

de Man, Paul. 1983. *Blindness and Insight: Essays in the Rhetoric of Contemporary Criticism.* Minneapolis: University of Minnesota Press.

———. 1986. "'Conclusions': Walter Benjamin's 'The Task of the Translator.'" In *The Resistance to Theory,* 73–105. Minneapolis: University of Minnesota Press.

Derrida, Jacques. 1967a. *De la grammatologie.* Paris: Éditions de Minuit.

———. 1967b. *L'écriture et la différence.* Paris: Éditions du Seuil.

———. 1972. *Marges de la philosophie.* Paris: Éditions Galilée.

————. 1987. "Des tours de Babel." In *Psyché: Inventions de l'autre*, 203–35. Paris: Éditions Galilée.

de Vogüé, Adalbert, trans. 1989. Introd. to *Commentaire sur le premier livre des Rois*, by Gregory the Great. Sources Chrétiennes, 1:18–136. Paris: Éditions du Cerf.

————. 1996. "L'auteur du commentaire des rois attribué à Saint Grégoire: un moine de Cava?" *Revue Bénédictine* 106:319–31.

de Vrégille, Bernard. 1967. "Écriture sainte et vie spirituelle." In *Dictionnaire de spiritualité*, 4:169–76.

Dilthey, Wilhelm. 1924. *Die geistige Welt. Gesammelte Schriften*, vol. 5–60. Ed. V. G. Misch. Leipzig and Berlin: B. G. Teubner.

Dolto, Françoise. 1977. *L'Évangile au risque de la psychanalyse*. Paris: Éditions Universitaires.

Donner, Johann Jacob Christian, trans. 1858. *Homers Odyssee*. Stuttgart: Hoffmann'sche.

Dufour, Médéric, and Jeanne Raison, trans. 1965. *L'Odyssée*. Paris: Garnier Flammarion.

Dugas-Montbel, Jean-Baptiste, trans. 1870. *Odyssée et Poèmes Homériques*. 3rd ed. Paris: Firmin Didot.

Ebener, Dietrich, trans. 1983. *Homer, Werke in zwei Bänden*. Vol. 2. Berlin: Aufbauverlag.

Eco, Umberto. 1979. *Lector in fabula*. Milan: Bompiani.

Escarpit, R. 1970. *Le littéraire et le social. Eléments pour une sociologie de la littérature*. Paris: Flammarion.

————. 1973. "Littérature." In *Dictionnaire international des termes littéraires*, 47–53. Paris-La Haye: Mouton.

Fagles, Robert, trans. 1996. *The Odyssey*. New York: Penguin Books.

Figal, Günter. 1996. *Der Sinn des Verstehens*. Stuttgart: Philipp Reclam.

Fish, Stanley. 1980. *Is There a Text in This Class? The Authority of Interpretive Communities*. Cambridge, MA: Harvard University Press.

Fitzgerald, Robert, trans. 1961. *Homer: The Odyssey*. New York: Doubleday.

Flaubert, Gustave. 1971. *Madame Bovary*. Paris: Garnier.

Foucault, Michel. 1969. *L'archéologie du savoir*. Paris: Gallimard.

————. 1970. *The Order of Things. An Archaeology of the Human Sciences*. New York: Vintage Books.

————. 2002. "What Is an Author?" In Irwin 2002, 9–22.

Frege, Gottlob. 2001. "On Sense and Nominatum." In *The Philosophy of Language*, ed. A. Martinich, 199–211. New York: Oxford University Press.

Gadamer, Hans-Georg. 1960. *Wahrheit und Methode*. Tübingen: Mohr.

————. 1965. "Hermeneutics and Historicism." In Gadamer 1998, 505–41.

————. 1998. *Truth and Method*. 2nd ed. New York: Continuum.

————. 1999. "Rhétorique, herméneutique et critique de l'idéologie. In *Herméneutique et philosophie*, 83–108. Paris: Beauchesne.

Giguet, P., trans. 1880. *Oeuvres complètes d'Homère*. Paris: Hachette.

Gillet, Dom Robert. 1975. Introd. to *Morales sur Job*, by Grégoire le Grand, trans. A. de Gaudemaris, 7–109. Paris: Éditions du Cerf.

Gracia, Jorge. 2000. "Relativism and the Interpretation of Texts." *Metaphilosophy* 31:43–62.

———. 2001. *How Can We Know What God Knows? The Interpretation of Revelation.* New York: Palgrave.

———. 2002. "A Theory of the Author." In Irwin 2002, 161–89.

Grass, Günter. 1962. *The Tin Drum.* Trans. R. Manheim. New York: Pantheon Books.

———. 1963. *Cat and Mouse.* Trans. R. Mannheim. New York: Harcourt, Brace, and World.

———. 1965. *Dog Years.* Trans. R. Manheim. New York: Harcourt, Brace, and World.

———. 1991. "Der vitale und vulgäre Wunsch, Künstler zu werden." In *Die 'Danziger Trilogie' von Günter Grass. Texte, Daten, Bilder,* ed. V. Neuhaus and D. Hermes, 11–33. Frankfurt: Luchterhand.

Gregory the Great. 1849. *Homiliae in Evangelium.* Patrologia Latina 76, ed. Jacques-Paul Migne. Paris: Garnier.

———. 1963a. *Canticum canticorum.* Corpus Christianorum. Series Latina 144. Turnhout, Belgium: Brepols.

———. 1963b. *Librum primum Regum expositionum libri vi.* Corpus Christianorum Series Latina 144. Turnhout, Belgium: Brepols.

———. 1971. *Homiliae in Hiezechihelem prophetam.* Corpus Christianorum Series Latina 142 Turnhout, Belgium: Brepols. English translation: *The Homilies of Saint Gregory the Great on the Book of the Prophet Ezekiel.* 1990. Ed. Juliana Cownie, trans. Theodosia Gray. Etna, CA: Center for Traditionalist Orthodox Studies.

———. 1979. *Moralia in Iob.* Corpus Christianorum Series Latina 143, 143A, 143B. Turnhout, Belgium: Brepols, 1979. English translation: *Morals on the Book of Job.* 1844–50. Oxford: J. H. Parker.

———. 1982. *Magni Registrum Epistularum.* Corpus Christianorum Series Latina 140. Turnhout, Belgium: Brepols.

Grice, H. P. 2001. "Logic and Conversation." In *The Philosophy of Language,* ed. A. P. Martinich, 165–75. New York: Oxford University Press.

Guignon, Charles. 2002. "Truth in Interpretation: A Hermeneutic Approach." In Krausz 2002a, 264–84.

Guillén, Claudio. 1993. *The Challenge of Comparative Literature.* Trans. C. Franzen. Cambridge, MA: Harvard University Press.

Habermas, Jürgen, ed. 1977. *Hermeneutik und Ideologiekritik.* Frankfurt: Suhrkamp.

———. 1984. *The Theory of Communicative Action. Reason and the Rationalization of Society.* Trans. T. McCarthy. Vol. 1. Boston: Beacon.

Hagen, Kenneth. 1985. "The History of the Scripture in the Church." In *The Bible in the Churches: How Different Christians Interpret the Scriptures,* ed. K. Hagen, 3–34. New York: Paulist Press.

Hammond, Martin, trans. 2000. *Homer, The Odyssey.* London: Duckworth.

Hampe, Roland, trans. 1979. *Homer, Odyssee.* Stuttgart: Philipp Reclam.

Hegel, G. W. F. 1970. *Phänomenologie des Geistes*. Frankfurt: Suhrkamp.

Heidegger, Martin. 1950. "Der Ursprung des Kunstwerkes." In *Holzwege*, 1–72. Frankfurt: Klostermann.

———. 1959a. *Unterwegs zur Sprache*. Pfullingen, Germany: Neske.

———. 1959b. *An Introduction to Metaphysics*. Trans. R. Mannheim. New Haven, CT: Yale University Press.

———. 1962. *Being and Time*. Trans. J. Macquarrie and E. Robinson. New York: Harper and Row.

———. 1976. "Was ist Metaphysik?" In *Wegmarken*, ed. F.-W. Von Herrmann, 103–21. Frankfurt: Klostermann.

———. 1984. *Sein und Zeit*. 15th ed. Tübingen: Niemeyer.

———. 1989. *Beiträge zur Philosophie. Vom Ereignis*. Gesamtausgabe 65. Frankfurt: Klostermann.

Hirsch, E. D. 1967. *Validity in Interpretation*. New Haven, CT: Yale University Press.

———. 1976. *The Aims of Interpretation*. Chicago: University Press of Chicago.

Hogan, Patrick Colm. 1996. *On Interpretation. Meaning and Inference in Law, Psychoanalysis, and Literature*. Athens: University of Georgia Press.

Hugh of Saint-Victor. 1879. *De scripturis et scriptoribus praenotatiunculae*. Patrologia Latina 175, ed. Jacques-Paul Migne. Paris: Garnier.

———. 1880. *Eruditionis didascalicae libri septem*. Patrologia Latina 176, ed. Jacques-Paul Migne. Paris: Garnier.

Humboldt, Wilhelm von. 1963. *Schriften zur Sprachphilosophie*. Darmstadt: Wissenschaftliche Buchgesellschaft.

———. 1979. "Über die Verschiedenheit des menschlichen Sprachbaues und ihren Einfluss auf die geistige Entwicklung des menschengeschlechts." In *Werke*, Band 3 *Schriften zur Sprachphilosophie*, ed. A. Flitner and K. Giel, 368–756. Stuttgart: Cotta.

Husserl, Edmund. 1913. *Logische Untersuchungen*. Halle: Max Niemeyer.

———. 1970. *The Crisis of European Sciences and Transcendental Philosophy. An Introduction to Phenomenological Philosophy*. Trans. D. Carr. Evanston, IL: Northwestern University Press.

———. 1991. *Cartesian Meditations*. Trans. D. Carr. Dordrecht: Kluwer.

Irwin, William. 1999. *Intentionalist Interpretation. A Philosophical Explanation and Defense*. Westport, CT: Greenwood.

———, ed. 2002. *The Death and Resurrection of the Author*. Westport, CT: Greenwood.

Iseminger, Gary, ed. 1992. *Intention and Interpretation*. Philadelphia: Temple University Press.

Iser, Wolfgang. 1976. *Der Akt des Lesens. Theorie ästhetischer Wirkung*. Uni-Taschenbücher, 636: Literaturwissenschaft. Munich: Fink.

———. 2000. *The Range of Interpretation*. New York: Columbia University Press.

Jaccottet, Philippe, trans. 1982. *Homère, L'Odyssée*. Paris: François Maspéro.

Jakobson, Roman. 1959. "On Linguistic Aspects of Translation." In *On Translation*, ed. R. Brower, 232–39. Cambridge, MA: Harvard University Press.

James, Henry. 1983. *The Portrait of a Lady*. London: Dent. (Orig. pub. 1881.)

Juhl, P. D. 1980. *Interpretation. An Essay in the Philosophy of Literary Criticism*. Princeton, NJ: Princeton University Press.

Jünger, Friedrich Georg, trans. 1979. *Homers Odyssee*. Stuttgart: Ernst Klett.

Kayser, Wolfgang. 1992. *Das sprachliche Kunstwerk. Eine Einführung in die Literaturwissenschaft*. 20th ed. Tübingen and Basel: Francke.

Kessler, Stephan. 1995. *Gregor der Grosse als Exeget. Eine theologische Interpretation der Ezechielhomilien*. Innsbruck: Tyrolia.

Kleinknecht, Hermann. 1958. "Platonisches im Homer. Eine Interpretation von Odyssee XIII 187–354." *Gymnasium* 61:59–75.

Knapp, Steven, and Walter Michaels. 1992. "The Impossibility of Intentionless Meaning." In Iseminger 1992, 51–64.

Knox, Bernard. 1996. Introd. to *The Odyssey*, by Homer, trans. R. Fagles, 3–64. New York: Penguin.

Krausz, Michael. 1992. "Intention and Interpretation: Hirsch and Margolis." In Iseminger 1992, 152–66.

———. 2002a. "Interpretation and its Objects" In Krausz 2002b, 122–44.

———, ed. 2002b. *Is There a Single Right Interpretation?* University Park: Pennsylvania State University Press.

Kristeva, Julia. 1986. "Le mot, le dialogue et le roman." In *The Kristeva Reader*, ed. Toril Moi, 30–61. Oxford: Blackwell.

Lacoue-Labarthe, P., and J. L. Nancy. 1978. *L'absolu littéraire. Théorie de la littérature dans le romantisme allemand*. Paris: Éditions du Seuil. English translation: *The Literary Absolute*. Trans. P. Barnoud and C. Lester. Albany: State University of New York Press, 1988.

Lamarque, Peter. 2002. "The Death of the Author: An Analytical Autopsy." In Irwin 2002, 79–91.

Lattimore, Richard, trans. 1965. *The Odyssey of Homer*. New York: Harper and Row.

Lawrence, T. E., trans. 1991. *The Odyssey of Homer. Newly Translated into English Prose*. New York: Oxford University Press. (Orig. pub. 1932.)

Leconte de Lisle, Charles Marie, trans. 1923. *Odyssée. Traduction d'Homère*. Paris: Alphonse Lemerre.

Lefevere, André. 1975. *Translating Poetry. Seven Strategies and a Blueprint*. Assen, Netherlands: van Gorcum.

———. 1982. "Théorie littéraire et littérature traduite." *Canadian Review of Comparative Literature* 9:137–56.

———. 1992. *Translating Literature. Practice and Theory in a Comparative Literature Context*. New York: Modern Language Association of America.

Levinson. Jerrold. 1992. "Interpretation and Intention: A Last Look." In Iseminger 1992, 221–56.

Lévi-Strauss, Claude. 1967. *Les structures élémentaires de la parenté*. Paris: Mouton.

Lohmann, Johannes. 1960. "Über den paradigmatischen Charakter der sprachlichen

Kultur." In *Die Gegenwart der Griechen im neureren Denken. Festschrift für Hans-Georg Gadamer zum 60. Geburtstag*, 171–87. Tübingen: Mohr.

Lombardo, Stanley, trans. 2000. *Homer, Odyssey*. Indianapolis, IN: Hackett.

Lyotard, Jean-François. 1979. *La condition postmoderne*. Paris: Éditions de Minuit.

———. 1988. *The Differend*. Trans. G. vanden Abbeele. Minneapolis: University of Minnesota Press.

McNally, Robert. 1959. *The Bible in the Early Middle Ages*. Westminster, UK: Newman.

Mackail, J. W., trans. 1932. *The Odyssey*. Oxford: Clarendon.

Mandelbaum, Allen, trans. 1990. *The Odyssey of Homer*. Berkeley: University of California Press.

Mann, Thomas. *Buddenbrooks. Verfall einer Familie*. 1981. Frankfurt: Fisher.

Margolis, Joseph. 1974. "Works of Art as Physically Embodied and Culturally Emergent Entities." *British Journal of Aesthetics* 14:187–96.

———. 1980. *Art and Philosophy*. Brighton, UK: Harvester.

Markus, R. A. 1996. *Signs and Meanings: World and Text in Ancient Christianity*. Liverpool: Liverpool University Press.

———. 1997. *Gregory the Great and His World*. New York: Cambridge University Press.

Merrill, Rodney, trans. 2002. Homer, *The Odyssey*. Ann Arbor: University of Michigan Press.

Meunier, Mario, trans. 1961. *Homère, L'Odyssée*. Paris: Albin Michel.

Morris, Pam. 1993. *Literature and Feminism*. Cambridge: Blackwell.

Morris, William, trans. 1904. *Odyssey of Homer Done in English Verse*. London: Longmans, Green.

Mounin, Georges. 1963. *Les problèmes théoriques de la traduction*. Paris: Gallimard.

Murray, A. T., trans. 1931. Homer, *The Odyssey*. The Loeb Classical Library. London: William Hunemann; New York: G. P. Putnam's Sons.

Nehamas, Alexander. 1981. "The Postulated Author: Critical Monism as a Regulative Idea." *Critical Inquiry* 8:133–49.

———. 1987. "Writer, Text, Work, Author." In *Literature and the Question of Philosophy*, ed. A. Cascardi, 265–91. Baltimore: John Hopkins University Press.

Nicholas of Lyra. 1879a. *De commendatione sacrae Scripturae in generali*. Patrologia Latina 113, ed. Jacques-Paul Migne. Paris: Garnier.

———. 1879b. *De intentione auctoris et modo procedendi*. Patrologia Latina 113, ed. Jacques-Paul Migne. Paris: Garnier.

Nietzsche, Friedrich. 1984. *Zur Genealogie der Moral. Eine Streitschrift. Werke III*. Frankfurt: Hullstein.

Novitz, David. 2000. "Interpretation and Justification." *Metaphilosophy* 1/2:4–24.

———. 2002. "Against Critical Pluralism." In Krausz 2002a, 101–21.

O'Loughlin, Thomas. 1998. *Teachers and Code-Breakers: The Latin Genesis Tradition, 430–800*. Instrumenta Patristica, vol. 35. Turnhout, Belgium: Brepols.

Otto, Walter. 1951. *Gesetz, Urbild und Mythos*. Stuttgart: J. B. Letzlersche.

———. 1955. *Die Gestalt und das Sein. Gesammelte Abhandlungen über den Muthos und seine Bedeutung fur die Menschheit*. Düsseldorf: E. Diedrichs.

———. 1962. *Das Wort der Antike*. Stuttgart: E. Klett.

———. 1984. *Les dieux de la Grèce. La figure du divin au miroir de l'esprit grec*. Trans. C.-M. Grimbert and A. Morgant. Paris: Payot.

Palmer, George, trans. 1921. *The Odyssey of Homer*. Boston: Houghton Mifflin.

Personneaux, Emile, trans. n.d. Homère, *L'Odyssée*. 6th ed. Paris: Charpentier.

Pettersson, Torsten. "The Literary Work as a Pliable Entity: Combining Realism and Pluralism." In Krausz 2002a, 211–30.

Pinker, Steven. 1994. *The Language Instinct*. New York: William Morrow.

Plato. 1925. *Ion*. Trans. W. Lamb. Cambridge, MA: Harvard University Press.

———. 1987. *Republic*. Trans. Paul Shorey. Cambridge, MA: Harvard University Press.

Pope, Alexander, trans. 1848. *The Odyssey of Homer*. Hartford, CT: Silas Andrus and Son.

Rapisarda Lo Menzo, Grazia. 1986. "L'Écriture sainte comme guide de la vie quotidienne dans la correspondance de Grégoire le Grand." In *Grégoire le Grand. Colloques Internationaux du CNRS*, ed. Jacques Fontaine, Robert Gillet, and Stan Pellistrandi, 215–26. Paris: CNRS.

Rees, E., trans. 1977. *The Odyssey of Homer*. Indianapolis, IN: Bobbs-Merrill.

Ricoeur, Paul. 1975. *La métaphore vive*. Paris: Éditions du Seuil.

———. 1984. *Time and Narrative*. Chicago: Chicago University Press.

———. 1986. *Du texte à l'action. Essais d'herméneutique II*. Paris: Éditions du Seuil.

———. 1990. *Soi-même comme un autre*. Paris: Éditions du Seuil.

———. 1991. "Life in Quest of Narrative." In *On Paul Ricoeur. Narrative and Interpretation*, ed. D. Wood, 20–33. New York: Routledge.

Rieu, E. V., trans. 1946. *Homer, The Odyssey*. New York: Penguin Books.

Rorty, Richard. 1998. *Truth and Progress: Philosophical Papers 3*. Cambridge: Cambridge University Press.

Rosen, Stanley. 1987. "The Limits of Interpretation." In *Literature and the Question of Philosophy*, ed. Anthony Cascardi, 210–41. Baltimore: Johns Hopkins University Press.

Ross, T. 1992. "Copyright and the Invention of Tradition." *Eighteenth Century Studies* 26:1–27.

———. 1996. "The Emergence of 'Literature.' Making and Reading the English Canon in the Eighteenth Century." *ELH* 63:397–422.

Rouse, W., trans. 1937. *The Story of Odysseus. A Translation of Homer's Odyssey into Plain English*. London: Thomas Nelson and Sons.

Sabato, Ernesto. 1950. *The Outsider*. Trans. H. de Onis. New York: Knopf.

———. 1968. "Sartre contra Sartre. La misión trascendente de la novela." In *Tres aproximaciones a la literatura de nuestro tiempo*, 63–93. Santiago, Chile: Editorial Universitaria.

———. 1981. *On Heroes and Tombs*. Trans. H. Lane. Boston: David Godine.

———. 1991. *The Angel of Darkness*. Trans. A. Huxley. New York: Ballantine Books.

———. 1997a. "A propósito del *Informe sobre ciegos*." In *Obra Completa*, ed. R. Ibarlucia, 947–51. Buenos Aires: Seix Barral.

————. 1997b. *Sobre héroes y tumbas*. In *Obra Completa*, ed. R. Ibarlucia, 111–520. Buenos Aires: Seix Barral.

————. 1997c. *El túnel*. In *Obra Completa*, ed. R. Ibarlucia, 21–109. Buenos Aires: Seix Barral.

————. 1999. *Antes del fin*. Barcelona: Seix Barral.

Saussure, Ferdinand de. 1985. *Cours de linguistique générale*. Ed. Tullio de Mauro. Paris: Payot.

————. 2002. *Ecrits de linguistique générale*. Ed. S. Bouquet and R. Engler. Paris: Gallimard.

Schaidenreisser, Simon. 1911. *Odyssea*. Ed. F. Weidling. Leipzig: Avenarius.

Scheffer, Thassilo von, trans. 1938. *Homer, Odyssee*. Leipzig: Dietrich'sche.

Schlegel, F. 1967. *Kritische Ausgabe*. Vol 2. *Charakteristiken und Kritiken*. I. 1796–1801. Ed. H. Eichner. Zürich: Thomas.

————. 1968. *Dialogue on Poetry*. Trans. E. Behler and R. Struc. University Park: Pennsylvania State University Press.

————. 1991. *Philosophical fragments*. Trans. P. Firschow. Minneapolis: University of Minnesota Press.

Schleiermacher, Friedrich. 1977. *Hermeneutics. The Handwritten Manuscripts*. Ed. H. Kimmerle, trans. J. Duke and J. Forstman. Atlanta: Scholars.

————. 1990. *Hermeneutik und Kritik*. Ed. Manfred Frank. Frankfurt: Suhrkamp.

————. 1996. *Schriften*. Ed. A. Arndt. Frankfurt: Deutscher Klassiker.

Schliemann, Heinrich. 1976. *Ilios: The City and Country of the Trojans; the Results of Researches and Discoveries in the Site of Troy and throughout the Troad in the Years 1871, 72, 78, 79*. New York: Arno.

Schröder, Alexander, trans. 1948. *Homers Odyssee*. Berlin: Suhrkamp.

Schwitzke, Heinz. 1960. *Irrfahrt und Heimkehr. Homers Odyssee nach dem Text des Lagers 437*. Freiburg: Walter.

Searle, John. 1979. *Expression and Meaning. Studies in the Theory of Speech Acts*. Cambridge: Cambridge University Press.

————. 1983. *Intentionality: An Essay in the Philosophy of Mind*. New York: Cambridge University Press.

————. 1992. *The Rediscovery of the Mind*. Cambridge, MA: MIT Press.

Sedlezki, Johann, trans. 1784. *Homers Odyssee*. Augsburg: Matthäus Riegers.

Shewring, Walter, trans. 1980. *The Odyssey; Homer*. Oxford: Oxford University Press.

Simion, Eugen. 1996. *The Return of the Author*. Trans. J. Newcomb and L. Vianu. Evanston: Northwestern University Press.

Smalley, Beryl. 1952. *The Study of the Bible in the Middle Ages*. New York: Philosophical Library.

Stecker, Robert. 1997. *Artworks. Definition, Meaning, Value*. University Park: Pennsylvania State University Press.

Steiner, George. 1975. *After Babel: Aspects of Language and Translation*. London: Oxford University Press.

Strawson, Peter. 2001. "On Referring." In *The Philosophy of Language*, ed. A. P. Martinich, 228–42. New York: Oxford University Press.

Taylor, Charles. 1985. *Philosophy and the Human Sciences. Philosophical Papers 2*. Cambridge: Cambridge University Press.

Thom, Paul. 2000. *Making Sense: A Theory of Interpretation*. Lanham, MD: Rowman and Littlefield.

Valdés, Mario. 1992. *World-Making: the Literary Truth-Claim and the Interpretation of Texts*. Toronto: Toronto University Press.

Vandevelde, Pol. 1994. *Être et discours. La question du langage dans l'itinéraire de Heidegger (1927–1938)*. Brussels: Académie royale de Belgique.

———. 1996. "Ontologie et récit selon Ricoeur. Une application a Günter Grass, *Les années de chien*." In *Les Études de Lettres* 3–4:195–213.

———. 1998. "La traduction comme interprétation. Une comparaison et quelques répercussions théoriques." In *Existentia* 3:1–26.

———. 1999. "Poetry as a Subversion of Narratives in Heidegger." *American Catholic Philosophical Quarterly* 72:239–54.

———. 2002. "L'interprétation comme acte de conscience et comme évènement. Une critique de Gadamer." In *Littérature et savoir(s)*, ed. S. Klimis and L. Van Eynde, 41–64. Brussels: Publications des Facultés universitaires Saint-Louis.

———. 2003a. "*Diuina Eloquia cum Legente Crescunt*: Does Gregory the Great Mean a Subjective or an Objective Growth?" *Rivista di Storia della Filosofia* 4:611–36.

———. 2003b. "Literatur und Wahrheit am Beispiel Ernesto Sabatos." In *Literatur als Phänomenalisierung*, ed. H. R. Sepp and J. Trinks, 30–63. Vienna: Turia and Kant.

———. 2003c. "Sens et langue chez Heidegger. L'aporie de la voie politique entre 1933 et 1935." *Études phénoménologiques* 37–38:149–74.

———. 2005. "A Pragmatic Critique of Pluralism in Text Interpretation. *Metaphilosophy* 36:501–21.

Vincentius of Lerins. *The Commonitorium of Vincentius of Lerins*, ed. R. S. Moxon. New York: Cambridge University Press, 1915.

Voss, Johann Heinrich, trans. 1980. *Homers Odyssee*. Ettville am Rhein, Germany: Rheingauer.

Wasselynck, Robert. 1964. "Les *Moralia in Job* dans les ouvrages de morale du haut moyen âge latin." *Recherches de théologie ancienne et médiévale* 31:5–31.

———. 1965. "L'influence de l'exégèse de S. Grégoire le Grand sur les commentaires bibliques médiévaux (VII–XIIe S.). *Recherche de théologie ancienne et médiévale* 32:157–204.

Webster, Peter Dow. 1959. "Franz Kafka's *Metamorphosis* as Death and Resurrection." *American Imago* 16:349–65.

Weiher, Anton, trans. 1990. *Homer, Odyssee*. 9th ed. Munich: Artemis.

Whorf, Benjamin. 1956. "Languages and Logic." In *Language, Thought, and Reality*, ed. J. Carroll, 233–45. Cambridge, MA: MIT Press.

Wimsatt, William, and Monroe Beardsley. 1946. "The Intentional Fallacy." *Sewanee Review* 54:468–88.

Wittgenstein, Ludwig. 1953. *Philosophical Investigations*. New York: Macmillan.
Wolterstorff, Nicholas. 1995. *Divine Discourse. Philosophical Reflections on the Claim that God Speaks*. Cambridge: Cambridge University Press.
Zinn, Grover. 1995. "Exegesis and Spirituality in the Writings of Gregory the Great." In *Gregory the Great: A Symposium*, ed. John Cavadini, 168–80. Notre Dame: University of Notre Dame Press.

Index